On the Rural

On the Rural

Economy, Sociology, Geography

HENRI LEFEBVRE

Edited by STUART ELDEN *and* ADAM DAVID MORTON

Translated by ROBERT BONONNO
with MATTHEW DENNIS
and SÎAN ROSA HUNTER DODSWORTH

UNIVERSITY OF MINNESOTA PRESS
MINNEAPOLIS • LONDON

The Publication History on pages 241–43 gives original and previous publication history for the writings compiled in this book.

Texts from *Du rural à l'urbain* by Henri Lefebvre copyright 1970, Éditions Économica.

Copyright 2022 by the Regents of the University of Minnesota

All rights reserved. No part of this publication may be reproduced, stored in a retrieval system, or transmitted, in any form or by any means, electronic, mechanical, photocopying, recording, or otherwise, without the prior written permission of the publisher.

Published by the University of Minnesota Press
111 Third Avenue South, Suite 290
Minneapolis, MN 55401-2520
http://www.upress.umn.edu

ISBN 978-1-5179-0468-5 (hc)
ISBN 978-1-5179-0469-2 (pb)

A Cataloging-in-Publication record for this book is available from the Library of Congress.

Printed in the United States of America on acid-free paper

The University of Minnesota is an equal-opportunity educator and employer.

31 30 29 28 27 26 25 24 23 22   10 9 8 7 6 5 4 3 2 1

When we contemplate a field of wheat or maize, we are well aware that the furrows, the pattern of sowing, and the boundaries, be they hedges or wire fences, designate relations of production and property.

— HENRI LEFEBVRE, *The Production of Space*

Contents

From the Rural to the Urban and the Production of Space   ix
    STUART ELDEN *and* ADAM DAVID MORTON

Notes on Translation   xlvii

Acknowledgments   li

1. Introduction to *From the Rural to the Urban* (1969)   1

2. Problems of Rural Sociology: The Peasant Community and Its Historical–Sociological Problems (1949)   17

3. Social Classes in Rural Areas: Tuscany and the *Mezzadria Classica* (1950)   37

4. Perspectives on Rural Sociology (1953)   59

5. Social Relations, Population Phenomena, and Labor Problems in the Agricultural Sector of Underdeveloped Countries (1954)   77

6. The Village Community (1956)   89

7. The Theory of Ground Rent and Rural Sociology (1956)   105

8. The Marxist–Leninist Theory of Ground Rent (1964)   115

9. Introduction to the Psychosociology of Everyday Life (1960)   151

10. The New Urban Complex: Lacq-Mourenx and the
    Urban Problems of the New Working Class (1960)   171

11. Experimental Utopia: For a New Urbanism (1961)   193

12. The Valley of Campan: A Study in Historical Sociology (1963)   205

Publication History   241

Index   245

From the Rural to the Urban and the Production of Space

Stuart Elden and Adam David Morton

Much of the focus of Anglophone scholarship on Henri Lefebvre has been as a theorist of everyday life, urban sociology, or the production of space.¹ This influence in radical geography, urban studies, cultural studies, and other fields has been especially evident since his death, which is not entirely surprising, given the pattern of translation of his work. Only a few of his books were translated into English in his lifetime, including *Dialectical Materialism, The Sociology of Marx, Everyday Life in the Modern World, The Explosion,* and *The Survival of Capitalism*.² In the year of his death, 1991, the first volume of *Critique of Everyday Life* was translated, along with *The Production of Space*.³ A few years later, *Introduction to Modernity* was translated by John Moore, and *Writings on Cities,* which included his book *The Right to the City* and some related essays, was edited and translated by Eleonore Kofman and Elisabeth Lebas.⁴ In the first decade of the twenty-first century, there have been a number of translations. Continuum (now part of Bloomsbury) published the translation of *Key Writings* and *Rhythmanalysis*; Verso the remaining two volumes of *Critique of Everyday Life*; and the University of Minnesota Press *The Urban Revolution* and *State, Space, World*.⁵ Most recently the University of Minnesota Press has published translations of *Toward an Architecture of Enjoyment*, edited by Łukasz Stanek, and *Marxist Thought and the City*; while Verso has brought out translations of two of Lefebvre's major theoretical works, *Metaphilosophy* and *Hegel, Marx, Nietzsche: Or the Realm of Shadows*.⁶

An Anglophone reader, then, now has access to many aspects of Lefebvre's multifaceted career. All his books on everyday life are available in English, as are nearly all his works on urban questions. *State, Space, World* samples his essays on political themes though is only a fraction of that work, which culminated in the four-volume study *De l'État*.[7] While situating Lefebvre appropriately within Western Marxism is still somewhat lacking in Anglophone debates, there have been notable contributions establishing this connection.[8] Many of Lefebvre's books on Karl Marx, as well as his engagements with existentialism or structuralism, remain untranslated, though a sense of their arguments can be found in pieces included in *Key Writings*.[9] His important book *La fin de l'histoire* will hopefully be the next theoretical work to be translated, which ideally would be followed by *La somme et le reste,* a sprawling autobiographical work first published in 1959.[10] While this would certainly not be all of Lefebvre's work in English, it would give a very comprehensive sample of most themes.

Yet, until the present collection, one key aspect of his work, his studies of rural sociology and political economy, has been neglected. While Lefebvre is a well-established figure in debates in Anglophone human geography, this is rarely because of his interest in rural questions.[11] Again, translation is a large part of the reason: only a few pieces of his work on this theme have appeared in English. The essay "Perspectives on Rural Sociology" (1953) from *Du rural à l'urbain* appeared in *Key Writings* in 2003 and appears here in a new translation.[12] Another essay, "The Theory of Ground Rent and Rural Sociology" (1956), was translated in *Antipode,* as the first collaboration of this book's two editors, and a prelude to the present work.[13] It is included here in a lightly revised version.

English-language readers could also turn to one essay in the first volume of *Critique of Everyday Life,* titled "Notes Written One Sunday in the French Countryside."[14] This piece includes Lefebvre's description of a small Pyrenean village, and especially its church, along with a discussion of festivals as a contrast to everyday rural life. As the title suggests, it is far from a scholarly piece, and it contains no references. Friedrich Nietzsche is briefly mentioned, as is the Dutch theologian Cornelius Jansen, but the notes conclude with the insights that Marxism and the dialectical method can give to this description.[15] Lefebvre suggests: "Using Marxist method, every cultivated and truly 'modern' man will soon be able to look at the irksome and incomprehensible mumbo-jumbo of our towns and villages, our churches and our works of art, and read them aloud, like an open book."[16] The essay forms an interesting contrast with the chapter "Notes on the New Town" in *Introduction to Modernity*, in which Lefebvre describes the urban development of Lacq-Mourenx.[17] As Lefebvre opens that essay, dated April 1960: "A few kilometers away from the tower blocks of the new town lies the sleepy old village where I live. Just a few minutes from my timeworn house, and I am surrounded by the derricks of a building estate [*cité*] without a past."[18] In a sense, what this present volume provides is the material Lefebvre wrote between the essay in *Critique of Everyday Life* and the one in *Introduction to Modernity*, not just in terms of chronology—the late 1940s to the early 1960s—but also in terms of tracking the transition from one form of life to another.

Lefebvre's Path to Rural Sociology as Production of Space

Lefebvre's early writings were in philosophy, with one of his first publications a long introduction to a translation of Friedrich Wilhelm Joseph von Schelling's *Philosophical Investigations into the Essence of Human Freedom*.[19] The translation was made by Georges Politzer, who would go on to shape French psychology profoundly, before being executed by the Nazis in 1942. Politzer was one of the members of the Philosophies group, named after the journal they founded, along with Georges Friedmann, Pierre Morhange, Lefebvre, and Norbert Guterman.[20] Guterman and Lefebvre would be instrumental in bringing Karl Marx's early writings to a French audience, publishing the first translations from his 1844 "Economic and Philosophical Manuscripts" in the late 1920s.[21] Guterman and Lefebvre were also important in the 1930s for producing selections of Karl Marx and G. W. F. Hegel's writings for a French audience, and for translating Vladimir Ilyich Lenin's notebooks on Hegel's dialectic, which came with a substantial coauthored introduction.[22] He knew the surrealists, and on some accounts was part of a famous group of intellectuals who attended Alexandre Kojève's lectures on Hegel's *Phenomenology of Spirit*.[23] Around some odd jobs, including a spell as a taxi driver and his military service, Lefebvre taught philosophy in *lycées* and wrote books on political and social issues, including *Le nationalisme contre les nations* in 1937 and *Hitler au pouvoir, les enseignements de cinq annees de fascisme en Allemagne* in 1938.[24] He also produced more explicitly theoretical works in this period, including *La conscience mystifiée* with Guterman in 1936 and the 1939 study *Nietzsche*, intended to defend him from the fascist misappropriation.[25]

After the German invasion of France, Lefebvre lost his teaching job as a result of his membership in the Parti communiste français (PCF, French Communist Party), left Paris, and headed to the Pyrenees. Lefebvre knew the Pyrenees well, having been born in Hagetmau, though he had spent much of his childhood in Brittany. As an adult, he spent much of his time at his mother's family home in Navarrenx in the Pyrenees, usually splitting his life between there and Paris.[26] During the war, he was involved in the resistance, though the exact nature of his contribution remains unclear.[27] He certainly used this time to do research on the history and sociology of the Pyrenees. After the war, this led him to enter the Centre national de la recherche scientifique (CNRS, National Centre for Scientific Research) to work on rural issues. While this was partly due to a need for employment, Lefebvre recalled that he was struck by "the gravity [*l'acuité*] of peasant problems in the modern world, in underdeveloped countries and also in socialist countries."[28] In 1954 he submitted his two doctoral theses to the Sorbonne—a primary thesis on peasant communities in the Pyrenees and a secondary thesis that was a detailed study of one valley, its people, geography, and history. The first, principal thesis was only published in 2014; the second as the book *La vallée de Campan* in 1963.[29] The theses were supervised by Georges Gurvitch, as his initial supervisor Maurice Halbwachs had died in the Buchenwald concentration camp.[30]

At the CNRS, Lefebvre deepened his analysis of peasant communities and social classes, and began work on sociological and political-economic issues.[31] Most of the pieces he published during this time are included in the present volume.[32] Several were in the CNRS journal *Cahiers internationaux de Sociologie*.[33] Lefebvre's plans were often ambitious and did not always come to fruition. He planned a history of rural France with the historian Albert Soboul, but this was never completed.[34] Only a few traces of his engagement with Soboul, a significant historian of the French Revolution, can be found.[35] There was another study planned, under the title *Manuel* (or *Traité*) *de sociologie rurale*, which was intended to be a major work. According to Lefebvre's biographer Rémi Hess:

> It contained a theorization of concepts of rents, ground revenues, the distribution of ground revenues, and the relation between rents and markets. It had an important part on agrarian reform, both theoretical and practical. It showed how agrarian reform, initially revolutionary, was slowly recovered [*récupérée*] in different countries, notably southern Italy, Mexico and Spain. There were also other cases examined where agrarian reform was not totally recovered, as was the case later, notably in Iran. Additionally, there were many studies of *terrain* in the *Traité*, in particular Tuscany and the Pyrenees.[36]

Given Lefebvre's interest in land reform in Russia and China dating back to the 1930s, it seems at least possible these countries too would have been discussed.[37] One of his conference papers from this period discusses Tunisia, and he promises future analyses of Brazil, the Middle East, and Indochina (included here as "Social Relations, Population Phenomena, and Labor Problems in the Agricultural Sector of Underdeveloped Countries" [1954]).[38] (Twenty years later, in the third volume of *De l'État*, he would provide an analysis that was genuinely worldwide, covering countries in Western Europe and the Eastern bloc, the United States and Mexico, as well as Chile, Algeria, Japan, Senegal, and China.[39]) Yet his planned comprehensive study on rural questions—Lefebvre apparently worked on it for three years—was never published and the manuscript lost. Hess tells the story of how a late draft was stolen from a car parked near the Panthéon in Paris. While a newspaper advert in *France Soir* offered a sizable reward for its return, the manuscript was never found, and Lefebvre never rewrote it.[40]

The story should probably be taken with some skepticism, though rural work certainly occupied Lefebvre for much of the 1950s. This was during a period when he became increasingly frustrated with the PCF. While the increasingly Stalinist hard line of the party was one reason, and another was the revelations coming out of Russia, there was also a frustration with the way his research topics were seen. In his preface to the third edition of *Du rural à l'urbain,* Hess recounts Lefebvre's interest in the history of peasant movements but says that "he found few interlocutors either inside or outside the party. For example, he wrote a work on ground rent which did not find an editor. In that work, he had studied ground rent [*la rente du sol*] but also the sub-soil [*du sous-sol*], which ultimately led him to questions of oil."[41] Lefebvre was apparently told that "to look at ground rent is not Marxist. It is Ricardian."[42]

His long and complicated relation with the party led him to turn to other questions too. He had served the PCF machine in 1946 with his biting critique of existentialism, as the communists saw the rise of Jean-Paul Sartre and others as a challenge that needed confronting. Lefebvre accused the existentialists of retreading ground the Philosophies group had traveled in the 1920s, only without the realization of the flaws he and his colleagues had long since overcome. Lefebvre was now also one of the key voices in France helping bring Marx to a wide, public audience. As well as the best-selling introduction *Le marxisme* in 1948, Lefebvre published a guide to Marx's thought, a collection of his writings with a long introduction, and *Logique formelle, logique dialectique* in 1947.[43] The last of these was the first volume of a projected series titled *À la lumière du matérialisme dialectique,* but it was the only one published. His views in the book departed sufficiently from party orthodoxy that he found himself criticized. A second volume, *Méthodologie des sciences,* was written but censored by the PCF. It appeared posthumously in 2002.[44]

In the late 1940s and 1950s, Lefebvre generally avoided these more contentious topics and instead wrote books on literary, artistic, and philosophical figures. These included studies of René Descartes, Denis Diderot, Blaise Pascal, François Rabelais, the poet and dramatist Alfred de Musset, and the painter Éduoard Pignon.[45] These books were ways to escape the scrutiny of the party, and yet to develop Marxist readings of these thinkers and their contexts nonetheless. He trod a fine line with this tactic. His book on aesthetics, eventually published in 1953, had been delayed by party censors for four years. It was finally allowed, partly due to a fabricated quotation from Marx that served as an epigraph.[46] He had fewer problems with his guide to Lenin's thought in 1957, a book he later repudiated, but his 1958 *Problèmes actuels du marxisme* criticized Stalinism, and led to a party tribunal at which he was suspended.[47] Eventually Lefebvre turned the suspension into an expulsion, and as he would claim, through the left rather than the right door.[48] He got many issues off his chest in *La somme et le reste* in 1959 and a revised edition of *Problèmes actuels du marxisme* in 1960.[49]

In the 1960s, his focus turned—as the title of his collection of essays suggests—from the rural to the urban. This collection was compiled by Marco Gaviria, who had been a student of Lefebvre's at the University of Strasbourg in the early 1960s and later commissioned *Toward an Architecture of Enjoyment* from Lefebvre in 1973. Lefebvre's turn to urban questions led to a series of works in which he cemented a reputation as a theorist of the first rank, most of which have been translated, including *The Right to the City*, *The Urban Revolution*, and *Marxist Thought and the City*, which culminate in the summation of *The Production of Space*. In that book, Lefebvre questions, "What of the part played by *land*, as concept and reality, in this context?"[50] Here he draws attention to *Capital*, vol. 3, and the focus on the "trinity" formula (land, labor, and capital) that transcends the capital-labor binary to bring in a third cluster of factors—land, the landowning class, ground rent, and agriculture—to address not simply the ownership of land but also underground and submarine resources as well as the breeding of livestock and the construction and buildup of land. "What excuse could there be today," Lefebvre then asks, "for not going back to this exemplary if unfinished work—not with a view to consecrating it in any way but in order to put questions to it?"[51]

Lefebvre explores some of these issues in more detail in writings translated in the present volume, and we return to his reading of Marx and the rural as production of space shortly. What we want to stress at this point is that the question of the rural never entirely disappears for Lefebvre: it is fundamental to his project of the political economy of space. Witness his statements in *The Production of Space* that "the history of space thus has its place between anthropology and political economy" and that "a new political economy must no longer concern itself within things in space, as did the now obsolete science that preceded it; rather, it will have to be a political economy of space (and of its production)." At the junction of the critique of the political economy of space is therefore included not only rural space and urban space but also a critique of the state and state powers.[52] Nonetheless, his shift of focus to urban and spatial questions coincided with a move from the CNRS to the University of Strasbourg in 1961 and then to the University of Paris X: Nanterre in 1965, where he taught until his retirement in 1973. In both Strasbourg and Nanterre, he was a professor of sociology. In 1962 he cofounded the Institut de sociologie urbaine (ISU, Institute of Urban Sociology) to conduct further empirical work.[53]

But there was a more significant reason for the move to study urban questions. Lefebvre's interest in rural problems led him to detailed studies of the region he knew best, the Pyrenees. In the commune of Lacq, not far from Navarrenx, natural gas deposits were discovered in 1951 and the wish to exploit this gas—along with the hydrogen sulfide within it—led to the establishment of a large extractive industry. Alongside the processing plant for the gas, aluminum and chemical factories were built. In order to house the workers, major building projects began in 1957 and 1958 near the small village of Mourenx.[54] Lefebvre recalls seeing the "first stones laid for the new town," which became for him "a small laboratory."[55] It is this transformation that Lefebvre discusses in the essay in *Introduction to Modernity* and in "The New Urban Complex: Lacq-Mourenx and the Urban Problems of the New Working Class" (1960) in the present volume. Hess suggests that the violence of the process—bulldozers through hedgerows, dynamite to prepare the ground—was particularly striking.[56] In Lefebvre's words, seeing the process led him to "begin studying urban questions *in vivo*, in *statu nascendi*." He adds, "I suspected that this irruption of the urban in a traditional rural reality was not simple local chance [*hasard*] but that it was linked to urbanization, to industrialization, to worldwide [*mondiaux*] phenomena."[57] The local phenomena, which he discussed in some detail, opened up general problems that would form key themes of his ongoing research.

As such, it is essential to recognize two things. First, Lefebvre was led to study the urban question because of observing a process of urbanization, a transformation. The urban is not a static, already existing object but something in the process of becoming. Second, Lefebvre came to this question because of an interest in rural problems. Some of his most detailed historical and empirical studies were of rural communities and economies. What might be deemed rural concerns remain at the core of capitalism and the production of space, and resource extraction, just as it was for Lefebvre, is crucial here. Consequently, the Anglophone tendency to privilege the urban in its reading of Lefebvre's work misses both his intention of approaching urban and rural sociology together and of seeing the process of transformation at stake in the production and organization of state space. It also privileges his work as a theorist, missing the empirical and historical work he did on both rural and urban questions.[58]

From the Rural to the Urban

The present book includes the specifically rural essays from Lefebvre's 1970 collection *Du rural à l'urbain*, along with some of the transitional texts from that book that trace the urbanization process. We have also included some supplementary pieces on rural questions to provide a comprehensive survey of Lefebvre's work on this theme. Anglophone readers already have a good number of Lefebvre's writings on specifically urban questions—notably *Writings on Cities*, *The Urban Revolution*, and *Marxist Thought and the City*. Nonetheless, we hope that in time the remaining essays of *Du rural à l'urbain* and other untranslated texts by Lefebvre on urban questions, particularly parts of *Espace et politique* from 1972, will be collected in another volume.[59]

Following Lefebvre's 1969 introduction, the chapters here begin with some of his initial works on the rural itself. Chapters 2, 3, and 4 are the first three chapters of *Du rural à l'urbain*, with chapters 5 and 6 added as supplements. In these chapters, as well as setting out the problematic he wants to explore, he also develops his approach to combining historical and sociological modes of inquiry. This approach has come to be called the "progressive-regressive" model, though that is Sartre's term for the approach, not Lefebvre's. Sartre discussed this approach in his "Questions of Method," the theoretical preface to his *Critique of Dialectical Reason*. He declared that he had "nothing to add to this passage, so clear and so rich, except that we believe that this method, with its phase of phenomenological description and its double movement of regression followed by progress, is valid—with the modifications which its objects may impose upon it—*in all the domains of anthropology.*" He suggests that the only problem is that "Lefebvre has not found imitators among the rest of the Marxist intellectuals."[60] Rather than accept this generous praise, Lefebvre was critical, indicating that this was not his method but Marx's. Sartre was giving him undue credit, and instead should learn to read Marx properly.[61] Lefebvre says this is the insight Marx has that "human anatomy contains a key to the anatomy of the ape" and "the bourgeois economy thus supplies the key to the ancient, etc."[62] At the same time, historical examinations can help us explore the present, hence the importance of both steps. This is an approach that effectively combines history and sociology, the diachronic and the synchronic.[63] More broadly, several of the writings on the rural as production of space address historical sociology as a method. Recall this provocation in *The Production of Space*:

> The process of slicing-up, moreover becomes a "discipline" in its own right: the instrument of knowledge is taken for knowledge itself. The search for some unity here is confined to labored interdisciplinary or multidisciplinary montages which never manage to fit any of the pieces together.[64]

It is therefore perhaps unsurprising to observe Lefebvre emphasizing the complexity of peasant life by drawing attention to issues of *horizontal complexity* (focusing on agrarian formations and structures of the same historical period in terms of temporality) and *vertical complexity* (addressing how the rural world is constituted by the coexistence of formations of different periods in terms of spatiality). Hence:

The two complexities—the horizontal and the vertical, which we could also call the *historical*—intersect, cross, and act upon one another. This results in an interlinking of facts that can only be untangled by some form of solid *methodology*. We must simultaneously identify the objects and goals of rural sociology and define its relationship to the sciences and disciplines that will become its auxiliaries: human geography, political economy, ecology, statistics. ("Perspectives on Rural Sociology")

Something worth teasing out, then, is the historical sociological method on display throughout this collection of rural writings as the beginning of this examination of the production of space, which can be linked to wider interpretative and relational approaches such as the method of incorporated comparison shaping historical geographical studies. As Philip McMichael has elaborated, the method of incorporated comparison avoids the conventions of treating social phenomena as parallel cases and, instead, views comparable social phenomena as differentiated moments of a historically integrated process. Analysis can then involve the temporal multiple form of incorporated comparison based on focusing on instances as products of a continuously evolving process in and across *time* (e.g., particular parallel events in the evolution of the states system as part of an ongoing, general process of state formation that emerges within a world-historical process of late capitalism) or a spatial singular form of incorporated comparison based on focusing on variation in or across *space* within a world-historical conjuncture (e.g., by comparing combinations of peasant and market economies, slave and wage labor systems, metropolitan and colonial cultures).[65] There is then a spatio-historical dialectical method that links these writings on the rural as production of space to the relational method of incorporated comparison shaping historical sociological and geographical studies.[66]

These rural writings as production of space lead directly to a concern with political economy, especially as found in chapters 7 and 8. Chapter 8, "The Marxist–Leninist Theory of Ground Rent" (1964), has been added to the materials here, a Spanish text for which there appears to be no extant French original. This was originally a conference presentation from Mexico. We believe this to be a fragment of the material written for the "Manual of Rural Sociology," a project that was never finished or published. Although the text here has gone through the process of two translations—from lost French text to Spanish; from Spanish to English—we believe this is a valuable supplement to Lefebvre's discussions. This is because the essay is a decisive corrective to the reduction of Lefebvre to the production of urban space and presents, instead, a much broader critique of the political economy of space embedded in the rural-urban dialectic. As Lefebvre reminds the attentive reader, the specificity of the capitalist mode of production of space is revealed through a focus on "the 'land-labor-capital' relation, the constitutive trinity of capitalist society," which is something that animates these rural writings too.[67] While Lefebvre's writings on rural economy, sociology, and geography cannot be reduced to the analysis of ground rent, it is of course fundamental to the analysis, as this collection makes clear.

Subsequent chapters in this volume do explore the shift to the urban, in the examination of the *urbanization* of a region (around Lacq, and the building of the new town of Mourenx) and in relation to everyday life—seen in chapters 9, 10, and 11. A number of themes seem remarkably contemporary given recent events and current debates arising from increased inequalities in the twenty-first century. There is room to highlight two such examples here. First, it is noteworthy that Lefebvre singles out Honoré de Balzac, among others, for delivering "important documents on the life of the countryside in the nineteenth century" ("Problems of Rural Sociology" [1949]). Remember that Balzac was also an interest for Marx, too, with him noting that the novel *Les Paysans* was remarkable in the way it demonstrated the dominance of capitalist ways of thinking within the peasantry.[68] Of course, the literary economy of Balzac has become a major vehicle for Thomas Piketty and his depiction of property hierarchies, power, domination, ideology, and thus the presentation of "inequality with a verisimilitude and evocative power that no statistical or theoretical analysis can match."[69] Second, throughout the shift to the urban in this collection, there is an emphasis on monuments as a digest of everyday life. In an era when symbols around the world have been projected to center stage as sites of contestation—such as the statues of Confederate General Robert E. Lee in Virginia, or the civic monuments to Captain Cook and Major General Lachlan Macquarie in Sydney, in 2017; or the statues of Edward Colston in Bristol, Cecil Rhodes in Oxford, or King Leopold II in Antwerp, in 2020—then so do monuments and memorials continue to animate aspects of political economy here, too. Hence in "Introduction to the Psychosociology of Everyday Life" (1960), monuments are recognized as fetishized objects, turning some streets into museums so that space and time become stamped with the seals of abundance, of envy, and also of poverty and deprivation. Whereas, presciently in the context of the spaces of difference mobilized by Black Lives Matter, Lefebvre asks in "Experimental Utopia" (1961) whether monuments can overflow their social function: "Shouldn't we reinvent or imagine several monuments or several types of monuments?"[70]

As a further and final supplement to these materials, we include two chapters from Lefebvre's secondary doctoral thesis, *La vallée de Campan*, which as noted previously was published in 1963 but first presented to the Sorbonne in 1954. Lefebvre recalls it was written in Bagnères-de-Bigorre in the Pyrenees in 1941 and in Paris in 1952.[71] Lefebvre consulted a great deal of published and unpublished historical sources in making this sociological study. As Stanek discusses, although it was submitted as a thesis, it was initially commissioned by Georges-Henri Rivière, director of the Musée national des arts et traditions populaires. Lefebvre was part of the *chantiers intellectuels* (intellectual work sites) set up during the war, allowing research work to continue for those who had lost their jobs.[72]

Together, these materials comprise the first half of *Du rural à l'urbain*—all the rural essays, and three that track a transition; supplemented by "The Village Community" (1956); presentations, including one from Mexico that we believe is a fragment of a lost text; and some indicative material from one of Lefebvre's theses. Along with "Notes Written One Sunday in the French Countryside" from the first volume of *Critique of Everyday Life*, this gives the Anglophone reader access to the most significant of Lefebvre's writings on the rural and shows how these exemplify and lead to his more familiar work on urban questions and the production of space.

Lefebvre's focus does noticeably shift to urban questions, with little substantially on the rural after the 1950s. The second half of *Du rural à l'urbain* is on these urban topics, which as we have noted are already well represented in existing English translations. Yet of the second half of that book itself, only "Preface to the Study of the Habitat of the 'Pavilion'" is currently translated, in *Key Writings*.[73]

The key exception to this rough schema of seeing the 1950s as Lefebvre's rural period, and the 1960s as the beginning of his urban one, is a book on the Pyrenees published in 1965.[74] It was a commission from a Swiss publisher for a series on "Atlas des Voyages." Compared to the essays included here or the doctoral work, it was a more accessible book, mixing styles from dialogue to description, and its first edition was filled with landscape photographs, portraits, maps, and other images. Written for a popular audience, almost as a tourist guide, it is rightly described by Nick Entrikin and Vincent Berdoulay as "an attractive book, interestingly written and well-illustrated, but only marginally identifiable as a Lefebvrian scholarly text."[75] Lefebvre's widow, Catherine Régulier, recalled that while a major incentive for Lefebvre to write the book was to earn money, it was also to discuss his native region.[76] Régulier did not meet Lefebvre until the late 1970s, so this must be Lefebvre's own recollection of the project.

Lefebvre's work has been used in so many ways that it is impossible to summarize or survey these studies. However, it is worth noting that he has been used creatively in work looking at rural politics from the Negev desert to Chile, Mexico, and Colombia.[77] This has not always been using his rural work, but rather his more general theorizations of space and politics. A particularly striking example of this tendency is an essay by Keith Halfacree that develops a "Lefebvrian model of (rural) space" but does so without the use of his own writings on rural questions.[78] Rather, it builds its model mainly by using *The Production of Space*, and Halfacree even chides Lefebvre for a "relative neglect of the rural within his work."[79] Yet while some of Lefebvre's projects on the rural were abandoned, the books *Du rural à l'urbain*, *La vallée de Campan*, and *Pyrénées* testify to the importance of the theme. To these can be added the posthumously published principal thesis on peasant communities.

Three and a half books on the rural is only a "relative neglect" for someone of Lefebvre's productivity. It is to be hoped this collection will provide further inspiration and conceptual tools for theorists in the Anglophone world. It gives a good sample of his significant contributions to rural sociology, political economy, and the politics of land and what Karl Kautsky called "the agrarian question."[80] Let us now turn to suggest how Lefebvre's work on rural sociology might be situated within a wider critique of political economy.

Beyond Lifeless Abstractions with the Theory of Ground Rent

Whatever limitations exist with Lenin's *Materialism and Empirio-Criticism*, he nevertheless charts a compelling course through the twin issues of dialectics and abstraction. The approach to *integral philosophy* that he forges attempts to tread a pathway between relativism and materialism, with that tension pursued through dialectics. For dialectical materialism, there is no boundary between relative and absolute truth for the existence of truth is unconditional, while the striving for truth is historically conditional. To cite Lenin directly, dialectics *"contains* the element of relativism, of negation, of skepticism, but *is not reducible* to relativism. The materialist dialectics of Marx and Engels certainly does contain relativism, that is, it recognizes the relativity of all our knowledge, not in the sense of denying objective truth, but in the sense that the limits of approximation of our knowledge to this truth are historically conditional."[81] Hence dialectical materialism insists on the approximate, relative character of theory vis-à-vis matter and its properties; insists on the absence of absolute boundaries in Nature; and accepts its transformation through abstraction of the "psychical."[82] In sum, "that is why Marx and Engels laid the emphasis in their works rather on *dialectical* materialism than on dialectical *materialism*, why they insisted rather on *historical* materialism than on historical *materialism*."[83] Additionally, through his emphasis on integral philosophical materialism, Lenin is a parser of abstraction avoiding *dead abstraction*, based on general contextless reflection, or *lifeless abstraction*, which reduces the appearance of things to the thought concept.[84] Historical materialism offers a method based on *concrete abstraction* that traces the inner connection between the forms of appearance of capital and the core patterns or essence of surplus-value formation. Hence, for Marx, classical economics commits a *violent abstraction* of the law of value by basing it on immediate experience, for example by only focusing on the simple extension of the working day (absolute surplus value) rather than also appreciating the cutting of wages or reducing the cost of living (relative surplus value).[85] As Marx reiterates in the third volume of *Capital*, it is the inner connection that is revealed by his critique of political economy because "all economics up till now has either violently made abstraction from the distinctions between surplus-value and profit, between rate of surplus-value and rate of profit, so that it could retain the determination of value as its basis, or else has abandoned, along with this determination of value, any kind of solid foundation for a scientific approach, so as to be able to retain those distinctions which obtrude themselves on the phenomenal level."[86] Hence capital as the self-valorization of value "does not just comprise class relations, a definite social character that depends on the existence of labor as wage-labor," but reflects an inner movement through different circuits of production and consumption, not as a static thing but as an "abstraction in action."[87]

All these elements and their combination confront the reader in this collection and especially come to the fore in Lefebvre's writings on rural political economy and the theory of ground rent, which are in direct dialogue with Marx and Lenin. In his early study *Dialectical Materialism*, Lefebvre transcends dualism with a focus on *internal relations* and aims to restore dialectics to "truth within the total movement of reality and of thought, of the content and the form." Hence, in dialectical materialism, idealism and materialism are "not only re-united but transformed and superseded [*dépassés*]."[88] Consequently, "there can be no pure abstraction. The abstract is also concrete, and the concrete, from a certain point of view, is also abstract. All that exists for us is the concrete abstract."[89] In these rural writings, the connections to Marx and Lenin can be found not only on issues of philosophy and dialectics but also on wider concerns of method and concrete abstraction. In his pivotal essay "The Marxist–Leninist Theory of Ground Rent," which we have situated at the core of this collection, Lefebvre makes this clear: "The method used in the analysis and presentation of capitalist society moves from the abstract to the concrete. Let us be clear: from a scientific abstraction, albeit an objective and well-founded one, to reality in all its complexity."

How might more specific resonances within these texts connect to political economy, historical sociology, and agrarian and geographical studies? There are at least four themes that we want to highlight here: (1) agrarian reform and uneven development; (2) class relations; (3) the survival—literally, the afterlife—of noncapitalism; and, finally, (4) ground-rent theory itself. While we disaggregate them here, these are themes that have to be related intrinsically, in their totality, as indeed Lefebvre does throughout this collection.

Agrarian Reform and Uneven Development

Just as elsewhere, one of the main threads running through these essays is Lefebvre's recognition of the centrality of agrarian reform within conditions of uneven development. This focus on agrarian reform is, for Lefebvre, both a fundamental transformation of historical and social relations and constitutive of conditions of capitalist space. As he states in *The Production of Space*, "During the first half of the twentieth century, agrarian reforms and peasant revolutions reshaped the surface of the planet. A large portion of these changes served the ends of abstract space."[90] It is no coincidence, then, that discussion of agrarian reforms in this collection led to wider reflections on uneven development, highlighting the transition from the rural to the urban across the world scale. Hence the "law" of uneven development is something that is stressed throughout history, shaping agrarian relations in China, Mexico, Egypt, Italy, Japan, and India as well as, of course, in France across the essays "Problems of Rural Sociology" and "Perspectives on Rural Sociology." Framing this focus is the condition of primitive accumulation, whereby "the era of the peasant grows distant in time and space" as a consequence of the forceful expropriation and extirpation of direct subsistence producers from their land and their transformation into wage laborers that only have their labor to sell (see "Introduction to *From the Rural to the Urban*" [1969]). Agrarian reform here is posited as "modifying the relations of production" without transforming them, leading Lefebvre to ask: "Why was the course of worldwide revolution deflected in this way?" Perhaps the most teasing link to be established here is to the contradictory combination of revolution-restoration that Antonio Gramsci posited as emblematic of a passive revolution, referring to an insurrectionary force that is domesticated, resulting in both the transformation (revolution) and the persistence (restoration) of different conditions shaped by ruptures in social property relations.[91] As already established, Lefebvre delivers a supersession—a transformation and transcendence—of idealism and materialism with his formulation of historical materialism. Equally, in these essays Lefebvre shows how he should be situated within a pantheon of theorists who have brought about a supersession—a transformation and transcendence—of understandings of agrarian reform and uneven development. Witness the description of Lacq-Mourenx in the Pyrénées-Atlantiques as the "Béarnaisian Texas" and the fulcrum of the transition from the rural to the urban in France; or the historical crystallization of the *mezzadria classica* sharecroppers in Tuscany reflecting not a transformation of feudal relations "but rather a failure, a cessation, even a regression of that transformation" (see "Social Classes in Rural Areas" [1950]); or the emphasis on the *refeudalization* of relationships and the struggles over territory in the Campan Valley (see "The Valley of Campan" [1963]). It is therefore vital to see Lefebvre alongside Marx and Lenin, or Gramsci and Leon Trotsky, as theorists who address agrarian reform, conditions of uneven development, and deflected (or passive) revolution within the transition to capitalism.

Class as Process

Taking class relations as a process, a further rich seam through these essays is revealed, and it is one worth mining. Certainly, the spotlight on the peasantry signals long-standing debates about the "death of the peasantry" and, especially in Latin America, in addressing the magnetic poles of *campesinistas* (emphasizing peasantization) and *decampesinistas* (stressing depeasantization or proletarianization of the peasantry) in the transformation of agrarian structures to capitalism as a mode of production.[92]

The essay "Social Classes in Rural Areas" sets up, however, a series of fertile connections on the process of class formation. Honing in on the agrarian structure of sharecropping in Tuscany and the crystallization of the *mezzadria classica,* Lefebvre attempts to trace both the persistent framework of agrarian feudalism *and* the coming into existence of capitalism. Here the *braccianti* come to the fore as seasonal salaried workers, as

> the constitution of a class from initially sporadic elements having only a secondary function. Larger in number, indispensable, having acquired a degree of technical skill, living together in small communities, the *braccianti* see themselves as a distinct group, as a *class*. They form their own distinct associations, their own unions; they are becoming an important element in social and political life. ("Social Classes in Rural Areas")

Subsequently, in the same essay it is stated that "the class of the *braccianti* is constituted, acquires an awareness, an ideology. It exists at a certain stage or level of maturity."

These insights and more are pivotal in a twofold sense. First, they reveal an approach to class as a *process* based on observed behavior over time rather than as a static, structural definition. This analysis has important parallels to the *emergentist* theory of class that has been recognized in the work of E. P. Thompson. Rather than upholding a static model of capitalist productive relations from which classes and consciousness derive and correspond to, Thompson places emphasis on emergent processes of class formation. This means analyzing contexts within which particular communities experience new structures of exploitation and points of antagonistic interest, even though forms of class consciousness—involving a conscious identity of common interests—may not have immediately formed.[93] Therefore, Thompson does not "see class as a 'structure,' nor even as a 'category,' but as something which in fact happens (and can be shown to have happened) in human relationships."[94] Second, this emphasis on class as a process of becoming relates to Gramsci's own methodological criteria on the history of subaltern classes.[95] This entails a twofold approach to unraveling contestations over state space by initially identifying the "objective" formation of subaltern social classes within developments and transformations of the relations of production.[96] Historical and contemporary research then needs to incorporate, as much as possible, a consideration of the mentalities and ideologies of subaltern classes, their active as well as passive affiliation to dominant social forms of political association, and thus their involvement in formations that might conserve dissent or maintain control.[97] Additionally, such a method entails focusing on the formations that subaltern classes themselves produce (e.g., trade unions, workers' cooperatives, or peasant associations), which press claims or assert autonomy within the existing "relations of force." Questions of historical and political consciousness expressed by subaltern classes can then be raised. As Gramsci writes, "the history of subaltern social groups is necessarily fragmented and episodic," to the extent that "subaltern groups are always subject to the activity of ruling groups, even when they rebel and rise up."[98] What emerges, then, is a methodology of subaltern class analysis embedded within the uneven and combined developments of the agrarian landscape in the transition to capitalism. It is the role of the *integral historian* to produce a conception of space "that can only be dealt with monographically, and each monograph requires an immense quantity of material which is often hard to collect."[99] Hence the contrast between the advocacy of *integral history* (understood relationally and intrinsically) and the rejection of extrinsic history (focusing on economic forces held as external to history).[100] The integral history of subaltern class analysis (evident in Lefebvre's approach to rural sociology) might then be linked to understandings of the state in its integral sense— referring to the changing geographies of state intervention across extended territorial-, place-, and scale-specific dimensions.[101] One outcome from this focus on rural sociology might then be a methodology that pulls together integral philosophy, integral history, and integral state space.

Lefebvre's work on rural questions thus spans work akin to regional geography, political economy, and ecology. To make use of these distinct approaches, the methodological challenge of connecting *sociology* and *history* in their relations of internality is awarded prominence.[102] Lefebvre is interested in developing an approach that avoids simply bolting history onto sociology, or the absorption of one by the other, and instead studies rural sociology that takes on the social process *as a whole*. This method of integral history, rural sociology, or *historical sociology* is then constituted through several moments that are (1) descriptive, (2) analytic–regressive, and (3) historical–genetic. The result is a specifically Marxist methodological approach to integral state space that moves through a regressive, historical analysis of the conditions of possibility of the present, thus using the past to make sense of the present, then using the present to understand the past, and a progressive analysis open to the future, to the possible.[103] In Lefebvre's own words, the benefit is that "we see then that the peasant contribution to the history of ideologies—confused, diffused, formulated by city dwellers—has been considerable" in shaping integral aspects of state space, including "the study of ideas, which is to say, to philosophy" ("Perspectives on Rural Sociology").

The Survival of Noncapitalism

This approach then leads to an important emphasis on the survival of noncapitalism within the complex of the rural and the urban.[104] Here Lefebvre frequently returns to revealing the survivals and revivals of peasant life in terms of the structures of feudal social property relations *and* their ideological forms manifest in the sediments of agrarian myths, folklore, or religion. Agrarian communities, therefore, do not simply dissolve in "the transition from bonds of consanguinity to bonds of territoriality" ("Perspectives on Rural Sociology").[105] Rather, there can exist the strengthening of peasant communities and the presence of "deep-seated residues" in the transformation from collective ownership to private property that necessitates more concerted sociohistorical study of peasant communities. Hence, "historical and sociological analyses intersect the study of folklore and the development of myths" ("Problems of Rural Sociology"). The importance of focusing on rural communities in the process of dissolution and their survival as "archaic remnants and 'sociological fossils'" ("Perspectives on Rural Sociology") once again connects to wider historical–sociological themes of uneven development and the political economy of state formation. The link to Gramsci is again clear in terms of the common stress on the "epistemological significance" of class struggle, revolving around shaping state and subaltern class intersubjectivities internally related to the emergence of capitalism.[106] For Gramsci, this entailed tracing the residues of "common sense"—taken-for-granted "beliefs, superstitions, opinions, ways of seeing and of acting"—whether in popular folklore or superstitions, religious beliefs, or practices that are transformed in the attempt to engender a "modern outlook."[107] The principal worldview of peasant producers' common sense is therefore splintered in the first instance in terms of religion, with differences existing between the peasantry, the petits bourgeois, and town workers, women, or intellectuals.[108] Subsequently, the constitution of the human subject is composed of very contradictory ideological formations with common sense standing between elements of folklore and modern philosophy, science, and economics. Identity here is protean; "it contains Stone Age elements and principles of a more advanced science, prejudices from all past phases of history at the local level and intuitions of a future philosophy," often based on educational practices intended to call modernity into existence through the rudiments of natural science, a belief in objective laws, civic rights and duties, and the disciplining of work.[109] Such are the similar "sociological fossils" that attract Lefebvre's attention in these writings on the rural, the agrarian question, and the persistence of the peasantry with the uneven development of capitalism ("The Village Community," "The Valley of Campan"). At the fulcrum of that focus is the theory of ground rent and its transformation as a condition within the framework of feudalism to ground rent in the capitalistic sense, which is now the fourth and final original aspect to highlight in these writings on the rural as production of space.

The Theory of Ground Rent

The somewhat sotto voce discussion of Marx and Lenin on uneven development, land ownership, and capitalist exploitation of agriculture becomes a crescendo in "The Marxist–Leninist Theory of Ground Rent." Here the emphasis on the afterlife of feudalism reappears, with Lefebvre noting that a "semifeudal mode of production still stubbornly persists and survives" within French agrarian capitalism, through a constellation of factors marked by uneven development, overproduction, and permanent agricultural crisis. These factors are also confronted at the worldwide scale, too, within the overall crisis of capitalism. The nuance and detail that is added here, though, is the focus on ground rent specifically as an enduring legacy of feudalism and the need to engage the Marxist theory of ground rent, which is a "particularly complex and difficult theory and hard to get to grips with." "Ground rent," states Lefebvre in this essay, "is the only theory of *Capital* that goes beyond the study of capitalism and its laws" and merits sustained attention. Here the dialogue in the rural writings takes a crucial turn to Marx and especially the third volume of *Capital*, specifically in the focus on surplus profit and ground rent, as well as a set of writings by Lenin that includes *The Development of Capitalism in Russia*.[110] One particular puzzle for Lefebvre is how a monopoly that results from the historical form of landed property enables certain people to develop an economic value from this monopoly and thus valorize it within capitalist production. As Marx states, "The monopoly of landed property is a historical precondition for the capitalist mode of production and remains its permanent foundation."[111] How does feudal landed property and agriculture become subjected to capital and how does this transformation impact on capitalism as a mode of production? For Marx, "ground-rent is thus the form in which landed property is economically realized, valorized."[112] For Lefebvre, this distinction between landed property with its feudal origins and capitalist landlords is essential to understanding the competing roles of landowners and capitalists. The former lay claim to a monopoly of a piece of the earth, exacting a tribute and then subsequently a price, and the latter exact "improvements" on the land through a monopoly of capitalist exploitation with such capital investments arising in and impacting on differential surplus profits and the organic composition of capital. These issues, Lefebvre notes, animated Marx so much so that "just before his death, he had already begun researching a huge number of documents in reference to Russia" ("The Marxist–Leninist Theory of Ground Rent"), which appeared subsequently as *The Ethnological Notebooks of Karl Marx*.[113] It can also be found in pivotal commentaries about the "peripheries" of capitalism and the multilinear geographical scope of his critique of political economy.[114] The significance of these themes continues today in debates about primitive accumulation, decolonization, landownership, privatization, nationalization, the "new" international division of labor, and the role of the state.

Without the space here for a fuller exposition, some definitional guidance may nonetheless be helpful in navigating this essay on ground rent. The monopoly of landed property sets a barrier to the investment of capital because it commands a rent, a transfer of a portion of commodity prices and thus surplus profit, from the capitalist to the landowner in the form of a payment of absolute ground rent. Hence, "the monopoly to a piece of the earth enables the so-called landowner to exact a tribute, to put a price on it."[115] Following from that, "land pays ground-rent only when the individual produce price of its product is below the production price that governs the market, giving rise to a surplus profit that is transformed into rent."[116] Without the abolition of landed property, this barrier of the monopoly of landed property to the unrestricted valorization of capital remains. That is why, says Marx, there is a contrasting situation enacted through the violent expropriation of colonialism and through principles such as *terra nullius*:

> What makes a colony a colony—and here we are referring only to agricultural colonies proper—is not just the amount of fertile land. . . . It is rather that this land is not appropriated, is not subsumed under landed property.[117]

By contrast, with the economic valorization of landed property and the development of ground rent, surplus profits may accrue in two differential forms. First, if there are different portions of land that result in unequal productive amounts, as a result of the fertility of the soil and/or location, then this is recognized as Differential Rent I. Second, if there are additional and successive capital investments made on the same land and thus both capital and labor are involved in "improving" the land, then this is referred to as Differential Rent II because, "after the capital investment has been made, the land bears the rent not because capital has been invested in it but rather because the capital investment has made the land a more productive field of investment than before."[118] Here the metabolic interaction between capital and nature is transformative, and human labor as "a new and additional element goes into capital" on the land.[119]

The transition to capitalism in which the persistence of the old regime of landed property remains and the remnants and survivals of feudalism are evident, including their cultural forms, also presents itself in at least two different pathways. This is where Lenin enters the dialogue concerning the development of capitalism in Russia. He first describes the "Junker road," which is based on the persistence of the landlord economy whereby serfdom is retained and then slowly transformed into a capitalist "Junker" economy: "The basis of the final transition from labor-service to capitalism is the internal metamorphosis of feudalist landlord economy. The entire agrarian system of the state becomes capitalist and for a long time retains feudalist features."[120] In these instances, there is the retention of landed proprietorship alongside the executors of bourgeois revolution, leaving a predominant role for the liberal-monarchist bourgeois and landlord. His second model is the "peasant road," which is based on the persistence of peasant farming whereby the landlord economy is broken up by revolution, destroying the relics of serfdom and large landownership and leading to the free development of small peasant farming and the expropriation of the landlords' estates in the interests of the peasantry: "The entire agrarian system becomes capitalist, for the more completely the vestiges of serfdom are destroyed, the more rapidly does the differentiation of the peasantry proceed." Although infinite and diverse combinations may arise from these pathways, the destruction of landlordism is seen to unfold in the latter variant by "the speediest and freest development of the productive forces on a capitalist basis," because of the predominant role of the proletariat and the peasant masses vis-à-vis the neutralizing and unstable or counterrevolutionary bourgeoisie.[121]

For Lefebvre, all these strands of landed property, absolute and differential rent, and the alternative pathways embedded in the transition to capitalism come to bear on the role of the theory of rent and monopoly capitalism. The monopoly of land ownership is supplemented by the monopoly of capitalist exploitation with the two aspects of the "double monopoly" sitting in uneasy tension. As Lefebvre states, "There may be a fight between the monopoly of land ownership and that of exploitation to keep, to increase, or to lower absolute rent. There may be a fight for the distribution of differential rent" ("The Marxist–Leninist Theory of Ground Rent"). Nationalization of the land could be regarded as one response to this tension. However, this is why this essay on ground rent is so important to ongoing present-day debates on land ownership, privatization, and the role of the state and public landownership. In Lefebvre's assessment, "nationalization could do no more than abolish absolute rent by transferring it to the state." Nationalization of the land is therefore regarded as a category of bourgeois capitalist society because the nationalization of land may abolish absolute rent but it allows differential rent to remain: "In this way the theoretical concept of nationalization cannot be examined outside the theory of ground rent." It is to these class struggles and antagonisms over landownership between landed proprietors, land privatizers, and nationalization conferred in state ownership that this essay speaks. Land and its presuppositions and appurtenances in the form of ground rent show no signs of losing relevance, especially under the sway of privatizations and the "new enclosures" marked by neoliberalism.[122]

Conclusion: No Space Is Utterly Abolished

We have already indicated some of the themes that would concern Lefebvre in the 1960s and into the 1970s as he turned more and more to urban questions. Yet, as ever in his career, he was running multiple research themes in parallel. The republication of the first volume of *Critique of Everyday Life* in 1958, with a new preface as long as the original book, was followed by the second volume in 1961. The final volume appeared in 1981. His major theoretical statement *Metaphilosophy* was published in 1965, along with some other significant studies of Marx around the same time, including *The Sociology of Marx* in 1966; the two-volume *Œuvres choisis*, along with Guterman, in 1963 and 1966; and a standalone introduction to Marx in 1964.[123] *Everyday Life in the Modern World* was published in 1968.

The 1970s saw more urban studies, *The Production of Space*; *Hegel, Marx, Nietzsche* the four-volume book on the state, the critique of structuralism, and other works. The project on the state also continues his interest in the process of *mondialisation*, a becoming worldly or worldwide, which both anticipates and differs from the discussion of globalization (the French now use *globalisation* and *mondialisation* often interchangeably). This exhausting publication schedule continued until his death in 1991, with *Elements of Rhythmanalysis* appearing posthumously in 1992. Unlike many of his contemporaries, there has not been an extensive program of posthumous publication—Lefebvre published much more in his lifetime than many authors, but none of his lecture courses have appeared, and there is no publicly accessible archive of his papers, save for a few texts in the Guterman archive at Columbia University and some teaching records elsewhere.

For the Anglophone reader, this is perhaps not a major issue at present, since much of Lefebvre's work remains untranslated and therefore awaits discovery. This process of discovery or rediscovery is even the case for many French readers, since so many of Lefebvre's books are out of print. Lefebvre's rural work, however, is still largely available in French, even if relatively forgotten. This collection seeks to remedy both the accessibility and the neglect in the Anglophone world, finishing with Lefebvre's cue that "no space disappears completely, or is utterly abolished in the course of the process of social development—not even the natural place where that process began."[124] This is an insight that applies as much to the rural as the urban in the ongoing and contested production of space.

We have included a map to help orient readers in terms of the key places Lefebvre mentions and some other major towns in the region of the Western Pyrenees, including Hagetmau, where he was born, and Pau, where he died. But this is obviously a flattened cartographic representation, which does not give a sense of the topography, land use, or transport connections. These elements of space as it is inherited, organized, and lived are crucial, and hard to represent appropriately. Indications of the uneven development of the region are entirely lacking. The analysis Lefebvre makes helps add detail into this kind of picture, and so the map

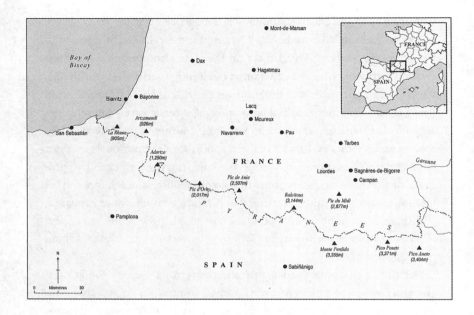

should be taken as an initial indication, and far from a comprehensive representation of rural economy, sociology, and geography.

Notes

1. For surveys of his work generally, see Rob Shields, *Lefebvre, Love & Struggle: Spatial Dialectics* (London: Routledge, 1999); Stuart Elden, *Understanding Henri Lefebvre: Theory and the Possible* (London: Continuum, 2004); and Andy Merrifield, *Henri Lefebvre: A Critical Introduction* (London: Routledge, 2006). Most of the other books on Lefebvre in English have a more restrictive focus on urban questions of space, of which the best is unquestionably Łukasz Stanek, *Henri Lefebvre on Space: Architecture, Urban Research, and the Production of Theory* (Minneapolis: University of Minnesota Press, 2011).

2. Henri Lefebvre, *Dialectical Materialism,* 2nd ed., trans. John Sturrock (Minneapolis: University of Minnesota Press, 2009 [1939]); Henri Lefebvre, *The Sociology of Marx,* trans. Nobert Guterman (London: Penguin, 1968 [1966]); Henri Lefebvre, *Everyday Life in the Modern World,* trans. Sacha Rabinovitch (Harmondsworth: Allen Lane, 1971 [1968]); Henri Lefebvre, *The Explosion: Marxism and the French Upheaval,* trans. Alfred Ehrenfeld (New York: Modern Reader, 1969 [1968]); Henri Lefebvre, *The Survival of Capitalism,* trans. Frank Bryant (London: Allison & Busby, 1976 [1973]).

3. Henri Lefebvre, *Critique of Everyday Life: Volume 1, Introduction,* trans. John Moore (London: Verso, 1991 [1947]); Henri Lefebvre, *The Production of Space,* trans. Donald Nicolson-Smith (Oxford: Blackwell, 1991 [1974]).

4. Henri Lefebvre, *Introduction to Modernity: Twelve Preludes,* trans. John Moore (London: Verso, 1995 [1962]); Henri Lefebvre, *Writings on Cities,* ed. and trans. Eleonore Kofman and Elisabeth Lebas (Oxford: Blackwell, 1996), including texts from 1966 and later.

5. Henri Lefebvre, *Key Writings,* ed. Stuart Elden, Elisabeth Lebas, and Eleonore Kofman (London: Continuum, 2003); Henri Lefebvre, *Rhythmanalysis: Space, Time and Everyday Life,* trans. Stuart Elden and Gerard Moore (London: Continuum, 2004 [1992]); Henri Lefebvre, *Critique of Everyday Life: The One-Volume Edition,* trans. John Moore and Gregory Elliott (London: Verso, 2014 [1947, 1961, 1981]); Henri Lefebvre, *The Urban Revolution,* trans. Robert Bononno (Minneapolis: University of Minnesota Press, 2003 [1970]); Henri Lefebvre, *State, Space, World: Selected Essays,* ed. Stuart Elden and Neil Brenner, trans. Gerald Moore, Stuart Elden, and Neil Brenner (Minneapolis: University of Minnesota Press, 2009).

6. Henri Lefebvre, *Toward an Architecture of Enjoyment,* ed. Łukasz Stanek, trans. Robert Bononno (Minneapolis: University of Minnesota Press, 2014); Henri Lefebvre, *Marxist Thought and the City,* trans. Robert Bononno (Minneapolis: University of Minnesota Press, 2016 [1972]); Henri Lefebvre, *Metaphilosophy,* ed. Stuart Elden, trans. David Fernbach (London: Verso, 2016 [1965]); Henri Lefebvre, *Hegel, Marx, Nietzsche: Or the Realm of Shadows,* trans. David Fernbach (London: Verso, 2020 [1975]).

7. Henri Lefebvre, *De l'État,* 4 vols. (Paris: UGE, 1976–78).

8. Two pioneering studies were Mark Poster, *Existential Marxism in Post-War France: From Sartre to Althusser* (Princeton, N.J.: Princeton University Press, 1975); and Michael Kelly, *Modern French Marxism* (Oxford: Blackwell, 1982). See also Elden, *Understanding Henri Lefebvre,* especially chapter 1; Kanishka Goonewardena, Stefan Kipfer, Richard Milgrom, and Christian Schmid, eds., *Space, Difference, Everyday Life: Reading Henri Lefebvre* (New York: Routledge, 2008); Benjamin Fraser, ed., *Toward an Urban Cultural Studies: Henri Lefebvre and the Humanities* (London: Palgrave, 2015); and Michael E. Leary and John P. McCarthy, eds., *The Routledge Handbook of Henri Lefebvre, The City and Urban Society* (London: Routledge, 2019).

9. See, in particular, Henri Lefebvre, *L'existentialisme,* 2nd ed. (Paris: Anthropos, 2001 [1946]); Henri Lefebvre, *Le marxisme* (Paris: Presses Universitaires de France, 1948); Henri Lefebvre, *Marx* (Paris: Gallimard, 1964); Henri Lefebvre, *Au dèla du structuralisme* (Paris: Anthropos, 1971).

10. Henri Lefebvre, *La fin de l'histoire* (Paris: Éditions de Minuit, 1970); Henri Lefebvre, *La somme et le reste,* 3rd ed. (Paris: Meridiens Klincksieck, 1989 [1959]).

11. A significant exception is Nick Entrikin and Vincent Berdoulay, "The Pyrenees as Place: Lefebvre as Guide," *Progress in Human Geography* 29, no. 2 (2005): 129–47. See Elden, *Understanding Henri Lefebvre*, 127–47.

12. See Lefebvre, *Key Writings*, 111–20.

13. Henri Lefebvre, "The Theory of Ground Rent and Rural Sociology," trans. Matthew Dennis, ed. Stuart Elden and Adam David Morton, *Antipode* 48, no. 1 (2016): 67–73. This was prefaced by Stuart Elden and Adam David Morton, "Thinking Past Henri Lefebvre: Introducing 'The Theory of Ground Rent and Rural Sociology,'" *Antipode* 48, no. 1 (2016): 57–66, the themes of which have been developed for this introduction.

14. Lefebvre, *Critique of Everyday Life: Volume 1*, 201–27.

15. As John Moore indicates, Lefebvre wrote his diploma thesis on Jansen and Pascal, under the supervision of Léon Brunschvicq. See Lefebvre, *Critique of Everyday Life: Volume 1*, 272n8.

16. Henri Lefebvre, *Critique de la vie quotidienne I: Introduction*, 2nd ed. (Paris: L'Arche, 1958 [1947]), 238; Lefebvre, *Critique of Everyday Life: Volume 1*, 224.

17. Lefebvre, *Introduction to Modernity*, 116–26.

18. Henri Lefebvre, *Introduction à la modernité: Préludes* (Paris: Les Éditions de Minuit, 1962), 121; Lefebvre, *Introduction to Modernity*, 116.

19. Henri Lefebvre, "Introduction: Le même et l'autre," in *Recherches philosophiques sur l'essence de la liberté humaine et sur les problèmes qui s'y attachment*, by Friedrich Schelling, trans. Georges Politzer (Paris: F. Rieder, 1926), 7–64. Lefebvre's essay is untranslated, but Schelling's work appears as *Philosophical Investigations into the Essence of Human Freedom*, trans. Jeff Love and Johannes Schmidt (Albany: State University of New York Press, 2006).

20. On this period, the best accounts are Bud Burkhard, *French Marxism between the Wars: Henri Lefebvre and the "Philosophies"* (New York: Humanity Books, 2000); and the work of Michel Trebitsch, notably "Les mésaventures du groupe Philosophies, 1924–1933," *La revue des revues*, no. 3 (Spring 1987): 6–9. For Lefebvre's recollections, see "A Group of Young Philosophers: A Conversation with Henri Lefebvre," Bernard-Henri Lévy *Adventures on the Freedom Road: The French Intellectuals in the Twentieth Century*, trans. Richard Vesey (London: Harvill, 1991), 131–38.

21. See Karl Marx, "Travail et propriété privée," *La revue marxiste*, no. 1 (February 1929): 7–28; Karl Marx, "Notes sur les besoins, la production et la division du travail," *La revue marxiste*, no. 5 (June 1929): 513–38; Karl Marx, "Critique de la dialectique hégélienne," *Avant-Poste*, no. 1 (June 1933): 33–39, and no. 2 (August 1933): 110–16.

22. Karl Marx, *Morceaux choisis*, introduced by Henri Lefebvre and Norbert Guterman, selected by P. Y. Nizan and J. Duret (Paris: Gallimard, 1934); G. W. F. Hegel, *Morceaux choisis*, trans. Henri Lefebvre and Norbert Guterman (Paris:

Gallimard, 1938); Vladimir Lenin, *Cahiers de Lénine sur la dialectique de Hegel*, rev. ed., trans. Henri Lefebvre and Norbert Guterman (Paris: Gallimard, 1967 [1938]).

23. Marina Galletti and Alastair Brotchie, "Chronology," in *The Sacred Conspiracy: The Internal Papers of the Secret Society of Acéphale*, by Georges Bataille, ed. Marina Galletti and Alastair Brotchie (London: Atlas Press, 2017), 94.

24. Henri Lefebvre, *Le nationalisme contre les nations*, 2nd ed. (Paris: Meridiens Klincksieck, 1988 [1937]); Henri Lefebvre, *Hitler au pouvoir, les enseignements de cinq annees de fascisme en Allemagne* (Paris: Bureau d'Editions, 1938).

25. Henri Lefebvre and Norbert Guterman, *La conscience mystifiée*, 3rd ed. (Paris: Éditions Syllepse, 1999 [1936]); Henri Lefebvre, *Nietzsche*, 2nd ed. (Paris: Editions Syllepse, 2003 [1939]).

26. See René Lourau, "Préface: L'espace Henri Lefebvre," in Henri Lefebvre, *Pyrénées*, 2nd ed. (Pau: Cairn, 2000 [1965]), 9–13, 11.

27. See Rémi Hess, *Henri Lefebvre et l'aventure du siècle* (Paris: A.M. Métaillée, 1988), 112–16.

28. Lefebvre, *La somme et le reste*, 550.

29. Henri Lefebvre, *Les communautés paysannes pyrénéennes* (Bagnères-de-Bigorre: Société Ramond / Cercle Historique de l'Arribière, 2014), published posthumously; Henri Lefebvre, *La vallée de Campan: Étude de sociologie rurale*, 2nd ed. (Paris: Presses Universitaires de France, 1990 [1963]).

30. Stanek, *Henri Lefebvre on Space*, 9.

31. Hess, *Henri Lefebvre et l'aventure du siècle*, 165–68.

32. There are a few related pieces not collected by Lefebvre in *Du rural à l'urbain* and not included as supplements in this book. See Jean Ballard, André Chamson, Henri Lefebvre, Armand Lunel, Charles Parain, and Albert Soboul, "Opinions sur le regionalisme," *Annales de l'Institut d'études occitanes* 5 (1950): 6–14; and Henri Lefebvre, Jean Daric, Paul Gemaehling, Theodore Caplow, Paul Leuilliot, and Jean Stoetzel, "Structures familiales comparées," in *Villes et campagnes*, ed. Georges Friedmann (Paris: Armand Colin, 1956), 327–62.

33. As well as pieces included here, from this period see Henri Lefebvre, "Marxisme et sociologie," *Cahiers internationaux de Sociologie* 4 (1948): 48–74; Henri Lefebvre, "La notion de totalité dans les sciences sociales," *Cahiers internationaux de Sociologie* 18 (1955): 55–77; and Henri Lefebvre, "De l'explication en économie politique et en sociologie," *Cahiers internationaux de Sociologie* 21 (1956): 19–36.

34. Hess, *Henri Lefebvre et l'aventure du siècle*, 169–70; Michel Trebitsch, "Preface," in *Critique of Everyday Life: Volume 1*, xxv.

35. See the discussion in Ballard et al., "Opinions sur le régionalisme"; Lefebvre's contribution to the discussion that follows Albert Soboul, "La communauté rural (XVIIIe–XIXe siècle): Problèmes de base," *Revue de synthèse* 7 (1957): 283–316, especially 310–12; and Henri Lefebvre, "What Is the Historical Past?," *New Left Review* 90 (1975): 27–34, originally published as "Qu'est-ce que le passé historique?,"

Les Temps Modernes 161 (1959): 159–69. The latter is a review of Soboul's *The Sans-culottes: The Popular Movement and Revolutionary Government, 1793–1794*, trans. Remy Inglis Hall (Princeton, N.J.: Princeton University Press, 1972). For a discussion, see Stanek, *Henri Lefebvre on Space*, 5–8.

36. Hess, *Henri Lefebvre et l'aventure du siècle*, 169.

37. See Hess, *Henri Lefebvre et l'aventure du siècle*, 166–67; and Rémi Hess, "Presentation de la troisième edition," Henri Lefebvre, *Du rural à l'urbain*, 3rd ed. (Paris: Anthropos, 2001 [1970]), v–xxvi, xix–xx.

38. This important piece appears in none of the main bibliographies of Lefebvre's work (Hess, Shields, Elden, Stanek). For a brief discussion of the conference at which it was presented, see Pierre George, "Deux Congrès internatioaux sur les problèmes de population et de développement économique," *Bulletin de l'Association de Géographes Français*, nos. 245–46 (1954): 138–46.

39. Lefebvre, *De l'État*, 3:269–371.

40. Hess, *Henri Lefebvre et l'aventure du siècle*, 169–70; Stanek, *Henri Lefebvre on Space*, 15.

41. Hess, "Presentation de la troisième edition," xx; see also Hess, *Henri Lefebvre et l'aventure du siècle*, 167–68.

42. Quoted in Hess, *Henri Lefebvre et l'aventure du siècle*, 168. For a detailed discussion of how a richer notion of land in Adam Smith is reduced to merely rent in David Ricardo, see Leo Steeds, "Earth, Property, Territory: The Birth of an Economic Conception of Land" (PhD diss., University of Warwick, 2020).

43. Henri Lefebvre, *Le marxisme* (Paris: Presses Universitaires de France, 1948); Henri Lefebvre, *Pour connaître la pensée de Marx* (Paris: Bordas, 1947); Henri Lefebvre, *Marx et la liberté* (Genève-Paris: Trois Collines, 1947); Henri Lefebvre, *Logique formelle, logique dialectique*, 2nd ed. (Paris: Anthropos, 1969 [1947]).

44. Henri Lefebvre, *Méthodologie des sciences: Un inédit* (Paris: Anthropos, 2002).

45. Henri Lefebvre, *Descartes* (Paris: Éditions Hier et Aujourd'hui, 1947); Henri Lefebvre, *Diderot ou les affirmations fondamentales du matérialisme*, 2nd ed. (Paris: L'Arche, 1983 [1949]); Henri Lefebvre, *Pascal*, 2 vols (Paris: Nagel, 1949 and 1954); Henri Lefebvre, *Rabelais*, 2nd ed. (Paris: Anthropos, 2001 [1955]); Henri Lefebvre, *Musset*, 2nd ed. (Paris: L'Arche, 1970 [1955]); Henri Lefebvre, *Pignon* (Paris: Édition Falaise, 1956).

46. Henri Lefebvre, *Contribution à l'esthétique*, 2nd ed. (Paris: Anthropos, 2001 [1953]) For a discussion, see Lefebvre, *La somme et le reste*, 536–39; and Elden, *Understanding Henri Lefebvre*, 85–86.

47. Henri Lefebvre, *Pour connaître la pensée de Lénine* (Paris: Bordas, 1957); Henri Lefebvre, *Problèmes actuels du marxisme* (Paris: Presses Universitaires de France, 1958). For the repudiation, which is in part because Louis Althusser praised the book, see the discussion in Henri Lefebvre and Catherine Régulier, *La revolution n'est plus ce qu'elle etait* (Paris: Libres-Hallier, 1978), 103–4.

48. Henri Lefebvre, *Le temps des méprises* (Paris: Stock, 1975), 89–97.
49. Henri Lefebvre, *Problèmes actuels du marxisme*, 2nd ed. (Paris: Presses Universitaires de France, 1960 [1958]).
50. Henri Lefebvre, *La production de l'espace*, 4th ed. (Paris: Anthropos, 2000 [1974]), 372; Lefebvre, *The Production of Space*, 323.
51. Lefebvre, *La production de l'espace*, 375; Lefebvre, *The Production of Space*, 325.
52. Lefebvre, *La production de l'espace* 138, 345, 399–400; Lefebvre, *The Production of Space*, 116, 299, 346.
53. Stanek, *Henri Lefebvre on Space*, ix, 19–20.
54. On this, with some plans and archive photographs, see Stanek, *Henri Lefebvre on Space*, especially 106–16.
55. Lefebvre, *Le temps des méprises*, 222.
56. Hess, *Henri Lefebvre et l'aventure du siècle*, 176.
57. Lefebvre, *Le temps des méprises*, 222.
58. Stanek, *Henri Lefebvre on Space*, is excellent on the detailed research that lay behind, and led to, his more famous theories of space.
59. Henri Lefebvre, *Espace et politique: Le droit à la ville II*, 2nd ed. (Paris: Anthropos, 2000 [1972]). Some parts of this book are already in English: "Reflections on the Politics of Space," in Lefebvre, *State, Space, World*, 167–84; and "Introduction" and "Institutions in a 'Post-technological' Society," in Lefebvre, *Writings on Cities*, 185–97, 198–202. The latter is an incomplete translation of the French chapter. The chapter "Engels and Utopia" was included in later editions of *La pensée marxiste et la ville*, having been cut from the original due to word limits (see Lefebvre, *Espace et politique*, 81n). It is translated in Lefebvre, *Marxist Thought and the City*, 95–108. One other chapter of *Du rural à l'urbain* is partly translated in Lefebvre, *Key Writings*, 121–35.
60. Jean-Paul Sartre, "Questions de méthode," in *Critique de la raison dialectique* (Paris: Gallimard, 1985 [1960]), 50–51n1; Jean-Paul Sartre, *Search for a Method*, trans. Hazel E. Barnes (New York: Vintage, 1968), 51–52n8.
61. Henri Lefebvre, "Introduction to *From the Rural to the Urban*," in *Du rural à l'urbain* (Paris: Anthropos, 1970), 7–20; Lefebvre, *Le temps des méprises*, 143–44; Lefebvre, *La Production de l'espace*, 79–80n1; Lefebvre, *The Production of Space*, 66n37, where he objects to the method being attributed to Sartre himself.
62. Karl Marx, *Grundrisse: Foundations of the Critique of Political Economy*, trans. Martin Nicolaus (Penguin: Harmondsworth, 1973), 105. See also Henri Lefebvre, *Une pensée devenue monde: Faut-il abandonner Marx?* (Paris: Fayard, 1980), 99–100.
63. For a helpful discussion, see Michael Kelly, "Towards a Heuristic Method: Sartre and Lefebvre," *Sartre Studies International* 5, no. 1 (1999): 1–15.
64. Lefebvre, *La Production de l'espace*, 386; Lefebvre, *The Production of Space*, 335.

65. Philip McMichael, "Incorporating Comparison within a World-Historical Perspective: An Alternative Comparative Method," *American Sociological Review* 55, no. 3 (1990): 385–97.

66. Adam David Morton, *Revolution and State in Modern Mexico: The Political Economy of Uneven Development*, updated ed. (Lanham, Md.: Rowman & Littlefield, 2013), 244–46; Gillian Hart, "Relational Comparison Revisited: Marxist Postcolonial Geographies in Practice," *Progress in Human Geography* 42, no. 3 (2018): 371–94.

67. Henri Lefebvre, *La survie du capitalisme: La reproduction des rapports de production*, 3rd ed. (Paris: Anthropos, 2002 [1973]), 3; Lefebvre, *The Survival of Capitalism*, 8.

68. Karl Marx, *Capital: A Critique of Political Economy*, vol. 3, trans. David Fernbach (London: Penguin, 1981), 130. There is a contribution to literary economy in Balzac's work that, as David Harvey has noted, depicts a spatial patterning of social order so that his novels "focus on processes of social change after the restoration of monarchy on 1814 and frequently lament the failure to accomplish a 'real' restoration of progressive aristocratic, Catholic, and monarchical power in the wake of the catastrophic end of Empire." See David Harvey, *Paris, Capital of Modernity* (London: Routledge, 2003), 52. Among other writings, the short story *Le Chef-d'œuvre inconnu* (*The Unknown Masterpiece*, 1831) by Balzac also had significant influence on Marx as the poet of the dialectic. See Francis Wheen, *Marx's "Das Kapital": A Biography* (London: Atlantic Books, 2006), 1–6. Balzac was a constant reference for Lefebvre, with discussions in *Contribution à l'esthétique*, especially 84–87, and many of his novels used to illustrate points in *Introduction to Modernity*. In *Hegel, Marx, Nietzsche* (211n22/190n26), in a French twist to the modern myth, Lefebvre suggests that a typing monkey will eventually produce *La comédie humaine*, the multivolume work that contains most of Balzac's literary output.

69. Thomas Piketty, *Capital in the Twenty-First Century*, trans. Arthur Goldhammer (Cambridge, Mass.: Belknap Press of Harvard University Press, 2014), 2; Thomas Piketty, *Capital and Ideology*, trans. Arthur Goldhammer (Cambridge, Mass.: Belknap Press of Harvard University Press, 2020), 15.

70. See also Adam David Morton, "The Architecture of 'Passive Revolution': Society, State and Space in Modern Mexico," *Journal of Latin American Studies* 20, no. 1 (2018): 117–52.

71. Lefebvre, *La vallée de Campan*, 220.

72. Stanek, *Henri Lefebvre on Space*, 5–7. For a discussion of the Campan study, see Stanek, *Henri Lefebvre on Space*, 53–57.

73. Lefebvre, *Key Writings*, 121–35. The translation omits a short passage (128). The book this prefaced was a product of work at the ISU. See Henri Raymond, Nicole Haumont, Marie-Geneviève Dezès, and Antoine Haumont, *L'Habitat Pavillonnaire* (repr., Paris: L'Harmattan, 2001 [1966]).

74. Henri Lefebvre, *Pyrénées* (Lausanne: Editions Recontre, 1965). The second edition (cited in n. 26) is largely unillustrated.

75. Entrikin and Berdoulay, "The Pyrenees as Place," 138. Subsequent parts of this essay provide a summary of the book.

76. Entrikin and Berdoulay, "The Pyrenees as Place," 138, citing an interview with Catherine Régulier, March 9, 1999.

77. Yuval Karplus, "The Production of Space: A Neglected Perspective in Pastoral Research," *Environment and Planning D: Society and Space* 31, no. 1 (2013): 23–42; Mara Duer, "The Right to Belong to the Land: Coloniality and Resistance in the Araucanía" (PhD diss., University of Warwick, 2017); Chris Hesketh, *Spaces of Capital / Spaces of Resistance: Mexico and the Global Political Economy* (Athens: University of Georgia Press, 2017); Teo Ballvé, *The Frontier Effect: State Formation and Violence in Colombia* (Ithaca, N.Y.: Cornell University Press, 2020); Martín Arboleda, *Planetary Mine: Territories of Extraction under Late Capitalism* (London: Verso, 2020).

78. Keith Halfacree, "Rural Space: Constructing a Three-Fold Architecture," in *Handbook of Rural Studies*, ed. Paul Cloke, Terry Marsden, and Patrick Mooney (London: SAGE, 2006), 44–62, quote on 44.

79. Halfacree, "Rural Space," 49.

80. Karl Kautsky, *On the Agrarian Question*, trans. Pete Burgess (London: Zwan, 1988 [1899]).

81. V. I. Lenin, *Materialism and Empirio-Criticism: Critical Comments on a Reactionary Philosophy* (Moscow: Foreign Languages Publishing House, 1952 [1908]), 135.

82. Lenin, *Materialism and Empirio-Criticism*, 270.

83. Lenin, *Materialism and Empirio-Criticism*, 344. As reaffirmed by Antonio Gramsci, *Selections from the Prison Notebooks*, ed. and trans. Quintin Hoare and Geoffrey Nowell-Smith (London: Lawrence and Wishart, 1971), 465: "It has been forgotten that in the case of a very common expression [historical materialism] one should put the accent on the first term—'historical'—and not on the second, which is of metaphysical origin. The philosophy of praxis is absolute 'historicism,' the absolute secularization and earthliness of thought, an absolute humanism of history."

84. Lenin, *Materialism and Empirio-Criticism*, 235, 277.

85. Marx, *Capital*, 3:421. See also Derek Sayer, *The Violence of Abstraction: The Analytic Foundations of Historical Materialism* (London: Basil Blackwell, 1987).

86. Marx, *Capital*, 3:268–9.

87. Karl Marx, *Capital: A Critique of Political Economy*, vol. 2, trans. David Fernbach (London: Penguin, 1992), 185.

88. Henri Lefebvre, *Le matérialisme dialectique* (Paris: Presses Universitaires de France, 1971 [1940]), 26, 27, 78; Lefebvre, *Dialectical Materialism*, 22, 23, 84–85. It is

noteworthy that Bertell Ollman, *Alienation: Marx's Conception of Man in Capitalist Society*, 2nd ed. (Cambridge: Cambridge University Press, 1976), 276, includes, in a canon of theorists, Lefebvre as a contributor to the philosophy of internal relations. Witness also Ollman's earlier praise for Lefebvre as a dialectician that held "no-boundary interaction" in his theorizing, meaning that "the relations between parts of a system which possesses no truly separate parts can only be internal relations." Bertell Ollman, "Review: Henri Lefebvre," *The Sociology of Marx*, trans. Norbert Guterman," *American Journal of Sociology* 74, no. 9 (1969): 436.

89. Lefebvre, *Le matérialisme dialectique*, 82; Lefebvre, *Dialectical Materialism*, 77.

90. Lefebvre, *La production de l'espace*, 68; Lefebvre, *The Production of Space*, 55.

91. See Gramsci, *Selections from the Prison Notebooks*, 106–14. This theme is expanded on in Adam David Morton, "The Continuum of Passive Revolution," *Capital & Class* 34, no. 3 (2010): 315–42. Although Lefebvre is rather dismissive of Gramsci's development of the philosophy of praxis and his emphasis on the "Modern Prince" of the party in Lefebvre, *The Sociology of Marx*, 37—perhaps because of his break with the French Communist Party—this stance becomes more nuanced later. In tracing the constitution of capitalistic space, Gramsci becomes situated within the reconnaissance of space: "Is it conceivable that the exercise of hegemony might leave space untouched? Could space be nothing more than the passive locus of social relations, the milieu in which their combination takes on body, or the aggregate of the procedures employed in their removal?" Lefebvre, *La production de l'espace*, 18; Lefebvre,*The Production of Space*, 11.

92. Eric Hobsbawm, *Age of Extremes: The Short Twentieth Century, 1914–1991* (London: Michael Joseph, 1994), 289–93; Roger Bartra, *Agrarian Structure and Political Power in Mexico*, trans. Stephen K. Ault (Baltimore, Md.: Johns Hopkins University Press, 1993); Alain De Janvry, *The Agrarian Question and Reformism in Latin America* (Baltimore, Md.: Johns Hopkins University Press, 1981).

93. E. P. Thompson, "Eighteenth-Century English Society: Class Struggle without Class?," *Social History* 3, no. 2 (1978): 133–65. See also Morton, *Revolution and State in Modern Mexico*, 208, 268; Andreas Bieler and Adam David Morton, *Global Capitalism, Global War, Global Crisis* (Cambridge: Cambridge University Press, 2018), 43–44.

94. E. P. Thompson, *The Making of the English Working Class* (London: Penguin, 1968), 8.

95. Gramsci, *Selections from the Prison Notebooks*, 52–55.

96. Gramsci, *Selections from the Prison Notebooks*, 52.

97. Gramsci, *Selections from the Prison Notebooks*, 52.

98. Gramsci, *Selections from the Prison Notebooks*, 54–55.

99. Gramsci, *Selections from the Prison Notebooks*, 55.

100. Gramsci, *Selections from the Prison Notebooks*, 56n5.

101. Neil Brenner, *New State Spaces: Urban Governance and the Rescaling of Statehood* (Oxford: Oxford University Press, 2004), 77–80.

102. See Lefebvre, "De l'explication en économie politique et en sociologie," 35–36.

103. Elden, *Understanding Henri Lefebvre*, 216, 243. See also Ari Jerrems, "'An Opening Toward the Possible': Assembly Politics and Henri Lefebvre's Theory of the Event," *Global Society* 34, no. 2 (2020): 224–44.

104. See Chris Hesketh, "The Survival of Non-capitalism," *Environment and Planning D: Society and Space* 34, no. 5 (2016): 877–94.

105. In the prolegomenon to the more detailed exposition of primitive accumulation in Karl Marx, *Capital: A Critique of Political Economy*, vol. 1, trans. Ben Fowkes (London: Penguin, 1990 [1867]), 877–95, and the role played by the Duchess of Sutherland, note that Marx also tracks the transformation of feudal patriarchal property relations and the condition of consanguinity within the Scotch-Gaelic clan system and its transformation into private property in his dispatches for the *New-York Tribune*. See Karl Marx, "The Duchess of Sutherland and Slavery" (February 8–9, 1853), in *Dispatches for the New York Tribune: Selected Journalism of Karl Marx*, ed. James Ledbetter (London: Penguin, 2007), 113–19.

106. See Gramsci, *Selections from the Prison Notebooks*, 365; and Adam David Morton, *Unravelling Gramsci: Hegemony and Passive Revolution in the Global Political Economy* (London: Pluto Press, 2007), 61–63.

107. Gramsci, *Selections from the Prison Notebooks*, 34, 323.

108. Gramsci, *Selections from the Prison Notebooks*, 420.

109. Gramsci, *Selections from the Prison Notebooks*, 33–35, 324.

110. Marx, *Capital*, 3:751–950; V. I. Lenin, *The Development of Capitalism in Russia* (Moscow: Foreign Languages Publishing House, 1974 [1899]).

111. Marx, *Capital*, 3:754.

112. Marx, *Capital*, 3:756.

113. Lawrence Krader, ed., *The Ethnological Notebooks of Karl Marx* (Assen: Van Gorcum & Com., 1974).

114. See Theodor Shanin, ed., *Late Marx and the Russian Road: Marx and the "Peripheries" of Capitalism* (New York: Monthly Review Press, 1983); and Kevin Anderson, *Marx at the Margins: On Nationalism, Ethnicity and Non-Western Societies* (Chicago: University of Chicago Press, 2010).

115. Marx, *Capital*, 3:762.

116. Marx, *Capital*, 3:882.

117. Marx, *Capital*, 3:890.

118. Marx, *Capital*, 3:880.

119. Marx, *Capital*, 3:879.

120. Lenin, *The Development of Capitalism in Russia*, 32.

121. Lenin, *The Development of Capitalism in Russia*, 33.

122. See Brett Christophers, *The New Enclosure: The Appropriation of Public Land in Neoliberal Britain* (London: Verso, 2018).

123. Karl Marx, *Œuvres choisis,* 2 vols., ed. Henri Lefebvre and Norbert Guterman (Paris: Gallimard, 1963–66); Lefebvre, *Marx*.

124. Lefebvre, *La production de l'espace,* 463; Lefebvre, *The Production of Space,* 403.

Notes on Translation

The texts that follow have been translated by Robert Bononno, with two exceptions. Chapter 7 was translated by Matthew Dennis, initially for the journal *Antipode,* and Sîan Rosa Hunter Dodsworth translated the Spanish text in chapter 8. As editors, we have tried to render these texts consistent in terminology. At times, Bononno smooths over the idiosyncrasies of Lefebvre's expression, getting rid of some of the peculiar punctuation and other oddities, such as the way he sometimes describes himself as "the author (ego)," which becomes simply "I." In this way, we think that often Lefebvre reads better in English than he did in his original French. As fascinating and important as Lefebvre is, he is not the greatest prose stylist. Through the exercise of translation, Hunter Dodsworth often commented on the "oral" quality of the prose, with it reading like it was dictated. The story that Lefebvre did indeed dictate many of his books to female typists is quite well known.

A few notes on conceptual terms may be helpful. *Propriété* is translated as both "estate" and "property," depending on the sense; the related term *propriétaire* is translated as "owner." *Exploitation* is translated as "exploitation," as in one person exploiting another. It is also the French term for "farm," however, so it has been translated as this where appropriate and generally marked in the text. Related to this, Lefebvre also uses two terms for "farmer": *exploitant* (most frequently) and *agriculteur* (more rarely). These have both been translated as "farmer," although occasionally *exploitant* has been translated as "profiteer" when Lefebvre uses both terms in the same sentence or when he seems to be emphasizing the exploitative nature of the farmer to those who work for him.

Le monde, le mondial, and *l'échelle mondiale* have been translated as "world," "the worldwide," and "world scale," following established practice with Lefebvre. Although today these words are often used interchangeably with *le globe* or *globale*, Lefebvre marks the difference more carefully. When Lefebvre uses *global*, this has a sense of the "general" rather than "global." In his writings later than those collected here, he always talks of *mondialisation* and not of *globalisation*, as a process of becoming worldly or worldwide. The world for Lefebvre is a scale, whereas the general is a level of analysis, not a scale. For this reason, it is also important to distinguish between *niveaux* (levels) and *échelles* (scales). Lefebvre's fullest discussion of this question can be found in a key chapter of *The Urban Revolution*.[1]

Lefebvre also distinguishes between *la vie quotidienne* (everyday life), *le quotidien* (the everyday), and *quotidienneté* (everydayness), as do the translations here, especially chapter 9. This contrasts with other translations, where *le quotidien* has often been translated as "everyday life" and *quotidienneté* as "the everyday," and follows the practice found in previous translations of Lefebvre's work, including *Key Writings* and *The Critique of Everyday Life*.

We have also taken on the laborious task of checking and completing Lefebvre's references. Like many of his generation, Lefebvre was notoriously careless with his references, which were often not provided, sometimes failed to provide key information, or made errors in what was given. We have tried to provide accurate references, including to English translations where available. Minor errors in references have been cleaned up for consistency. We, and Robert Bononno, have also added some explanatory references that we hope are helpful and not excessive. These notes are indicated as translator or editor notes; unlabeled notes are Lefebvre's own. Quotations from non-English texts in the introduction or notes without an English reference are translated by the editors.

Note

1. Henri Lefebvre, *The Urban Revolution*, trans. Robert Bononno (Minneapolis: University of Minnesota Press, 2003), 77–102. The same chapter is also partly translated in Henri Lefebvre, *Key Writings*, ed. Stuart Elden, Elisabeth Lebas, and Eleonore Kofman (London: Continuum, 2003), 136–50. For discussions and developments, see, for example, Neil Brenner, *New Urban Spaces: Urban Theory and the Scale Question* (Oxford: Oxford University Press, 2019).

Acknowledgments

We would like to thank the journal *Antipode* for its initial support of our work, and for allowing us to reprint chapter 7, as well as the Independent Social Research Foundation (ISRF) Flexible Grants for Small Groups Competition (FG2) for the project "Henri Lefebvre's Writings on Rural Sociology, Ground Rent and the Politics of Land," which funded the translation work. The financial support of the University of Sydney's Faculty of Arts and Social Sciences (FASS) Research Support Scheme as well as the Centre for International Security Studies (CISS), directed by James Der Derian, and the Institutional Research Support Fund at the University of Warwick are also gratefully acknowledged. We warmly thank our translators, Robert Bononno, Matthew Dennis, and Sîan Rosa Hunter Dodsworth for their work in rendering Lefebvre's often unwieldy prose into readable English. We also thank Oliver Davis, Natalie Bouchard, and Inanna Hamati-Ataya for their help with two of the notes, and Neil Brenner, Andy Merrifield, Bruno Siqueira Fernandes, and Łukasz Stanek for their support and enthusiasm for Lefebvre's work. Chris Orton of Durham University's Cartography Unit drew the map. We are grateful to Jason Weidemann and his colleagues at the University of Minnesota Press for their support with this volume, and their patience over its long gestation. Sheila McMahon copyedited the text, Lisa Scholey compiled the index; Daniel Ochsner and Neil West coordinated the production.

CHAPTER 1

Introduction to
From the Rural to the Urban

These essays, published between 1949 and 1969, summarize a twenty-year journey (France's embrace of "modernity") interspersed by various milestones.[1]

My point of departure was the study of philosophy and its critique, conducted simultaneously. I taught philosophy, continued to read Nietzsche, as always (with Nietzsche it has always been a fight, ever since adolescence, the struggle between angel and demon), and Marx and Hegel.[2] Periodically, and with their various appearances, Husserl, Heidegger, and, of course, Freud. None of which unfolded, especially after becoming a part of the Communist movement (and communism, that is to say, the Party, which, in 1928, was then a movement), without increasingly deep contradictions. These were initially unsettling, then stimulating, at least until they became sterile.

What was coming into view, through philosophy itself, was the critique of philosophy. "Theoretical man," refuted, rejected by Nietzsche, coincided with the philosopher. For many years there was something disturbing about this refutation, which risked slipping into the irrational, a claim made even more dangerous by fascism. But at the same time (after 1930), the works of Marx's youth were discovered, disseminated, translated, and slowly assimilated.[3] This led to a revival of Hegelianism, the theory of contradictions, of dialectics, alone capable of guiding thought in the midst of the chaos of contradictions at a time when we were slipping into war. And what did those texts of Marx say, what did they contain? The process of philosophy. Although Marxism is more than a theory of political economy (an economism), it cannot claim to be a philosophical system. Along with economism, philosophism began to crumble. So, what is Marxism? How can we define historical materialism, dialectical materialism, and their relationship? Considered philosophically, Marxism can only be considered from the standpoint of dialectics (Hegelian) and, yet, cannot be viewed as an improved version of Hegelianism. Materialist systematization has the same drawbacks as the older, idealist systemizations. Throughout those years, when dogmatism grew stronger, and already Stalinist, when the sense of system was confused with the sense of organization, with the sense, dare I say, of the party, when Marxism became institutionalized and an official ideology, when the threatened movement froze in place instead of spreading, throughout those years doubt crept into the "essence" of Marxist thought. Only recently emergent and recognized, the concept of alienation was already being contested by those who should have adopted it. They saw it as an additional danger. Some went so far as to claim that the concept provided fuel to the menacing fire of the "class enemy." Why? Because the concept of *alienation* already contained a political component. It could be used to characterize political alienation, alienation by the State, and by the party. Already, Stalinism, as such, at the very interior of Marxism, was the target: from such concepts, it could be *defined*. Marxism? Maybe it didn't provide a philosophy, a system, a definitive model of thought and action but a way forward, namely, the *realization of philosophy through its radical critique*.

Philosophy, while necessary, is neither sufficient nor self-sufficient. This is the conclusion that emerged from experience (politics, practice, and theory together) during those years. Such considerations didn't interrupt the war but they did staunch its public expression. Was it merely a question of adding a scientific varnish to philosophy? No. This addition, this complement to classical philosophy (speculative, contemplative), this superficial correction of philosophical illusions, is the attitude of the liberal bourgeoisie. It's the preparation for an *agrégation* in philosophy (a science certificate).[4] But this is a pathetic compromise, one that has been substituted for the real problem: the confrontation between the *philosophical world* and the *nonphilosophical world*, especially between the most boldly abstract thought and, therefore, the broadest in scope, and everyday life. The depth of philosophical analysis goes all the way down to the roots. Philosophical critique, which becomes a critique of philosophy, therefore claims to be radical. But the roots were planted in a different soil, the everyday.

Where is philosophy to be found? In brilliant, celebrated books. Nonphilosophy? In literature, among the poets, the tragedians. And everyday life? Everywhere. Elsewhere. Unwritten, poorly described, it must be experienced in situ. But where do we begin? How do we end this separation between philosophical presence and its absence, between the profound and the superficial?

In 1948 the CNRS [Centre national de la recherche scientifique], whose scope had grown under the influence of Georges Gurvitch, enabled me to make the transition from "pure" philosophy to the study of social practice and everydayness [*quotidienneté*]. Yet a very specific problem continued to dominate (and appears to continue to dominate) all the others—that of the peasants, the peasantry, agricultural production and industrialization in this context. This raises a number of questions.

(a) Why did the worldwide revolution, initially centered on the industrialized countries, and anticipated as such by Marxist theory, "theorized," why did it move toward agricultural countries, where the problems of primitive accumulation and of industrialization were beginning to become an issue? Why was the course of worldwide revolution deflected in this way?

(b) Under what conditions do the peasants cease to be a neutral or reactionary element in the complex interplay of social and political forces? When are they a "supplementary force," when and how do they release revolutionary virtualities? What are the limits of this development?

(c) Where exactly do the difficulties of agricultural production in the construction of socialism stem from?

For ten years this problematic at the world scale has inspired research that requires a center, a point of application, a nearby access point that might serve as a reference. And which is found in a detailed examination of a location on French soil. That place is the western region of the Pyrenees.⁵ This introduces a curious disproportion between research's worldwide ambitions and the size of the laboratory.

It turns out that a series of investigations of peasant communities (and their traces in the valleys of the Pyrenees) supports and encompasses an investigation of *agrarian reform* (its various modalities, its political contexts, its revolutionary virtualities and their eventual exhaustion) on a planetary scale; an investigation whose theoretical basis can be found in the Marxist theory of *ground rent* [*rente foncière*].

Ten years of work. The publications (articles) represent only a miniscule portion of the information gathered for the purposes of establishing a general theory. This effort was never concluded. It failed. Not only because it would have required a group, a team, to successfully conclude the project, but especially because the "subject" slipped away. The importance of agrarian reform, that of the peasant question, gradually diminished. The (revolutionary) potentials of the peasantry were exhausted after having reached their peak in China. With Fidel Castro and the Cuban Revolution, they made a final effort, which generated hope when it was already too late. And that was not all. In spite of the repeated attempts and promises, I never had the opportunity to study the peasant question in the large socialist countries. I amassed an enormous amount of documentation on the peasant question and agrarian reform in Latin America, Italy, and the Islamic states but had no interesting data on the USSR. And this in spite of the fact that I was a member of the CP [Communist Party]. Wouldn't the question itself have made me suspect? I never set foot on the sacred soil of the "socialist homeland." Moreover, no one ever made use of my knowledge of the peasantry, or agrarian problems, of reforms past, present, or possible, of the transition between the archaic and socialism.

Decisions are made, here and there, both empirically and politically. The Leader decides. Then, of what use is Marxist thought? None. It is already an institution, a teaching, a pedagogy, a political ideology, a prevailing system. In ten years and in twenty countries, I presented a thousand papers on philosophy, on dialectical materialism.[6] There was no appeal to concrete knowledge, although, pretty much everywhere, for better or worse and, often, for rather worse than better, questions concerning the peasantry were settled, agrarian reforms were introduced, and the last peasant revolutions were concluded. Was I going to abandon Marxism? Was I going to grow melancholy? No. I had no desire to look ridiculous.

Moreover, the peasant question doesn't exhaust the relationship between "philosophy and the nonphilosopical world." Everyday life is there, overwhelming but not without its advantages; it changes, is slowly and surely confirmed as *everydayness* within the sometimes stupefying and fascinating vividness of *modernity*. It affirms its triviality, its capacity for collapse, its swampy depths.

Two new and supportive truths have slowly come to light. First, Marx's primary focus was on the theory of *production*, through his affirmation of the primacy and determinant character of the relations of production and property as well as the subordinate nature of *distribution* (of "goods" or merchandise produced as well as the overall surplus value drawn from exploitation of the proletariat) in the society he analyzed, competitive capitalism. He ignored a whole set of phenomena concerning needs, demand, and social control, consumption and its possible organization. Second, these phenomena assumed increasing importance. In a way that was both spontaneous and planned, they were used (a *class strategy*) to substitute *something else,* supporting this class strategy, for the thought, the consciousness, the action that Marx theorized. This was a new situation that needed to be examined in order to understand what transpired during the twentieth century and what remained of Marxist thought. But how? The solution was to study *everyday life,* the site of change: programmed needs, the use of manipulation to model practice, but also the presence of "matter" and residues that escaped the powers and forms that imposed their models. The everyday is an unparalleled site of ambiguity: satisfaction and dissatisfaction, triviality and boredom within the sparkling armature of modernity (see *Critique of Everyday Life,* volume 1, 1946, and, in the present collection, "Introduction to the Psychosociology of Everyday Life," 1960).[7]

Since then, that is over the past ten years, a handful of far-left ideologues have taken possession of the ideas and outlook found in *Critique of Everyday Life*. They have come to conclusions that have little in common with the book's premises; in other words, they have behaved dogmatically, by extrapolation and ideological excrescence. For them, everyday life becomes a privileged site, a place of struggle and revolutionary transformation. As far as they are concerned, the metamorphosis of everyday life would soon, even immediately, give way to a completely new and transfigured form of social life.

That control over nature would morph into the appropriation of life and desire as part of a profound transformation is indeed an assertion of the radical critique of everyday life. Nor should we forget that the programmed everydayness, that of today, is tied to a class strategy that modifies the relations of production without transforming them, that introduces new elements into practice through consumption and the market. Everyday life serves the expansion of the world of commodities and the world of the State. But at the same time, society as a whole is transformed and, from an industrial society, becomes an urban one. Within the urban context, everyday life, which is established under pressure from social relations and the existing order, can change and serve the appearance of another life. In this context and only in this context, from which it cannot be separated.

Yet other, very "right-wing" ideologues, serving an epistemology and a rigidly fixed way of thinking, assert that everyday life is merely a detail, a superficial modality of capitalist society. This "lived experience" would not give rise to any concept; it would be unworthy. For them there has been nothing new in *praxis* since Marx, Lenin, or Trotsky. Against these new dogmatists, we can state that neither everyday life nor urban society are purely and simply *superstructure*, expressions of the relations of capitalist production. They are those things, but they possess something additional and different than institutions and ideologies, though they possess certain characteristics of ideologies and institutions. The world of commodities, with its logic and its language, is generalized in everyday life to the point that everything serves as a conduit for it, along with its significations. Would it be merely an ideology, a superstructure, an institution?

Am I now going to seize this opportunity to complain that some have attempted to overwhelm me from the left while others have attempted to destroy me from the right? Not at all. That I am being attacked in this way means that I occupy a central position. But every central position is under threat, tactically or strategically. Tactically: my position is turned around, surrounded, with the assault being conducted from the right and the left. Strategically: there is never a single center, and every center can experience a general or partial displacement of centrality. As for the virulence of the attacks, that can be guaranteed. A center such as this is located in the midst of assailants; it is not, therefore, the "happy medium" of mediocre and pathetic memory. Let others straddle the "correct" *line*, always correct!

But I want to return to what's been accomplished, to the path we've been following. We've come to a fork in the road. It is not the byproduct of the pathfinder, of his reflections or his fantasy. It arises from a new object, a modification in practice, which is drawing attention to itself.

Here in the Pyrenees, not far from where I was born, a New Town has risen. The product of industrialization and modernization, the glory of France and the Republic, Lacq-Mourenx rises, a cluster of new buildings endowed with enigmas rather than classical beauty. Bulldozers come and go over the soil of this so-called Béarnaisian Texas. A few steps from the most modern undertaking in France, among the derricks and the smoke, arises what will become a Town. It is the transition from the rural to the urban that is taking place, is being prepared before our very eyes and for our consideration. This raises another question. The problems pile up, intensify: the fate of a land marked by history, peasant traditions, and the peasants themselves. Industrialization has taken hold of lands that, until recently, had been abandoned. Urbanization, whose importance has continued to grow unabated, transforms the past. These towers, rising above the forests, opposite the mountains, are a challenge and a question. A challenge to the past, a question for the future. From the outset, this was not an attempt to erase an earlier social text; something more and different has been taking place, making itself known, signifying its presence—the urban. A page turns. A different social text is being written. Thus the first roof of the first workshop, or the first shelter of a worker separated from the means of production were signifiers. Already surpassed, but still all around us, the era of the peasant grows distant in time and space. Industrialization, far more contemporary and still consequential, is already no more than context and pretext. Urbanization supplants it as a problematic before supplanting it thematically and in the construction of categories (concepts). Already, new divisions of sociohistorical time are gaining headway. For example, differences appear between the peasant era, the industrial era, and the urban era, with a break (*relative* discontinuity) between the predominance of the countryside and agricultural production, with its specific relations of production and their problems—the predominance of the industrial enterprise, its rationality—and, finally, the predominance of the "urban" and its problematic.

The urban era doesn't magically make the contradictions and conflicts of the industrial era go away. Similarly, the latter has not abolished the conflicts and contradictions of the previous era. Conflict implies problems and "problematic." The problems get resolved or destroy the context in which they arise. The questions posed by agriculture in the world, by the peasantry, will be resolved or that world will collapse. Likewise for the era of industrial domination, with its own conflicts and contradictions. The city, its expansion, urban society and the "urban" that emerges, superimpose their contradictions on those of the industrial and agricultural eras, giving rise to an inextricable dilemma and a highly complex "problematic." Which contradictions can be said to *drive* growth and development (drive, which is to say, eventually destroy)? All of them. Urban contradictions, such as the conflict between *integration* and *segregation*, between forms of centrality (between centrality as form and its contents), between the urban and the State, do not neutralize those that spring up from the relations of capitalist production, between private property and socialization of the process of production, between proletariat and bourgeoisie. On the contrary, they aggravate them, making the solution all the more difficult.

II

Every article that appears here bears a date.

There are few questions as difficult (and insoluble) as those concerning the priority and precedence in the use of words, in the access to ideas. The origin of ideas (and ideologies) is generally buried in the obscurity of roots and emergences. It is commonly known that the same idea often arises in several places at the same time, and sometimes in apparently incompatible forms. The best ideas escape their authors. They emigrate outside the system, if there is one. They enter the public domain, social awareness, become commonplace. Some say that they prostitute themselves. But these are good ideas and that's how they work. Yet, from time to time, there are surprises. For example, there are those who publicly repudiate the private property of ideas to suddenly lay claim to a given word with the righteous attitude of a legitimate owner. To those who would not stoop to such confrontations, dates provide some relevant information.

Here, it would be more interesting to distinguish the shifting sands of the vagaries of thought, of uncertainties. For example, the dialectical relationship, conflict-laden and mobile, between *desire* and *need* is not always clearly grasped, notwithstanding the permanence, in spite of ideological pressures, of the rejection of a "philosophy of need" formulated on the basis of Marxist thought. Such fluctuations, dated and recontextualized, are not without sense. At certain moments, a confidence, an accumulation of exaggerated hope, has been invested in "sociology," given the increasingly obvious failure of philosophy. And yet I have always clearly and forthrightly stated that sociology is subject to its own form of criticism, that fragmentary knowledge can never claim to be total, that the socio-critical prevails over the socio-technical, and that totality is a problem (as soon as neither philosophy nor a fragmentary science have access to it).

Wouldn't the key be found in the direction, the path indicated and covered by these texts?

Although they are not logically interconnected and do not seek to construct a system, a common attitude runs through them. It is true that there is no overall key here for it is found *elsewhere*: in the dialectical logic itself attached to a conception of formal logic (as *tautology*, filled by a content, which occurs or arises throughout the process). Yet here we can recognize the process of thought that is threatened and sometimes broken. It seeks a path. And it finds it, but not without difficulty, exhausting its strength in a kind of tragic optimism (which it struggles to legitimize by confronting it with understanding). It moves between:

(a) *The thesis of closure,* of the closed society, finalized or closed off. (The system that proclaims itself, that closes by enclosing itself. The structure that wishes to rule. The plenitude that seeks to establish itself.)

(b) *The thesis of the void* [*la béance*] during a substantial metamorphosis. (Emptiness [*Le vide*]. The hope of explosion, a terminal catastrophe, the closed system exploding and bursting into pieces.)

A constant intent animates this research: to identify and reveal the opening, overcome the obstacles, create the breach. The point of thought is constantly directed at the system, which it calls "Stalinism" or "political philosophy" or "socio-logic" or "ideo-logic." This attitude is legitimized elsewhere, in the realm of Logic and the Logos, where it has been shown that because *logical form* is empty (tautological), it implies nothing about content. On this basis we can deduce nothing, conclude nothing. Between form and content there is a hiatus, an abyss crossed by bridges (mediators and transitions). When we try to use *form* to define content, isolate it, and enclose it within limits, we engage in *vitiated form*. Which explains the violent nature of the controversies surrounding the idea.[8]

These remarks highlight the drawbacks of such a collection of essays. While it traces an itinerary, the real significance (to the extent that it exists) lies elsewhere, in the "books" that deliver or claim to deliver what is essential. The continuities and moments, the themes and references need to be identified.

Consequently, these articles do not offer a tentative system but a *countersystem*: a nearly permanent critique and self-critique, heightened attention toward domination. Critical (active) negation of the system that strives to be absolute, that claims to be a philosophical and political model, requires constant vigilance directed toward "subsystems," institutions and ideologies, the systematization of values and decisions—and an equally permanent self-critique. As someone said concerning these texts, it is Penelope who extends the deadline by undoing the work of day every evening. Why? Because another day, another dawn will begin. Together with its own hope, its own despair. This deadline, is it that of the last word, the last instance and the last thought, that of the domination that seeks to establish itself? All of them! So every article has its objective (polemic) and its object (scientific), while also indicating a moment, a guidepost. Their succession doesn't follow any kind of logical interconnection but a development intercut with metamorphoses. The modifications that these objects and objectives undergo at the same time as the "subject" are not subjective. Their reasons are to be found in changes (to society and to knowledge) or in the critique of permanence and change. The kind reader may see a progression here, a succession of emergences: theories, problems, concepts.

So if each text carries a date, it must be considered not only as a function of its context but as a function of the overall movement. The context, most often, is evoked or suggested. The overall movement, for better or worse, is difficult to read because of its complexity. The growth of the urban problematic, the structuralist mode and its decline, these are the "objective" dates that characterize this movement.

The dispersion of these texts is in one sense only apparent. They have a theoretical center: the "country-city" relation, which is a dialectical relation, an incompatible opposition that tends to surpass itself whenever the ancient countryside and the ancient town are simultaneously reabsorbed into the generalized "urban fabric." What defines "urban society" is accompanied by the slow degradation and disappearance of the countryside, the peasantry, and the village, together with a dispersal, an uncontrolled expansion of what was once the Town.

Today, it is no longer a question of dreaming of a "new urbanism." That dream may have made sense ten years ago. The key question at this time is to go as far as we can with the radical critique of so-called urbanist projects, marked by a twofold stigmata: the action of the State and the expansion of the "world of commodities." Today, urbanism, like psychoanalysis and Marxism, has become institutional, further subjecting it to the blows of a redoubled critique.

Hopefully, the arrows will remind the (kind) reader not to forget that they point to either side of the road and even to the end of the road.

III

A few more words.

With this series of essays, will the future reader acknowledge that their author cannot be classified as a philosopher or a specialist of any given "discipline" (sociology, history, etc.)? Which would make him unclassifiable. From philosophy, he hopes to retain the need for questioning and radical critique, while avoiding its systematic focus and tendency for abstraction; he also hopes to continue the work of philosophy so that truth declares itself without forcing it to reveal or conceal itself, and so sense can be expressed spontaneously (so that those involved and those affected speak, articulating the sense of objects, acts, and situations). As for the fragmentary sciences, including sociology, they have a strong tendency to turn ideological, even "scientifically" ideological. If they are not coupled with constant criticism and self-criticism, grave consequences can follow; in such cases, we must continue to harass the sociologist, the historian, the psychologist without respite.

Concerning this "unclassifiable" character, several misunderstandings have arisen, which I will attempt to clarify.

(a) Jean-Paul Sartre, in his *Critique of Dialectical Reason*, attempted to use one of the articles reproduced here (concretely but modestly devoted to rural questions and rural sociology) as the first (methodological) model of a "progressive-regressive" approach that integrated sociology and history from a dialectical perspective. While I am grateful, the reader (well-meaning or spiteful) will find no proof, no sign of an identity or even an analogy between the approach outlined here and that of existentialism.[9] The path that leads from philosophy to metaphilosophy is incapable of accommodating that of a philosopher, no matter how esteemed, who maintains and perfects philosophical categories along the way.[10]

The text cited by Sartre is unfortunately much too short. It was written at a time when a hopeless terrorism was prevalent on all sides (on the "capitalist" side as well as on the "socialist" and "communist" side). To escape the pressure, what else could be done other than extending Marx's thought without acknowledging the source? Marx called this the "analytic-regressive approach" in the well-known fragment in which he states that mankind enlightens the ape and the adult the child; that the present enables us to understand the past and capitalist society enables us to understand earlier societies because it *develops* essential categories from them.[11] Thus capitalist ground rent enables us to understand feudal rent, the soil rent of antiquity, and so on.

The passage cited, if we are to understand it correctly, should be compared to the texts that Marx sought to develop but could never complete. It is completely "Marxist."

(b) To continue with this text, the recurrent *analytic-regressive* moment precedes a *historic-genetic* moment, during which thinking returns to the actual, based on a revealed past, comprehended in and for itself. This methodological precept, which is not without interest, implies no solidarity with the systematization obstinately pursued by Lucien Goldmann under the name of "genetic structuralism." Either the term concerns an elucidation and refinement of the process of Marxist thought, which raises no objection but results in no new terminology either; or it designates another systematization (and primarily a systematization, whereas Marx did not leave us with a system but a principle for critiquing systems). This systematization, which is not unrelated to the vogue for structuralism, will then be dragged along with the decline of this ideology.

(c) The reader may observe, from the very first pages of this collection, the frequent use of an essential concept: *structure*. I write about the legitimate use of this concept, as well as others that are methodologically and theoretically essential: form, function, level. The controversy with structuralism, the subject of a second collection of essays, certainly does not prevent us from using the concept.[12] Quite the contrary. Structuralism makes poor use of the notion of *structure* and obscures it to the point of its destruction. By using it for reductive purposes, it grafts an ideological growth to it. To criticize structuralism implies a methodological rather than a superfluous or reductive use of structural analysis.

(d) The first texts in this collection (1949) manifest a strong confidence in history. During these past twenty years, this confidence has grown dim, and is now nonexistent. On this point, which is not without interest or importance, the malevolent reader may take pleasure, at the author's expense, in identifying the systems of his disillusion, the signs of failure. The benevolent reader will note the contradiction, not unique to the author, between the disappointing findings and the effort to remain optimistic and reveal a path.

H. Lefebvre
November 10, 1969

How can I find the words to thank Mario Gaviria, who located and selected these texts, classified and revised them?[13] In particular, he was kind enough to include reports of talks, of which no more than an outline existed, and identify the ideas contained in them. For that, I am profoundly grateful.

H. L.

Notes

[*Du rural à l'urbain* (Paris: Anthropos, 1970), 7–20.—*Eds.*]

1. [Since only the "rural" parts of the book have been translated here, the essays range from 1949 to 1961, with supplemental pieces from 1956, 1963, and 1964.—*Eds.*]

2. [See Henri Lefebvre, *Hegel, Marx, Nietzsche: Or the Realm of Shadows*, trans. David Fernbach (London: Verso, 2020).—*Eds.*]

3. [Lefebvre and his colleague Norbert Guterman were crucial to their French reception, translating and introducing them in short-lived journals. See Karl Marx, "Travail et propriété privée," *La revue marxiste* 1 (February 1929): 7–28; Karl Marx, "Notes sur les besoins, la production et la division du travail," *La revue marxiste* 5 (June 1929): 513–38; and Karl Marx, "Critique de la dialectique hégélienne," *Avant-Poste* 1 (June 1933): 33–39, and *Avant-Poste* 2 (August 1933): 110–16. Lefebvre and Guterman went on to compile Karl Marx, *Morceaux choisis*, ed. Henri Lefebvre and Norbert Guterman (Paris: Gallimard, 1934); and Karl Marx,

Œuvres choisis, 2 vols., ed. Henri Lefebvre and Norbert Guterman (Paris: Gallimard, 1963–66.—*Eds.*]

4. [The *agrégation* is the qualification that allows people to teach, often initially in *lycées* and then later in universities.—*Eds.*]

5. [Lefebvre wrote a general book on the region, *Pyrénées* (Lausanne: Rencontre, 1965; 2nd ed., Pau: Cairn, 2000), on which he also wrote his doctoral dissertations, published as *Les communautés paysannes pyrénéennes* (Bagnères-de-Bigorre: Sociéte Ramond / Cercle Historique de l'Arribère, 2014), and *La vallée de Campan: Étude de sociologie rurale* (Paris: Presses Universitaires de France, 1963; 2nd ed., Paris: Presses Universitaires de France, 1990). We include parts of *La vallée de Campan* as chapter 12.—*Eds.*]

6. [See Henri Lefebvre, *Le materialisme dialectique,* 6th ed. (Paris: Presses Universitaires de France, 1971), translated by John Sturrock as *Dialectical Materialism* (London: Jonathan Cape, 1968), reissued with an introduction by Stefan Kipfer (Minneapolis: University of Minnesota Press, 2009).—*Eds.*]

7. [Henri Lefebvre, *Critique de la vie quotidienne I: Introduction,* 2nd ed. (Paris: L'Arche, 1958), translated by John Moore as Henri Lefebvre, *Critique of Everyday Life,* vol. 1, *Introduction* (London: Verso, 1991).—*Eds.*]

8. See Henri Lefebvre, *Logique formelle, logique dialectique* (1946; repr, Paris: Anthropos, 1969); and the forthcoming collection of essays, Henri Lefebvre, *Au-delà du structuralisme* (Paris: Anthropos, 1971).

9. See Jean-Paul Sartre, "Questions de méthode," in *Critique de la raison dialectique* (Paris: Gallimard, [1960]), 41–42 [actually n. 1 across those pages, and 50–51n1 in the 1986 reprint. See Jean-Paul Sartre, *Search for a Method,* trans. Hazel E. Barnes (New York: Vintage, 1968), 51–52n8. In 1946, Lefebvre had produced a stinging critique of the movement: *L'existentialisme,* 2nd ed. (Paris: Anthropos, 2001).—*Eds.*].

10. [See Henri Lefebvre, *Métaphilosophie* (Paris: Éditions de Minuit, 1965; 2nd ed., Paris: Syllepse, 2000), translated by David Fernbach as *Metaphilosophy,* ed. Stuart Elden (London: Verso, 2016).—*Eds.*]

11. [This is a reference to Karl Marx, *Grundrisse: Foundations of the Critique of Political Economy,* trans. Martin Nicolaus (Penguin: Harmondsworth, 1973), 105. There are a number of other references one can highlight as relevant to Lefebvre's thinking on issues of historical method. These include: (1) Friedrich Engels, "The Part Played by Labour in the Transition from Ape to Man," which was an unfinished fragment of the *Dialectics of Nature* (see Friedrich Engels, "The Part Played by Labour in the Transition from Ape to Man" [1876], available at https://www.marxists.org/archive/marx/works/1876/part-played-labour/index.htm; (2) the famous passage by Marx and Engels that relays that the bourgeoisie "compels all nations, on pain of extinction, to adopt the bourgeois mode of production; it compels them to introduce what it calls civilization into their midst,

i.e., to become bourgeois themselves. In one word, it creates a word after its own image" (see Karl Marx and Friedrich Engels, *The Communist Manifesto: A Modern Edition* [1848], introduced by Eric Hobsbawm [London: Verso, 1998], 40); and (3) Marx's own comment, in the preface to the first edition of *Capital,* vol. 1, that "the country that is more developed industrially only shows, to the less developed, the image of its own future" (see Karl Marx, *Capital: A Critique of Political Economy* [1867], vol. 1, introduced by Ernest Mandel, trans. Ben Fowkes [London: Penguin, 1990], 91).

As Kevin Anderson, *Marx at the Margins: On Nationalism, Ethnicity, and Non-Western Societies* (Chicago: University of Chicago Press, 2010), 178, has detailed in relation to this passage, in the later French edition, from 1872 to 1875, the sentence is altered by Marx as "The country that is more developed industrially only shows, *to those that follow it on the industrial path,* the image of its own future" (emphasis added). Therefore, rather than a unilinear determinism, this methodological emphasis develops into a more nuanced multilinear understanding of social development.—*Eds.*]

12. [See Lefebvre, *Au-delà du structuralisme*; only one essay of this collection is in English: "Beyond Structuralism," in *Key Writings,* ed. Stuart Elden, Elisabeth Lebas, and Eleonore Kofman (London: Continuum, 2003), 37–41. Lefebvre reedited some of the essays as *L'idéologie structuraliste* (Paris: Anthropos, 1975).—*Eds.*]

13. [As our introduction notes, Mario Gaviria (1938–2018) was a student of Lefebvre's at the University of Strasbourg in the early 1960s, and later became a collaborator on various projects. Gaviria commissioned a manuscript by Lefebvre in 1973 that was only published posthumously: *Toward an Architecture of Enjoyment,* ed. Łukasz Stanek, trans. Robert Bononno (Minneapolis: University of Minnesota Press, 2014). Stanek's introduction to that volume gives much more detail on Gaviria and his links to Lefebvre.—*Eds.*]

CHAPTER 2

Problems of Rural Sociology
The Peasant Community and Its Historical–Sociological Problems

I

Of those—citizens, intellectuals, even historians or sociologists—who cross one of our villages, discover its original or uncertain face, marvel at its torpor or admire its "picturesqueness," how many know that this village cannot be reduced to an accidental hodgepodge of people, animals, and things, and that its examination reveals a complex organization, a "structure"?

The study of rural communities, throughout the world, reveals equilibria that are more subtle than we would have at first suspected: the proportions between the amount of arable land, forests, and pasturage and the groups of living creatures for whom the land provides subsistence. Such a study, moving from objective facts to the human facts that are connected with them, also reveals that material equilibria, although not expressly and rationally planned by people, are not blindly and mechanically obtained; they arise from an awareness, which is difficult to grasp and even harder to define, a curious mixture of prudence, initiative, suspicion, credulousness, and routine: peasant wisdom. And finally, analysis reveals cracks in this order, uncertainties in this "wisdom," more or less durable disequilibria resulting from more or less profound causes, which is to say, there are problems, needs, tendencies, conflicts, successful and unsuccessful adaptations.

This organism, which we are not always able to see, is there before our eyes, along with its structure and its horizon. As for the awareness of this organized community, it is concealed in the life of the individuals who share in it, as secret as the immediacy of sensible reality. Organization and awareness contain and continue a history. They have a past. A peaceful village, simply residing on a hillside, without any apparent enigma, existed and thrived in this place long before the familiar cities that only now support our hopes and dreams.[1] Yet another hamlet, having long ago descended into a rather dull and reticent torpor, continues its vehement struggle against lords, princes, and kings. There are few traces of this past; nothing of it remains. Nothing and yet everything—the very form of the village itself.

Their past noticeably marks our cities. On a Paris street, a building from the Middle Ages tears itself away from the surrounding "modernity" and maintains its distance in time. Juxtaposed structures, from Roman ruins to banks, reproduce the ages of history in space, the succession of eras. The past is inscribed in the wounds of the stones themselves. Yet in the village, the château surrounded by its fields, its farmers, and its sharecroppers, with its prestige and power, remains a very contemporary and very active element of rural life. The old feudal manor often resembles the patriarchal peasant home, and the "bourgeois" house appears to be a somewhat more "comfortable" version of a peasant home. The past, for those who do not analyze it, is often lost, dissipated in a present that is entirely present and outwardly manifest, or perceived as a single, anachronistic, and obsolete block. This gives *rural sociology* its difficult characterization as a science of the present that cannot do without history, for here as elsewhere, the historical persists and acts upon the present.

II

I would first note the scarcity of documents and literary texts informing us about peasant life, specifically during the periods when agriculture was still broadly predominant. This consequential fact shows that enormous fragments of reality disappear inside ideological expressions.

Without going further into the past, what remains of the seventeenth century?[2] A handful of technical works, such as Olivier de Serres's *Théâtre d'Agriculture* [1600]. Certain paintings (Le Nain). Some well-known texts, such as scenes from Molière's "Don Juan," La Fontaine's *Fables*, or a dark page from La Bruyère. And a few lesser-known texts such as Charles Sorel's *La Vraie Histoire comique de Francion*. That's about all.

In the eighteenth century, with the traditional reality of peasant life already a distant memory, it appears in literature with Rousseau. A new capitalist form of agriculture appeared, along with its theoreticians and ideologues—the physiocrats. However, we had to wait until the end of what some historians refer to, with slight exaggeration, as the "agricultural revolution" of the eighteenth century; we had to wait until the industrial "revolution" of the economy and the growing predominance of industry over agriculture, and of the city over the countryside, before the ideologues discovered peasant reality in and for itself. They achieved this just as it began to collapse—the beginning of a profound crisis—and as its traditional forms were beginning to disappear. How can we explain this sudden interest in peasant reality on the part of writers and historians? Was it melancholic regret in the face of the disappearance of patriarchal life, which possessed a certain beauty and grandeur in spite of its limitations, or an expression of the political importance assumed by the rural bourgeoisie and the landowners, the "notables"? Both probably. We may recall, without pushing the analysis too far, that two great writers—Balzac and George Sand—left us with important documents on the life of the countryside in the nineteenth century.

The honor of having initiated the scientific study of French peasant history falls to several great regional scholars, largely overlooked today, whose research, conducted during the second half of the nineteenth century, still retains considerable value: Léopold Delisle (Normandy), Charles de Ribbe (Provence), Jean-Auguste Brutails (Roussillon-Catalan), Jean-François Bladé (Gascony), Alcide Curie-Seimbres and Justin Cenac-Moncaut (the fortified towns of the Midi, the Pyrenees), and so on.[3]

Only barely in existence, rural history and sociology became the object of an audacious ideological abduction. If the doctrine of the physiocrats reflects the ideas and interests of the high, progressive bourgeoisie of the eighteenth century, the theories of Frédéric Le Play clearly express the concerns and goals of a bourgeoisie that had risen to power. If Le Play was interested in the peasantry, in family and rural communities, it was because he discovered "virtues" and moral "values" in them—stability, obedience, resignation. He said so expressly without even questioning whether those "moral" values might be at the same time and most notably "political" values. Le Play dreamed of restoring traditional communities, family and village, which were already crumbling. Studying these social facts in the Pyrenees, he dared suggest as a norm and model a family of fifteen people (the Melouga family in Cauterets) living in a three-room house, consuming three kilos of sugar and fifty liters of wine per year among them! The inconsistency of reactionary ideology appears luminously in such works; the bourgeoisie that grew wealthy with the extension of the market extolled at the same time, and for very clear political reasons, earlier forms of life that were external to industrial and mercantile economy.[4]

In spite of these defects, Le Play's monographs remain models of the genre in certain respects. The budget of the Melouga family—a document that works against its author—has never been surpassed for its precision and the detail of its sociological observations. Nonetheless, the fact remains that the empiricist, positivist, descriptive sociology of Le Play, which obscures normative and metaphysical claims that are more than suspect, brought about a succession of sociological and literary works devoted to peasant life, the least of which can be said about them being that they did nothing to advance scientific understanding.

Would it be tendentious to examine the state of research and the ensuing problem, in France and elsewhere, that is, its "politicization"? Not at all, because it is a fact, and a highly important sociological fact at that!

It should be noted that the "rightward" trend in the study of the peasantry (past, present, and future of the peasantry) has been and continues to be challenged by a "leftward" trend. In contrast to the studies that attempt to use empiricist descriptions to justify various moral, metaphysical, and political claims, there are historical works that address the vicissitudes and tendencies of reality, that is, objectively, works influenced by Marxism or expressly Marxist. Is there any point in stating the best-known names in this magnificent array of sociological historians, simultaneously documentary researchers and observers of living reality, who have so deeply enriched our understanding of the French countryside?[5]

It is also worth noting the considerable contributions of the school of *human geography*, although some works are hard to distinguish from a somewhat narrowly focused "geographism" and others contain vast regional encyclopedias, where we find a little of everything: geology, physical geography, descriptive studies of habitat and lifestyles, political economy, even history and sociology. And I'll note in passing the extent to which the very concept of "human geography" needs to be revised and more clearly defined.

For twenty years now, in France and elsewhere, including the French colonies, administrators, sociologists, ethnographers, and geographers have freed themselves of the philosophical prestige stemming from formal logic and the legal prejudices derived from Roman law. These prejudices falsified perspectives by claiming that any number of realities were absurd or simply barbarous: communal living, customary law, spontaneous thinking. In Africa, in Madagascar, in Indochina, and elsewhere investigators have discovered this reality under different names, a reality very close to our own: the village, peasants, and the peasant community (see the work of Labouret, Weulersse, Sicard, etc.).[6] The older works of [Henry James] Sumner Maine, and [Robert] Baden-Powell have been continued and enriched by such recent contributions.

Recently, in the United States, *rural sociology* has become a distinct science, a branch of general sociology, and is taught in universities. This may be explained by the serious problems posed by American agriculture. However, the contributions of the large-scale works of rural sociology do not always appear proportionate to their size. With respect to the rural community—the village—the authors of these works have studied, in great detail, with maps and diagrams, the exchange of services, the service areas served, in a given community, by the mail carrier, the doctor, the school, the "trading center," the temple, and so on. Or they study, sociometrically, the Sunday visits of neighboring families.[7] The descriptive and normative nature of this sociology is frequently manifested. The authors study, as if they were simple facts among other facts, the efforts of certain more or less institutional associations or organizations (committees, clubs, etc.) that would allow members of "rural communities" to "forget" differences in prestige, which is to say, wealth. Thus, Kolb and Brunner attribute, according to [Jacob L.] Moreno, a "therapeutic power" to everything that strengthens "community identification and consciousness." We can easily discern here, although with different terminology and under other conditions, the attitude of Le Play.[8] Overall, these sociologists resent the fact that they are examining a reality *without a past* and, so to speak, without historical density. This leads to the empirical, descriptive, ahistorical nature of their research.

In the USSR the study of peasant reality is necessarily associated with the effort to transform that reality, that is, with economic and political theory. Nonetheless, rural sociology has a subject, namely, the analysis of still living local or national traditions. It studies the concrete conditions of peasant life and the systems of culture produced by historical evolution and partially covered by agrobiology (crop rotation, etc.). Finally, numerous historical works have continued the study of village communities (*mir*) and the family (*dvor*), their formation, decline, and dissolution.[9]

III

We should first distinguish three aspects of the question or, rather, three related but impossible-to-confuse sociohistorical realities: (a) the largest community—the clan, association, or federation of villages;[10] (b) the village community or rural community itself; (c) the family community (the tacit community known to our historians, patriarchal family, *zadruga*, *dvor*, etc.).

The second of these three terms, namely the village community (the least studied of all community forms), is the one I am most interested in here. But it is important that we identify the concept and provide a definition that combines the different aspects revealed by analysis. (This definition, which may seem abstract and "a priori," concretely summarizes an earlier analysis and will enable us to further enrich it.)

1. The rural or village community is not a productive force or a mode of production. It is not a productive force although obviously associated with the development of productive forces: with the organization of working the land under specific technical (tools) and social (division of labor, cooperative methods) conditions.

All historians of the rural community have insisted on the fact that at a certain time (eighteenth century in France, the nineteenth to the first twenty years of the twentieth century in Russia) it hampered the development of productive forces by limiting the types of crops grown, by quashing progressive agrarian initiatives and individualism, by subjecting the individual to traditional constraints, by hampering the introduction of new crops and new tools, and so on. Georges Lefebvre, Henri Sée, and Marc Bloch have provided key documentation on this point.[11]

Historically in conflict with productive forces, the rural community cannot be identified with them. But nor is it a mode of production. For the village appears once a group of people, previously nomadic or seminomadic, become attached to the land. It disappears, according to the precise sense of the word, under certain conditions, primarily large-scale farming operations (in antiquity—Roman villas, latifundia; in the feudal period—the manorial domain; in the industrial era—large capitalist farms, socialist *sovkhoz*).[12]

The rural community maintained itself, defended itself, and disappeared or reshaped itself under very different modes of production: slave, feudal, capitalist, socialist. It has persisted, more or less alive, sometimes rising, sometimes falling, from the most distant past to the present day; not, of course, outside the vicissitudes of history and economic and political transformations but retaining its own life and history.

Therefore, it is a *form of community*, like the family, like the nation, which appear, change, develop, or dwindle under specific conditions determined by the advancement of productive forces and the mode of production, without, however, being identified with those determiners of the socialeconomic process.

2. The rural community is a type of *organic* community and cannot be reduced to a mechanical union of individual elements. Wherever mercantile exchange, money, the monetary economy, or individualism triumph,

the community dissolves, replaced by the reciprocal exteriority of individuals and the "free" labor contract. It brings together, organically, not individuals but partial and subordinate communities, families (themselves of different kinds but inseparable from the organization of the community).

We might be surprised to rediscover here the old distinction between "organic" solidarity and the "mechanical" solidarity of sociology.

This organic solidarity within the community historically precedes "mechanical" solidarity, which represents the dispersion, dissolution, and atomization through "pure" individualism of the organic community. Such organic solidarity does not follow from mechanical solidarity unless it is reconstituted along new lines following a period of dissolution.

3. Obviously, within the concept of the rural community, we cannot make an abstraction of the form of ownership. Where property triumphs in the sense of Roman law (quiritarian property), the community tends to disappear or disappears completely. This triumph of private property, of the "jus utendi et abutendi," merely represents an abstract limiting case; wherever private (individual) property has been proclaimed, the rights of the family, or the nation, or the State have, in fact, limited it.

On the other hand, absolute "collective" ownership is also only a limiting case. Ever since the most distant past, goods consumed and a certain portion of the implements used have been objects of private appropriation. The same will hold true in the most distant future, to the extent that our economic, political, and sociological knowledge allows us to predict. The absence of this distinction, both simple and obvious, between the means of production and goods consumed, has confused and continues to confuse many questions concerning ownership. In fact, all societies have been situated and continue to be situated between these abstract limits: collective property and private property, more or less near one or the other limit. Based on the variable relation between these terms, we can identify a principle of classification for the forms of community:

Collective property and undivided property. These should be carefully distinguished. The words "collective property" refer to a form of social organization in which there is not yet, or not at all, any private appropriation. In the past, the social form of the clan devoted to hunting and gathering, to fishing, came close to this limit case. But the words "collective property" also refer to the eminent domain that some types of communities make use of, leaving to their elementary groups (families or villages in some cases) the enjoyment, use, usufruct, the effective possession of the land. For example—until certain late forms, such as the eighteenth-century *mir* and afterward—whenever there was a periodic redistribution of the land, when the apportionment to every elementary group was treated only as a provisional grant, in many cases this was still sometimes referred to as collective property.

The words "undivided property," on the contrary, refer to that portion of the land that is not, or not yet, assigned to elementary groups, while private property has already stabilized. The undivided property coexists with private property, in spite of the profound conflict between these two terms. Thus, already established owners throughout the world historically had a tendency to eat away at or divide among themselves the undivided property of rural communities (such as the "commons" in English history and French communal lands at the end of the eighteenth century). Pasturage, mountains, forests, water, remained, and continue to remain, partly undivided property in the French rural community. At the scale of the family, the patrimony and the home often remained undivided property of the family community (although in this case, ownership status generally evolved very quickly, becoming the individual property of the head of the family, the "paterfamilias" of Roman law). Every community has its own practical basis in collective or undivided property; that much is self-evident.

Division by equal shares. Village communities, within the context of a larger association—family communities in the context of the village community; individual members in the context of the family community—sometimes have equal rights to collective or undivided assets. In this case, if there are provisional allotments, they receive equal shares, either periodic or final. In the event of the dissolution of the community, they assume equal shares of the property.

Division by unequal shares. The same groups or group elements can have, or be assigned (sometimes by trickery or violence, or by a natural process of differentiation), unequal rights. For example, in the context of the larger unit, village communities received a benefit proportional to their population, or their wealth, or their strength. In the context of the village community itself, families received shares (temporary or final) proportional to the number of mouths to feed, or to the farming implements held, or to the number of livestock owned, or to their share of expenses, or even to acquired wealth (species wealth when the monetary economy was established). Similarly, in the smaller context of the family, certain members—women, daughters, younger children, and children in general—could lose their rights to the benefit of a more favored family member: the father, the eldest male child, sometimes the eldest female child or the youngest boy.

4. This analysis of property relations in no way exhausts the concept of the rural community. It also comprises *collective disciplines* that are extremely varied in terms of their forms and their robustness. The study of these disciplines introduces the sociologist into the concrete life of peasant groups: village shepherds and, sometimes, the "collective" sheep pen of pastoral communities; organized migratory herding; fields arranged in sectors or "fields," with regulated plantings. These included the use of crop rotation and open pasture lands, where fields are open to all the animals in the community, beginning with the grass around the house. These are only some of the most familiar cases of collective disciplines, the closest to us in time and space, and still observable in many parts of rural France. In our modern agricultural cooperatives, which, in a sense, reconstitute (on a new technical, economic, and political foundation) the organized community, the individualism of the nineteenth century again leaves room for collective disciplines.

It is important that we avoid thinking of these disciplines in the Durkheimian terms of obligation and sanction. These disciplines had and still have a practical foundation. Those who so desired, except for certain periods of "hardening" of the community, have always been able to withdraw from them. But was there any advantage to that independence? Let's look at a specific example. In all rural communities, even those that are collapsing, even those maximally individualized, *relations of proximity* are of extreme importance. Their form and content differ: sometimes they are purely practical (mutual assistance on large-scale projects, known as "souhaitage" in the Gâtinais region of central France and "arban" in the Limousin and the Marche); sometimes practical with a highly developed element of ritual (Basque country and Béarn, where the neighbors play an official role in family ceremonies, marriages, and burials); sometimes almost exclusively sumptuary (as in the reciprocal visits studied by American sociologists). Almost always, proximity relations had or retain a practical foundation. From what we have seen, in the old rural communities of France, work on contiguous plots and mutual assistance in this work necessitated that crops be planted simultaneously; not because of any collective attitude or entity but for very simple reasons. The practical requirement had an equally practical penalty: the independent worker, left to himself, would have seen his plot invaded by the community's livestock if he had taken the unfortunate initiative of removing his land from the crop rotation system. But isn't it also for practical reasons, rather than mysterious traditions, that plots of land have uniform shapes, a shape that has intrigued both historians and sociologists? In the ancient community, given the absence of boundary markers—hedgerows, enclosures—a uniform shape avoided, to the extent possible, quarrels over property limits, arguments, and lawsuits.

If true, we can speak of disciplines rather than collective obligations. We can speak of coordinated crop rotation rather than forced crop rotation, which suggests the idea of a collective constraint—excluding certain particular cases—foreign to traditional peasant wisdom.

5. These modes of organization always tend to bring about governing functions. At first, these are almost exclusively technical: a general meeting of the community or a limited meeting of the heads of families, in which their powers were delegated to certain members known for their knowledge, initially the elders but later various notables. This technical council ruled on calendar dates (harvests, grape harvesting, departure of migratory herds); coordinated collective activities, discussed various events; oversaw the planning of festivals and customary rites. Therefore, the council largely controlled the organization of the community *over*

time (the calendar of work and holidays) and *in space* (distribution of plots of land and shares; distribution of labor affecting the community as a whole).

But these functions, initially assigned (democratically) to individuals representing the community, over time became indistinguishable from functions of a different kind: *political* functions. There were several aspects to these functions: defense of the community against outside pressures and dangers; arbitration within the already differentiated community between interest groups and social classes, either existing or nascent; and the power exercised on the community by one of its members or by an outside element in the name of a superior State.

We are led, therefore, to a definition: the rural (peasant) community is a social group organized according to historically determined modalities, a group of families tied to the land. These elementary groups, on the one hand, possess the collective or undivided assets of the community and, on the other, various "private" assets, in variable but always historically determined proportions. They are connected through their collective occupations and appoint—as long as the community retains a life of its own—leaders who are assigned to direct tasks of a general interest to the community.[13]

IV

And what about the *problems* presented by the sociohistorical reality thus defined, some of which are the result of the definition itself and some of which are partly clarified or resolved by it?

1. *Problems of origin.* Can we, historically and sociologically, associate forms of peasant communities with some originary, primitive, elementary, undifferentiated group? The lack of a distinction, as we saw earlier, between instruments (means of production, the land itself being one of those means of production) and consumer goods (immediate or not) has confused discussions about *primitive communism*. This hypothesis, in spite of the objections, which specifically relate to the lack of the distinction noted above, remains today the most satisfactory.

We must also determine the precise conditions by which nomadic or seminomadic groups became stationary. Extensive historical and ethnographic documentation has been accumulated, which awaits its theoretical expansion, concerning the invention of agriculture (most likely, by women), its initial progress, the itinerant crops planted by seminomadic groups, the movements of those groups, the combination of agricultural labor with livestock raising (and also with warfare, pillage, and the capture and use of slaves). More specifically, with regard to the village community, the question of origin can be expressed as follows: is it the result of the dissolution or breakup of the primitive group (clan) or of an association of elementary groups (family communities)?

It seems that, presented abstractly, the question would be a false and insoluble one. In certain cases, under certain historical conditions, there was probably some dispersion, differentiation, or breakup of the primitive group; the village would then be formed on the basis of a preexisting community. In other cases—land clearing, decentralization, conquest, increasing density of the population in a given area—the village may have been formed through the association of more restricted family groups. The history of the Russian peasant community, the *obshchina* (primitive community), the *mir* (an administratively constituted community), of the clearance and colonization of vast areas in southern Russia, appears to demonstrate both types of formation, always under specific historical and sociological conditions.

2. *Problems of descent, succession, and sociological causality.* Against the simplistic evolutionism of the late nineteenth century, represented especially by Émile de Laveleye, we must acknowledge that the "evolution" of the peasant community has been more complex and more inconsistent than initially believed.[14] These first theoreticians, Laveleye especially, had the great merit of anticipating the unity of the problem, the successive forms of community. But the analogies they established now appear to us to be rather hasty. For example, Laveleye compared the ancient French "tacit community" with the Balkan *zadruga* and Russian *mir*, associating them all with the primitive community. But we now know that

the *mir* was an administrative creation of czarist power in the eighteenth century, based, it is true, on an ancient peasant tradition. Here, State power decided, like the followers of Frédéric Le Play, to arrest a moving reality for its own benefit. As for the tacit community and the *zadruga*—family communities rather than village communities like the *mir*—these differ profoundly from the others because of the role and authority of the head of the family.

The historian and sociologist can no longer accept the hypothesis of continuous evolution (which Engels had already superseded [*dépassé*] in the nineteenth century). The peasant community in France had already experienced transformation and differentiation, and had begun to dissolve by the time the Romans arrived. Caesar acknowledges this when he notes the existence among the "Gauls" of local or regional chieftains and client groups. Roman law, the Roman concept of property, the establishment of vast domains, accentuated this disaggregation and likely led to the partial disappearance of the peasant community. But it reestablished itself (the "villa" giving way to the "village") or solidified itself wherever it had been preserved during the slow dissolution of ancient society, and especially following the settlement of invading barbarians. These brought about a renewal of the community, *not because they were Germanic but because they were "barbarian," that is to say, closer to primitive society.* This important historical and sociological fact can be demonstrated by an analysis of a series of texts, including the Lex Romana Visigothorum; The Opinions of Julius Paulus, Breviary of Alaric, containing the Liber or Forum-Iudicum, and the Visigothic laws of Recceswinth, Wamba, etc. A historical and sociological analysis of these texts and of the influence in southern France (and Spain) of this compromise between Roman and barbarian (customary, community) law appears to satisfactorily demonstrate a reconstitution or strengthening of the peasant community (agro-pastoral) in the area in question. In the past, historians frequently erred by treating Visigothic law as *Germanic* law rather than as *barbarian* customary law.

Contemporary sociological findings clearly demonstrate the complexity, the interconnection of human phenomena. Today, we find deep-seated residues and even a certain consolidation of the patriarchal family. In this family type, the unbroken transmission of inheritance given to the father of the family (paterfamilias) is the fundamental goal of its organization. The right of the eldest son remains, and to preserve it we turn to the Civil Code, putting aside inheritance laws (this has been officially corrected in recent legislation). In the Basque country, in Béarn and Bigorre, this preservation of the patriarchal family is also joined to strong elements of the village community. Elsewhere we find extreme individualization, which leads, in the family and in the village, to the disappearance of communal attitudes as well as communal ownership. However, the widespread cooperative movement—itself complex, highly varied, and with its own conflicting tendencies—is a sign of a reconstitution of the village community on an entirely new technical, economic, and political basis.

In spite of the variety and interconnection of forms, in spite of the discontinuities that sever the sociohistorical process, the hypothesis of a causal succession of forms of ownership and community must be examined. It alone allows us to develop a scientific theory that can explain the facts. It alone enables us to dominate the sociological process, to discover an intelligible structure within it, and to thus absorb the analysis of concrete facts, historical and actual. Based on this hypothesis, the future of the group studied ranges from the primitive, undifferentiated community to its dissolution in the differentiated individual—from collective ownership to private property, from equality to inequality, from the organic communal group to its dispersion. But, *at the same time,* at various periods of history, and especially during our own, opposing tendencies have become apparent, tending toward the legal and social equality of individuals, and toward a reconstitution of the community along more or less novel foundations.

Thus, sociological theory can and must cooperate with history, with political economy, to reveal the *general law of the process* without omitting contingent or aberrant forms, and without neglecting the extreme complexity of the facts.

3. *Historical problems: the interaction of forms.* If the above is correct, there is nothing immutable, nothing eternal about the peasant community. Under certain conditions, it has disappeared or is disappearing. It may

disappear completely, dissolving into industrialized forms of agriculture (large capitalist farms or, although with an entirely different economic and social structure, the *sovkhoz*), so that we can no longer speak of the village or rural community in the precise sense of those terms. Like any historical reality, the peasant community has changed, strengthened, or dissolved. But under what conditions? That is the historical problem in all its magnitude.

We are barely beginning to reconstruct this history, to understand the bitter struggles, the battles waged by peasant communities against outside forces, against the feudalism of the Middle Ages or, later, the centralized state (a conflict that continues to this day in new forms and under various guises in large parts of the world: Africa, Asia, etc.).

Historians of our Middle Ages and the Ancien Régime focus almost exclusively on urban communes and cities. However, the peasant movement, at all times, has never been less important than the cities. It has preceded them, or accompanied them, or sustained them. We can attribute the decline and fall of the ancient world, and the end of feudal anarchy, to the fundamental effort of the peasant masses, grouped or regrouped in rural communities.[15] During the distant dawn of the modern age, in France and possibly elsewhere, we find a kind of "revolution of the serfs," an incomplete, sporadic, yet profound revolution, simultaneously economic, social, judicial, and political, sometimes violent, sometimes slow and deep, culminating in the partial emancipation of the peasant class and the partial possession of the land by the peasantry.

Of noteworthy sociological importance is the fact that it was not, or not only, social differentiation, the inequality of conditions, that split the community. This required the disintegrating action of the market economy as well as the skillful or brutal pressure of the state. Historical progress, here as elsewhere, is accomplished through the destruction of forms that once possessed grandeur and strength. Also worth mentioning, in passing, is the problem of the relationship between the peasant community and higher forms of the economy (the market economy, industrial, then capitalist, and, finally, socialist economy) as well as that of its relationship with the state. The rural politics of the Ancien Régime is a vast question, very little explored by historians, to mention only one aspect of the problem.

The *law of unequal development* of analogous forms and of the *interaction* of those forms (which coexist at different stages of their life) appears to be one of the great laws of history. While the peasant community in certain regions of France (north, east, center, the Pyrenees of the Midi) resumed a new life under the influence of the "barbarians," in other regions this reconstitution was incomplete or nonexistent. The influence of Roman law continued almost unabated along the Mediterranean coast of the Midi; and in the west, the dissolution of the community, and a very ancient individualism must have been accentuated through the belated clearing of this area of France. Yet there were interactions and reciprocal influences. From the eleventh and twelfth centuries, the Mediterranean influence began to reduce the influence of customary Pyrenean law in the region of Catalonia-Roussillon. If the hypothesis put forward here is correct, France would not have had several agrarian civilizations, whether determined by climate, technology, or ethnicity. There would only have been different degrees and modalities of dissolution or reconstitution of the peasant community.

We know what the problem is. I want to suggest considering the *historical–sociological study of the peasant community* as one of the main lines to follow in the interweaving of human facts.

4. *Other problems.* These include the problem of the conditions of the individual (women, younger children) in the peasant community, then and now, and problems related to awareness and ideology: peasant wisdom, the feeling of the sacred, the organization and ritualization of time and space in the community, and so on. Historical and sociological analyses intersect the study of folklore and the development of myths.

V

Thus, we see come into focus, in a specific sector, the perspectives of a sociology that is simultaneously scientific and concrete.

Today, there is nothing autonomous about peasant life. It can no longer evolve according to distinct laws; it is tied, in a multiplicity of ways, to the overall economy, to the life of the nation, to urban life, to modern technology. Yet the study of this rich and complex reality finds itself, in the past as well as the present, always face-to-face with the existence or extension of an original formation: the rural community. Nearly all our villages today, with the exception of recent trends, are communities in the process of dissolution.

In this brief study, I have tried to establish, or at least suggest, the possibility of an explanatory theory of this original formation, reconstructing and interlinking its successive moments, without separating them from general history and social life. And if it is true that the peasant community could be reborn today, on the basis of modern needs and modern foundations, nothing would be more interesting than that rebirth, from which might emerge a new meaning of the Earth.

Notes

[*Cahiers internationaux de Sociologie*, no. 6 (1949): 78–100, reprinted in *Du rural à l'urbain* (Paris: Anthropos, 1970), 21–40.—Eds.]

1. Some prescientific historians of the French countryside, such as Gaston Roupnel, have in all likelihood exaggerated the antiquity and perennity of our villages. They have discovered elements of the Neolithic almost everywhere, traces of a primitive community, thereby ceding to this myth of "primitivism" that weighs on our historical and sociological reasoning. These strange historians, in the name of history and a myth of origin, have even gone so far as to deny actual history!

2. The abundance of archived documents, unprepossessing and sordidly economical (all related to feudal rights and taxation), highlight the contrast between reality and the forms of awareness in a class society based on the oppression and exploitation of the peasantry.

3. We should also mention Eugène Bonnemère's *Histoire des paysans depuis la fin du moyen âge jusqu'à nos jours* (Paris, 1956), now somewhat outdated but still significant; and the fine work by Benjamin Guérard on the *Polyptyque de l'abbé Irminon de Saint-Germain-des-Prés* [2 vols. (Paris, 1844)].

4. It would be interesting to compare, both from the point of view of method (empiricist and normative on the one side; historical, materialist, and dialectical on the other) as well as from that of content (reactionary on one side, revolutionary on the other), Le Play's principal work with the works of Engels devoted to the peasant problem. The titles themselves are significant: *L'organisation de la famille, d'après le modèle éternel prouvé par l'observation des races* (Le Play) and *The*

Origins of the Family, Private Property, and the State (Engels). [Le Play's work was actually titled *L'organisation de la famille, selon le vrai modèle signalé par l'histoire de toutes les races et de tous les temps* (Paris: Alfred Marne et fils, 1871).—*Eds.*]

5. Not all the conclusions of the contemporary French historical school are equally solid. As in any advancing science, this may be the time for a revision. For example, in the south of France and even in Provence, when a rural farm grows in size and exceeds a certain amount of acreage, it often transitions from a two-year to a three-year crop rotation, simply because a third of the overall acreage, sown with wheat, potatoes, and so on, has met the needs of the farm. Is two-year crop rotation, then, a characteristic of southern French agriculture, determined by climate or by immemorial tradition? Wouldn't there also be the important question of the "structure" of the property? The question needs to be asked. And it is not the only one that might lead to a reconsideration of arguments that, not too long ago, seemed to have been settled once and for all.

6. I would specifically like to point out the work of Romanian sociologists, especially the fine, three-volume monograph published in 1938 on an archaic village (Nerej) in the montagnard region known as the Vrancea. Additionally, the research of historians of antiquity on the origins of the Greek or Roman city have advanced in the same direction. (See the various references in the work of [Louis] Gernet, and the *Annales d'Histoire Économique et Sociale* 9, 324 et seq.). [The first is a reference to H. H. Stahl, *Nerej: Un village d'une region archaïque; Monographie sociologique,* 3 vols. (Bucharest: Institut des Sciences Sociales de Roumanie, 1939). It is not clear what the reference to the *Annales* is intended to be, since volume 9 postdates Lefebvre's essay; and the ninth issue of the journal does not have this page range within it. The people he mentions are probably Henri Labouret, Jacques Weulersse, and Harald von Sicard.—*Eds.*]

7. See, for example, John H. Kolb and Edmund de S. Brunner, *A Study of Rural Society,* edited by William F. Ogburn (Boston: Houghton Mifflin Company, 1944), 313 et seq. Special mention should be made, however, of certain remarkable works, such as Paul Landis's *Rural Life in Process* [2nd ed. (New York: McGraw-Hill)], 1948. Almost singlehandedly, Landis has studied rural life in its unfolding. He describes villages of the European type in the northeast (concentrated habitat, organized crop rotation, communal life) and the French villages of the Mississippi. He has examined the problems of Blacks and poor whites in the Corn Belt. Landis also describes the indebtedness of poor and middle-class peasants (418), the lack of electricity (432), and the feudal nature of the plantations of the South.

8. The authors cited, moreover, come to what can be described as a cynical conclusion: "Unfortunately, such high ideals are yet to be realized in many a local rural community. On the debit side, some researchers report that even churches and schools perpetuate class lines and accentuate differences" (Kolb and Brunner, *A Study of Rural Society,* 23).

9. See the *Bulletin de l'Académie des Sciences de l'U.R.S.S.*, no. 2 (1947), which contains a lengthy report of the important work of B. D. Grebov on the history of the Russian peasant.

10. Like the *vrancea* studied by Romanian sociologists and the associations and syndicates of the valleys of the French Pyrenees.

11. [Three French historians, of whom Bloch is the best known as a member of the *Annales* school; Georges Lefebvre (no relation) was a historian of the French Revolution, and Henri Sée was an economic historian, especially of the Middle Ages.—*Eds.*]

12. [A *sovkhoz* was a Soviet farm, which along with the *kolkhoz*—a collective farm—were the two types of farms established in the USSR in 1917, becoming widespread from 1929 on. Collective farms were less subject to state control, made their own decisions on profits, but were obliged to meet quotas; state farms were owned by the state and workers were paid a salary: they became more and more common over time.—*Eds.*]

13. Compare this with the definition by Kolb and Brunner: "A rural community consists of the social interaction of the people and their institutions in the local area." Kolb and Bruner's definition taken from Charles Galpin, *Rural Social Problems* (New York: The Century Co., 1914). [In fact, this definition comes from Dwight Sanderson, *The Rural Community: The Natural History of a Sociological Group* (Boston: Ginn, 1932), 481.—*Eds.*]

14. *De la Propriété et de ses Formes primitives* (Paris: F. Alcan, 1877); *La Péninsule des Balkans* (Paris: F. Alcan, 1888). See also Maxime Kowalevsky, *Coup d'oeil sur l'évolution du régime économique et sa division en périodes* (Paris: V. Giard & E. Brière, 1896); *Passage historique de la propriété collective à la propriété individuelle* (Paris: Giard & E. Brière, 1895). [Émile de Laveleye, *Primitive Property*, trans. G. R. L. Marriott (London, 1878); Émile de Laveleye, *The Balkan Peninsula*, trans. Mrs. Thorpe (New York: G. P. Putnam's Sons, 1887). There appear to be no English translations of works by Maxime Kowalevsky, whose name is also transliterated as Maksim Kovalewsky or Kovalevskii.—*Eds.*]

15. The reader is asked to accept this proposition as a hypothesis that will be supported by facts—and possibly corrected by subsequent research.

CHAPTER 3

Social Classes in Rural Areas
Tuscany and the *Mezzadria Classica*

In studying agrarian structures, the economic determination of the classes in rural areas, and other relevant indices, Tuscany provides an excellent example. There are several reasons for this:

—it is an extremely old agricultural region, in which the rural landscape as well as the social structure have been developed and redeveloped many times, finally assuming an original form[1]
—ever since the end of the Middle Ages, Tuscany has preserved this original agrarian structure, essentially based on sharecropping (*mezzadria classica*), which became fixed, as if crystallized, in such a way that it was easily observable
—the documentation prepared by official agencies (Italian National Institute of Agrarian Economy) and union organizations is extremely precise and detailed

The agrarian structure in Tuscany illustrates the way the city, as an economic and political center, was able to control the countryside. Florence, Siena, Pisa, Lucca, Pistoia completely reshaped the surrounding countryside. Beginning in the thirteenth century, the old landowning aristocracy, of feudal origin, and the new urban aristocracy, whose origins were in trading and banking, reorganized their rural properties. The cities provided significant opportunities for agricultural products, but labor output and production had to be increased. The urban aristocracy had already spread to the surrounding areas, had broken the resistance of small feudal landowners and conquered or purchased their fiefdoms, thereby freeing the serfs. Those of the former landowners who managed to survive and the new owners replaced the earlier, servile use of the land with a more commercial arrangement. They eliminated exploitative land tenure and the seigniorial domain and instituted a system of *sharecropping*. The tenant farmer received half of the harvest, the other half being immediately available on the market. The advantage of this solution for the participants is obvious. On the seigniorial domain, the productivity of labor could only increase, the worker receiving no additional benefits. The serfs paid a fixed debt in kind or in cash, depending on the fluctuations of the market or the currency; the landowners sought to avoid such fixed payments, which could have led to the general liberation of the peasantry and the formation of a predominant class of small owners. In the sharecropping system, the peasant was free, a perpetual and hereditary holder of the concession to work the land. Therefore, he had an interest in increasing his labor and his productivity. On the other hand, the payment to the landowner was proportional to the output, and very high: basically half of the amount produced. Consequently, he benefited from any increase in productivity. The system was imposed in spite of the resistance of the peasantry. In one sense, it looked like progress. Yet it is important to emphasize that this progress was not so much the result of the *mezzadria* system itself as it was of the wealth of the cities and the expanded needs of urban markets.

Subsequently, sharecropping could have evolved toward capitalist exploitation to become a form of *tenant farming*. This evolution took place, as we know, in the north of Italy and the northern part of France, where sharecropping nearly disappeared. In Tuscany, however, the arrested development of the cities, their stagnation (following the shift of worldwide commerce toward the Atlantic), brought about the crystallization of the *mezzadria classica*.

Some theorists of the agrarian question still maintain that sharecropping was and remains a "peasant's paradise."

In fact, agriculture has changed radically since the distant past, when sharecropping could, in a way, be considered a solution. The increase in the productivity of labor and the soil, even their basic maintenance, assumes other conditions. The simple intensification of labor, the extension of the working day, the number of people working are no longer sufficient. The peasant or village wheelwright can no longer manufacture modern instruments. They have to purchase fertilizer and tools, and improve the soil—in short, they require capital. But the *mezzadria* system barred the peasant from accumulating capital and, consequently, productive investment in the land he cultivated. "Progressive" theoreticians of the agrarian question, therefore, consider sharecropping as a semifeudal system, a transition between precapitalist forms of agriculture and more evolved forms. Our following examination of the output of a sharecropping system shows that the sharecropper can only hope to maintain his already mediocre situation. Only the farmer, who pays the owner a fixed ground rent in cash, can accumulate capital, invest it productively, and partly benefit from that investment (assuming the rent is reasonable and the size of the farm sufficient, as well as its location, the nature of the soil, and so on).[2]

No economic movement from the city or the countryside would modify the agrarian structure in Tuscany for several centuries. It remained as it was during the age of the communes and of the urban aristocracy. During their decadence, a reflux of the urban population led to an increase in the rural population and a greater division of the lands given over to sharecropping, without altering the fundamental agrarian structure. This structure was consolidated much later through a resurgence of feudalism; use of the laws of *majorat* and *fideicommisum* allowed the great families to preserve their lands intact and even to expand them.

Having come into existence through the influence of capitalism, but within the persistent framework of agrarian feudalism, the *mezzadria classica* took root through the influence of literally anachronistic economic, social, and political relationships. Therefore, the *mezzadria* did not accompany a transformation of feudal relations but rather a failure, a cessation, even a regression of that transformation. It is hard to imagine today that we could conceive of it as a satisfactory system. Only a violently antiscientific (from the technical as well as the sociological point of view) state of mind can explain such an attitude.

The population of Tuscany is approximately three million, out of which 1.5 million live from agriculture alone (percentage by province: Arezzo, 66.5% of the population; Siena, 66.3%; Grosseto, 61.9%; Pisa, 51.8%; Pistoia, 46.7%; Lucca, 39.7%; Florence, 35.7%; Livorno, 27.6%). The territory as a whole is divided as follows: 59% hillsides, 30.7% mountainous, and only 10.3% consists of open plains (the lower basin of the Arno, the Grosseto plain, the valleys of the Apennines).

Overall, Tuscany comprises 2,216,000 hectares; local communities (State lands, communes, religious communities) hold 14.7% of the cadastral surface, or 325,460 hectares (consisting primarily of woods and pasture land).

If we consider small farms those that cover less than 10 hectares, we find that they represent 93.7% of the number of farms but only 19.2% of the land. However, 0.1% (one in a thousand) of owners hold 21.6% of the land and 0.2% (two in every thousand) possess 32.3%. Specifically, 164 agrarian land holders own 310,896 hectares; 1,700 large landowners hold 46% of the land; but 348,312 small owners occupy no more than 283,739 hectares. Thus, the domination of large land holdings is an incontestable fact. If we look at the average-size holding (10 to 50 hectares), whose origin is generally bourgeois and capitalist (not medieval), these account for only 17.6% of the surface area; frequently, large properties belonging to several individuals (members of the same family) are classified among the average property holdings based on the share of each individual in the total family holding.

The following table provides a detailed breakdown of the agrarian structure in Tuscany by farm and ownership category (figures provided by the National Institute of Agrarian Economy based on a study commissioned on April 26, 1946, by a ministerial decision). The table shows that the feudal or semifeudal form of land concentration is at its maximum in the province of Grosseto, near Latium. Agrarian landowners hold 45.4% of the land and small landholders (from 0 to 10 hectares) only 10.2%,

Categories (number and surface area by percentage)

		Total number	from 2 ha	2 to 5 ha	5 to 10 ha	10 to 50 ha	50 to 100 ha	200 to 500 ha	500 to 1,000 ha	> than 1,000 ha
Arezzo	Number	36,475	60.6	16.4	9.1	11.1	2.3	0.3	0.1	0.1
	Surface area	313,811	4.1	6.1	7.5	27.4	24.5	12.5	9.8	8.1
Florence	N.	34,845	63.9	13.4	8.1	10.8	2.8	0.7	0.2	0.1
	S.A.	368,022	2.8	4.1	5.4	22.2	25.0	21.0	12.0	7.5
Grosseto	N.	34,277	69.7	14.9	6.3	6.6	1.7	0.4	0.1	0.1
	S.A.	438,330	3.1	3.7	3.4	11.3	12.4	10.7	10.0	45.4
Livorno	N.	16,172	72.5	14.7	6.3	5.0	1.0	0.3	0.1	0.1
	S.A.	117,593	5.3	6.4	6.0	13.8	13.6	14.1	9.3	31.5
Lucca	N.	106,232	85.0	9.4	3.1	1.7	0.2	(very low %)		
	S.A.	170,351	22.8	18.4	13.3	19.3	8.6	3.6	4.0	10.4
Massa Carrara	N.	70,874	85.0	9.3	3.5	2.1	6.1	(very low %)		
	S.A.	110,135	22.8	18.4	15.8	23.7	5.4	5.2	4.3	4.4
Pisa	N.	30,369	76.8	10.9	5.3	5.1	1.3	0.4	0.1	0.1
	S.A.	233,150	4.4	4.5	4.9	13.9	16.4	15.7	11.6	28.6
Pistoia	N.	44,617	81.1	11.9	4.3	2.5	0.2	(very low %)		
	S.A.	92,692	16.8	17.9	14.0	22.2	10.7	5.2	6.2	7.0
Siena	N.	19,268	61.1	14.6	8.0	10.5	3.9	1.2	0.4	0.3
	S.A.	372,628	1.7	2.4	3.0	12.1	19.8	19.1	16.8	25.1
Tuscany	N.	393,192	76.9	11.7	5.1	4.8	1.0	0.3	0.1	0.1
	S.A.	2,216,712	6.2	6.6	6.4	17.6	17.2	13.7	10.7	21.6
			Small property			Average, large, and very large property				

although they compose more than 90% of all owners. In the countryside around Lucca, on the other hand, those same small landowners hold more than 54% of the land.

It is remarkable, and reflective of an entire economic, social, and political history of the region, that the domination of rural landowners is greater around the large cities (in the Florentine countryside, the concentration is as great as it is in Sicily) and increases rapidly as we move from north to south. Tuscany represents the transition between northern Italy ("modernized" by its market and industrial economy, by capitalism and the bourgeoisie) and a semi-medieval south. South of Siena, the predominance of large holdings is soon obvious. And the landscape changes, not only because of changes in the soil or climate but, especially, because of a different social structure. The green hilltops, crowned by cypress trees, the large, well-situated villages, the well-tended and vibrant countryside gives way to a depopulated, woodless region harboring a handful of poor villages. We approach a region both unprepossessing and ravaged by the influence of ancient Rome.

The region of Grosseto provides the investigations of sociologists with a form of agricultural exploitation of great interest, preserved as a kind of "sociological fossil" along with many other medieval holdovers. Communities of family sharecroppers of between sixty and eighty people live in a "large house" and farm sharecropped lands of 100 hectares and more. These are peaceful communities, *freresches,* similar to those that subsisted until the nineteenth century in the region around Thiers, in the Limousin, in Franche-Comté, in Lauraguais, and elsewhere in France.

The large properties and some of the average-size properties are divided into *poderi,* which constitute the farmed unit, the basic agricultural cell or smallholding. But the *poderi* themselves are frequently grouped into *fattorie* (47,830 *poderi* out of the 100,695 in Tuscany are part of a *fattoria*). To some extent, this arrangement explains the persistence of sharecropping in Tuscany. The *fattorie,* when the farmer is not too underdeveloped, provide sharecroppers with technical guidance and products that isolated peasants are unable to purchase. In this way, the peasants, when they manage to become small landowners, sometimes lose some of the technical elements leading to labor productivity. Having learned from experience, many of them have already abandoned this ancient peasant "ideal" of acquiring land. These facts play a large role in the pleas of traditionalists for sharecropping. In reality only a small number of landowners provide their sharecroppers with technical guidance and the instruments of production; overall, *as a class,* the landowners stubbornly refuse to invest capital in the *fattorie,* considered as business undertakings. For them, their portion of the harvest is intended to cover their personal expenses. It's clear that, as a class, they have had no further function in the process of production for several centuries. This allows them the greatest possible margin of "freedom"; the owner can choose to remain absent, live in the city or abroad, remain on the land, or interest himself in his property and his sharecroppers.

The domination of the agrarian landowners, who ensnared Tuscany in semifeudal relationships, is reflected in very concrete facts. For example, nearly everywhere, the roads leading out of the *poderi* terminate in the *palazzo* occupied by the owner or manager of the *fattoria*. The latter thus controls every movement of the sharecroppers, every wagon, every activity. Those who know the region acknowledge that many of the owners require their sharecroppers to seek their counsel and authorization before allowing their sons or daughters to marry. Additionally, unpaid labor and obligatory gifts (known as *oblighi* in the Middle Ages) to this day continue to place a burden on sharecropping contracts.

Landowners are "absentees" or live on their land, or confide the administration of their properties to a steward (manager of the *fattoria*). Occasionally, they would take over the responsibilities themselves. Numerous witnesses have claimed that this personal management has resulted in an oppressive paternalism. The activity of the superintendents and, to a greater extent, the owners led to their continual intervention in the life of the *famiglia colonica,* and they emphasized the intensification of labor far more than technical advancement (which requires investment). The number of agronomical engineers was low and sharecroppers relied on outmoded techniques, especially on *fattorie* where the owner lived and directed the work personally.

In Tuscany, *farmers* were of little importance. They cultivated only 2.7% of the surface area, a figure that included the small *affituari* and capitalist farmers. The latter type of activity was found mostly near cities (vegetable crops). Their conditions of existence changed considerably depending on the extent of the operation and the size of the investment involved.

Sharecroppers, however, accounted for 60% of the population given over to agriculture. The ambiguous nature of their economic existence is reflected in their social and psychological life. They are both entrepreneurs and workers. As entrepreneurs, they had access to a certain amount of capital (their share of the livestock, dead or alive) and delivered a portion of their output to the market. Therefore, they were dependent on the market, its fluctuations, and tended toward a form of mercantilism that distinguished them from the agricultural laborer. Yet, at the same time, they were workers who had to deal with a boss: the owner or his representative. Between the managers of the *fattorie* and the sharecroppers, conflicts were a common occurrence when it came to the management of the business as well as the evaluation and distribution of whatever was produced. The *mezzadria* was not an autonomous operation, an independent enterprise, which profoundly distinguishes the sharecropper from the small artisan-owner.

On the one hand, the *famigilia colonica* is a patriarchal family, and very hierarchical. The head of the family and the farm held the traditional and still respected title of *capoccia*. Many families have, for centuries, cultivated the same plot of land (it is forbidden to divide the units of the *mezzadria*, five to eight hectares if on a plain and more if located on a mountainside). Yet the sharecropper is not free; all the operations in which he is involved are entered into a sharecropping record, signed by both parties. For years, sharecropping has ceased to be, in principle, a hereditary and perpetual position, and syndicates of sharecroppers have demanded a precise definition of the "justifiable reasons" for breaking a contract and dismissal. Therefore, as entrepreneurs, sharecroppers have tended toward individualism. As workers, they resent the need to join together—to unionize to defend their common interests against those of the landowners.

The *braccianti* (agricultural proletarians; those who only have their labor to offer) form the most impoverished category of the rural population. Local witnesses attest to the fact that the class of *braccianti* has been altered and transformed in Tuscany over the past few decades. More accurately, the *braccianti* have become—in Tuscany—a class. Although there is little mechanization of agriculture, some progress has been made, and one can see threshers, harvesters, and other equipment in the region. The number of *braccianti* has increased and they have partly lost the aspect of being patriarchal servants, integrated into family life, living and dying for the same master (owner or sharecropper). They now live in small communities and go to work, in areas around the village, by bicycle. Additionally, through their ability to handle tools, they have acquired certain skills. Their number and the significance of their functions increase as the *fattorie* take on technical complexity. And here we find a remarkable phenomenon: the constitution of a class from initially sporadic elements having only a secondary function. Larger in number, indispensable, having acquired a degree of technical skill, living together in small communities, the *braccianti* see themselves as a distinct group, as a *class*. They form their own distinct associations, their own unions; they are becoming an important element in social and political life.

We can elaborate the social structure of rural Tuscany as follows:[3]

(a) Miscellaneous (cow herders, shepherds, *sensali,* or specialists in buying and selling livestock): 2,782 (0.4% of the active rural population)
(b) *Braccianti* (seasonal salaried workers or not): 89,556 (15%)
(c) Sharecroppers (managers and actively working family members): 364,096 (60.9%)
(d) Owner-operators (small landowners who are owner-occupants): 118,130 (19.8%)
(e) Tenant farmers (small farmers): 9,465 (1.6%)
(f) Capitalist farmers (who invest capital in an agricultural enterprise on land they do not own): 1,031 (0.2%)
(g) Employees and technicians: 3,690 (0.6%)
(h) Landowners (average or large-size): 8,888 (1.5%)

As previously shown, the rural population has no homogeneity and the expression "the peasant class" has no precise meaning. The peasantry, or rural population living off agriculture, comprises *classes* and groups, or categories that do not constitute a class. We can, however, speak of the class of landowners. Although small in number and playing no part in production, their economic, social, and political role is such that they constitute a class. It is impossible to study the region without coming across constant references to this class, without studying the class itself. The *braccianti,* and the sharecroppers, also constitute classes in Tuscany. But capitalist farmers (who in northern Italy, central and northern France, England, and elsewhere constitute a class) are too few in number in Tuscany, too insignificant, for us to call this category a "class." The same is true of technicians, administrators, and so on.

In other words, for there to be a *class,* a number of indices, of characteristics, must be combined: number or quantity, functional homogeneity, common interests and activities, awareness, ideology (qualitative indices). Also, a given index may not be present; if it is replaced by another, the group constitutes a class. Thus, the owners of landed property, a tiny percentage of the population, constitute a class because the strength, homogeneity, and unity of their actions and interests greatly exceed their numerical size.

On the other hand, these indices express tendencies and should not be treated as an undifferentiated mass, generally present or absent. In this way the class of the *braccianti* is constituted, acquires an awareness, an ideology. It exists at a certain stage or level of maturity.

For example, in Tuscany we find a class of agricultural workers, a class of small landholders, a class of sharecroppers, a class of landowners (which is itself divided into midlevel and more powerful landowners). Among these, the class of agricultural workers appears to grow, maintain and defend itself, that is, offer signs of life. The small landholders vegetate. The large landowners have, for a long time, been no more than a parasitic class, external to production (aside from a few isolated cases) but not external to social and political life, upon which they are a significant burden.

A direct study of the villages confirms the results of the analysis and more clearly isolates their significance.

Take San Gimignano, for example. It is a typical Tuscan town: the center is tightly clustered on a hillside, between old medieval walls, its population dispersed among the *fattorie* and *poderi*. The consolidated population comprises 3,778 persons and the dispersed population 7,509 (a total of 11,287, of which 5,798 are male and 5,489 are female). The population of the center comprises merchants, artisans, a number of midlevel property owners, physicians, pharmacists, teachers, and, finally, a large number of *braccianti*. The following table illustrates the social composition of the overall population.

	Men	Women
Laborers	169	—
Braccianti	629	—
Sharecroppers	2,631	1,368
"Small owners"	156	—
Artisans	204	3
Employees	268	71
Merchants	113	16
Students	61	31
Professionals	11	4
Property owners (non-operators)	97	70
Clergy	30	44
Retired	175	99
Children, schoolchildren	1,223	1,098
Homemakers	—	2,650

The smallholders [*petits propriétaires*] hold 156 farms, only 19 of which approach 10 hectares in size; 80 of them cover approximately 5 hectares. The sharecroppers, with their families, cultivate 743 *poderi* of between 6 and 8 hectares (that is, larger than the majority of the plots farmed by their owners). Some of these *poderi* belong to midlevel owners (one of whom owns 3 *poderi* of 18 hectares total, another 4 *poderi* of 68 hectares total, a portion of which is wooded, another 2 *poderi* with only 5.88 hectares in total, and so on); these are not grouped into *fattorie*. But the majority of them, grouped into *fattorie*, belong to the group of large landowners. This group contains some of the most celebrated names in history: the counts Guicciardini (family of the celebrated Guichardin), who hold 5,900 hectares in Tuscany, have 59 *poderi* of 510 hectares in total in San Gimignano.[4] The counts Strozzi hold 26 *poderi* covering 778 hectares (some of which is wooded).[5] A Swiss partnership, the Corti-Dante, holds 17 *poderi* covering 401 hectares; another company, the Pietrafitta, holds 33 *poderi* covering 411 hectares.

Among the employees of the *fattorie*, we find superintendents,[6] administrators, accountants, and a handful of "technicians" (drivers, mechanics) among the personnel of the companies, but no licensed agronomists. Based on statements by the local authorities, these administrative personnel of the *fattorie* also formed the cadres of the *fascio* when Mussolini was in power.

Since the Liberation, there have been 25 *fattorie* committees in San Gimignano (rural business committees), consisting of delegates elected by the sharecroppers. Roughly 50 small landowners belonged to the *Federterra*, a group of direct cultivators. And roughly 15 of the *fattorie* committees have obtained significant results: participation in the management of the *fattorie* considered as a rural business, control in the sharing of the goods produced, and so on.

Before returning to this important question (because characteristic of a change in social relations), I want to summarize the social structure of another important town, Poggibonsi.

Population: approximately 14,000 (the figure is imprecise because of the number of seasonal and unemployed workers who seek work elsewhere), including 7,150 grouped.

There are 167 very small farm owner-operators (46 of whom have less than one hectare; 76 with 1 to 2 hectares; 45 with 2 to 4 hectares); 45 small owners with 5 to 10 hectares; 29 with 10 to 20 hectares; 14 with 20 to 30 hectares; 7 with 30 to 40 hectares; 11 with 40 to 50 hectares; 11 with

50 to 100 hectares; 7 with 100 to 200 hectares; 5 with 200 to 300 hectares; 5 with 300 to 600 hectares; for a total of 299 owners; plus 270 *braccianti* and 480 *mezzadrile* families comprising 3,440 persons. In addition, there are approximately 1,500 industrial workers (glass works), including 500 unemployed.

It is remarkable that the data about production show that at Poggibonsi the large property cultivated by sharecropping produces only 1,000 to 1,200 kilos of wheat per hectare, whereas the small owners produce 2,400 to 2,500 kilos. Analogous proportions hold for the production of wine and oil.

To understand the current situation of the *mezzadria classica* and the new activity of the rural enterprise committees (from which the sharecroppers as an active class based on common interests are formed), we need to examine current legislation in the region.

After the Liberation, the sharecroppers succeeded in increasing their portion of the harvest from 50% to 60% (in France, sharecroppers, of which there are 180,000 to 200,000 in the southern half of the country, received two-thirds of the base product rather than half). Their organizations attempted to consolidate and even expand these advantages. Primarily, they demanded:

(a) A satisfactory settlement of the question of war damages (livestock seized or requisitioned at low cost; buildings that were destroyed or damaged)
(b) A definition of the "justifiable" reasons for firing
(c) Participation in the management of the company, and therefore the passage of legislation governing the *fattorie* [farm] committees and their transition from purely syndical organizations to management organizations
(d) The obligation, for the owner, to invest capital, to improve the soil, to modernize the farm, to improve tools and buildings
(e) Review of contracts on the basis of the contributions of each participant (see the following "theory of contributions")

However, in 1946, a law reduced the sharecropper's share to 57% of the produce of the current year, then to 55% for the following year. It abolished, in principle, the obligatory gifts and supplementary work (transporting wood, and so on). Finally, concerning the renewal of livestock herds, it reduced the sharecropper's portion to 30% of the expense; and each of them received a bonus of 2,000 lire per head of livestock saved from requisitions and seizures. The firing of sharecroppers was suspended. But a new law, passed on August 4, 1948, lowered to 53% the sharecropper's portion, with the threat to soon reintroduce the former division by halves. The question of obligatory gifts (*regalie oblighi*) was poorly resolved (only the supplementary work was eliminated). The ban on firing turned out to be extended for no more than a year. Finally, the owners found themselves forced to invest a specific amount (4%) of the product of the farm into upgrades, improvements, tools, and equipment.

The *fattorie* committees continued their activities in hopes of a strict application of these laws, especially the last, which the owners consistently avoided.

They took into their own hands the sale of farm products, livestock especially, directly extracting the legal percentage. In many cases, the owners refused the money given to them; in those cases the committees deposited it in a bank and managed the money themselves. They prevented the landowners from housing jointly owned livestock in their stables; they organized the resistance to traditional supplementary work, refused the obligatory gifts, which, in 1948, were solemnly carried to the hospitals of Florence.

It is highly unusual to see a modern organization (union, labor committee) operating under medieval conditions.

In San Gimignano, the legal 4% of the funds for improvements amounts to 25 million lire (9 million from the grain harvest, 2.4 million from oil, 6 million from wine, 7 million from livestock, 1 million from corn—estimates supplied by the mayor's office based on data provided by the *fattorie* committees). But in 1949 only 10 million lire were invested, which resulted in approximately 100 *braccianti* unemployed in San Gimignano, while the legal investment could have provided those unemployed workers approximately 29,000 days of work, that is, 290 days per year for each unemployed worker. "Full employment" could have become a reality, within the context of the present social structure, and in accordance with the law, if the class of owners didn't refuse, as a class, to apply the laws. Additionally, many sharecropper homes are falling into ruin or are quite obviously too small for the *famiglia colonica*; stables, granaries, roads, all are in poor condition.

This results in a highly interesting situation. The sharecroppers and their organizations are conducting activities that are both revolutionary and perfectly legal, directed against the obsolete (medieval) class of landowners. This produces unusual forms of activity. For example, the *backwards strike (sciopero al reversi)*. Called by the *fattoria* committee, the unemployed *braccianti* arrive in force on the lands that the owners refuse to improve. In spite of the presence of the owners, the superintendents, or their agents, the workers carry out the work; they then demand their salary (payable to the *legal* investment fund). In the backwards strike, the workers work against the wishes of the boss, and their work increases the productivity of the soil. This is doubly paradoxical when compared to the conventional notion of the strike. Thus, at Empoli, between Florence and Sienna, 70,000 cubic meters of grading, ditches, and other work has been carried out by the "strikers" under the direction of the *fattorie* committees. The latter paid the workers directly, withdrawing 4% from the money deposited by them into the bank and representing the sale of farm products. In all the areas of Tuscany where the committees are active, they have organized the planting of vines, the work of drainage or irrigation, the repair of buildings, and whatever else might be required. They even established, in individual locations, nascent production cooperatives for clearing the land and improving uncultivated or poorly cultivated soil, which assumes their presence on these lands notwithstanding the will of the owner. With this, though, the limits of current legal mechanisms have been reached.

This activity of the *fattorie* committees also demonstrates a profound transformation of social relations and ideas. The sharecroppers, often associated with the same plot of land and the same well-known family for centuries, often thought of themselves as a kind of peasant aristocracy.

Their life, harder than that of the small landowners, strengthened that ideology, symbolized by the patriarchal title of the head of the *mezzadrile* family. The committees, on the other hand, established an economic alliance, syndical in nature and, therefore, political in one way or another, with the poorest and most disdained category of laborers, the *braccianti*.

How then is the *mezzadria*, considered as a rural enterprise, organized and what is its economic situation? It's difficult to establish an exact accounting. We know that the peasant doesn't keep accounts and that rural accounting poses a number of difficult problems.

The following data are based on an interview with a sharecropper and a detailed inspection of an 8.24-hectare site in Poggibonsi (an area somewhat greater than the average sharecropped plot and much greater than the majority of small holdings). Approximately 4 hectares of cereal crops yield 7,000 kilos of grain, of which 53% was for the sharecropper in 1949 (the farmland was located on a slope of loose limestone soil whose yield was quite low due to the lack of fertilizer and proper equipment). About 75 bushels of wine were consumed in place or delivered to the owner; the sharecropper retained his share of 13,500 kilos of oil and 800 kilos of corn. Nine hundred kilos of potatoes and 2,500 kilos of fodder were consumed on site. The sale of livestock (pigs, calves) produced 110,000 lire, of which 53% went to the sharecropper, who also received the entire yield from poultry (50,000 lire). The farmer lived with his family (10 people) and spent 125,000 lire on salaries for the *braccianti* during periods of intense labor, and on miscellaneous purchases, especially fertilizer (far less than what was needed, the owner stubbornly refusing to pay for a portion of the fertilizer and tools and equipment). The year 1949 closed with a net profit of 15,000 to 20,000 lire for the sharecropper. He said he was satisfied with the results of that year and was able to pay back a portion of his debt, amounting to 45,000 lire. (The *sindaco* or mayor of the village and local secretary of the Federterra certified the accuracy of the sharecropper's statements, who was himself the secretary of a *fattoria* committee.)

The following is a description of the smallholding known as Castellucio, a hamlet in Pagnana, in Empoli. The *fattoria* belonged to a businessman who was more knowledgeable of technical matters than the majority of older landowners. Crop rotation (every eight years) was determined by an agronomist; manure was located far from the house, in pits of relatively modern design.

The house is square and, from a distance, in the valley of the Arno (near the Florence-Pisa main line), appears enormous. Up close, its dimensions are rather modest: one upper story, with the farm buildings on the ground floor. The house still bears the arms of its former feudal owners. Four families live here, unrelated, although one of them has lived here for more than 150 years, and two others for 75 and 50 years. Each family has three rooms of modest dimensions. The house groups together four *poderi* of 8 to 10 hectares (35 hectares in all), most likely formed, two or three hundred years ago, by dividing a property or smallholding that was farmed by a large rural family. The *fattoria* comprises 61 *poderi* of 500 hectares in all. Each family has its own house, stable, and storage area. The owner refuses to pay the legal 4% into the investment fund. A *fattoria* committee was formed; 5 elected members represent 58 of the 61 *poderi* (three families refused to join or withdrew after some secondary disagreement: having eaten the pigs the committee had planned to sell). This committee meets every week at the headquarters of the Federterra in Empoli. It has assumed responsibility for a large part of the administration of the *fattoria,* prepared plans for production, labor, and improvements. Its secretary maintains a register of all its decisions and activities. Before the Liberation, the landowner received the proceeds of nearly the entirety of the increase in livestock; therefore, he refuses to accept his legal share of the sale of livestock or pay his share of the general expenses. The *fattoria* committee manages fairly large amounts of money and uses the interest from the owner's share, more than the legal 4%, for improvements. By practicing the reverse strike, unemployed workers from Empoli came to plant vines along the borders of farmed plots. The plots are uniform, numbered, and crops are rotated every eight years, based on a chart displayed in each sharecropper's home. Plot 1, for example, currently covers 74 *ares* (1 *are* being equivalent to 100 square meters) of recently planted border vines.

The conflict with the landowner reached a critical point (May 1950). The prefect of police could not take any action against the committee, for it was completely within its rights. Instead, he offered to arbitrate the conflict by appointing an advisory commission responsible for examining and evaluating the work carried out. The committee, although it considered this action a step backward from the current legal situation, accepted. But the landowner and the federation of landowners rejected the offer of arbitration by the advisory committee and filed a complaint for violation of ownership. The court decided not to hear the motion and, consequently, recognized the legality of the committee's actions, including the reverse strike.

The "theory of contributions" attempts to accurately evaluate the operation of the *mezzadria* by quantifying the respective contributions of the landowner and the sharecropper. The soil and buildings are empirically evaluated, at the current rate based on the market for local real estate.[7] We also evaluate, at market prices, the contributions of living and dead livestock, the work of the sharecropper and the *famiglia colonica*, the harvest, and other factors.

Below, based on the "theory of contributions," is a summary of a farm run as a *mezzadria classica*. Aside from theory, this study (figures were provided by the sharecropper's union in the province of Florence) provides very accurate information about the life and organization of the smallholding.

General characteristics. Location: four kilometers from Florence on the road to Bologna. Limestone hills. Excellent viability. Mixed farming (grains, vines, pasture, fruit trees exposed to the wind, olive trees). Crop rotation every four years, alternating soil-improving and soil-depleting crops, determined by an agronomist on behalf of the landholder.

The sharecropper's house, located 200 meters from the Via Bolognese, will need repairs, along with the farm building itself (roofs are in poor condition).

Surface area. Eight hectares, 6,020 square meters, of which 4 hectares are for grain crops, 2 hectares for pasture (clover), 2 hectares for corn, 60 hectares for beans, 20 for potatoes, and 20 for miscellaneous crops (garden). There are 4,020 vines, 738 olive trees, 151 pear trees, 4 peach trees, 11 fig trees.

Livestock. Two dairy cows, 2 working cows, 1 donkey (no horse). *Dead stock.* Wagon, tank for transporting water, 2 watering pumps, 2 light plows.

Composition of the famiglia colonica. Grandfather (77), head of the farm; three married male children (Bruno, 46; Gino, 42; Carlo, 38). Their wives (Rita, 45; Anna, 38; Rosina, 36). Four children: 20, 14, 14, and 7 years of age.

Gross saleable production (April 1950)		
52 quintals of grain, or	364,000	lire
30 bushels of wine	195,000	—
7 quintals of oil	385,000	—
48 bushels of milk	273,000	—
2.94 quintals of meat (veal, pork)	133,300	—
19 quintals of fruit	108,300	—
plus miscellaneous crops (beans, etc.)		
Total	1,458,600	lire
Annual general expenses		
Feed for livestock (meal and hay)	47,500	lire
Bull	18,000	—
Veterinary, farrier	14,000	—
Workers' salaries (olive harvest, etc.)	30,000	—
Electricity	5,000	—
Fertilizer	36,600	—
Insecticides	36,000	—
Miscellaneous	20,000	—
Total	207,100	lire
Net proceeds	1,251,500	lire

Production factors. Property value, given its location near Florence: 4,400,000 lire. Current interest on long-term investments: 3.5%. Income from land resources or the fixed portion of constant capital: 145,000 lire. *Constant capital supplied by the landowner* (half of the livestock and tools, straw, hay, etc.): 593,200 lire. We can assume that this capital (the "circulating" portion of constant capital) is invested in industry. It returns 7% (current, empirically determined, average rate of profit).

The capital advanced by the landowner must, therefore, return a profit or interest of 41,524 lire, to which can be added 196,000 lire for taxes, for which the landowner is responsible, along with insurance, depreciation, and so on.

Constant capital provided by the sharecropper (share of livestock, tools, etc.): 435,000 lire, or at 7%, a return of 30,450 lire. To this should be added other expenses (fuel for threshing, etc.) amounting to 3,500 lire.

Variable capital. The work of the sharecropper and his family, assuming 600 hours of annual labor per hectare of wheat, 1,500 hours per hectare of corn, 150 hours for each hay cutting, 30 minutes per foot of vine, and so on (regional evaluation by analysts), for a total of 11,030 hours of labor, or 1,378 eight-hour days. The price of a day's labor is fixed, based on the average salary of the *braccianti* in the province, at 630 lire, making the salary for those 1,378 days of labor equivalent to 868,140 lire. To this should be added 50,000 lire as payment to the landowner for the technical supervision he provides (following the advice of an agronomical engineer).

Referring to the previous figures, we find that the net income (net proceeds less general expenses and production expenses) amounts to 39,386 lire, divided between the landowner and the sharecropper, who are considered to be associates in the undertaking.

The net proceeds should, therefore, be divided as follows:

(a) *For the landowner:* 461,317 lire (interest on fixed capital, plus his share of constant capital, plus the bonus for technical supervision, plus half the net income).
(b) *For the sharecropper:* 921,383 lire (payment for his labor, plus interest on his capital, plus his share of the net income).

Concerning general operating expenses (difference between gross output and net proceeds, which we have separated from production costs for greater clarity), these must also be split between the two associates.

Therefore, the sharecropper will receive goods amounting to 1,020,332 lire and the landowner 560,267 lire. The sharecropper's portion amounts to 64% of the total proceeds and that of the landowner 36%.

Similar analyses, taking into account the local circumstances (variations in the composition of capital), yielded the following results: In the Florentine plain, 51% to 64% of the proceeds must be allocated to the sharecropper; on the hillsides, 64%; on the mountainsides, 73% to 83% (the share of work increasing with respect to the value of the land and the equipment). In Lucca, on the low hills, 70%; on the Pisan plain, 64%, and so on.

It is clear, moreover, that the theory of contributions and the subsequent accounting are not free of criticism. The sharecroppers feel that they can easily provide the technical supervision for farming and that the bonus for supervision referred to above is an unacceptable concession. As for the landowners, they find the calculation of the number of hours worked and the payment of sharecroppers based on the legal workday of eight hours to be monstrous.

Nonetheless, the accounting summaries very accurately reflect the structure of the *mezzadria* and are the best source of accurate information about its organization and the life of the *famiglia colonica*.

The standard sharecropping contract prepared by the sharecroppers' union implies the theory of contributions (article 41 in the draft of 69 articles). Until now, the theory has not been accepted by government bodies. It would be useful, but take too long, to compare the standard contract prepared by the Federterra with current legislation and with the standard contract imposed in 1928 by the Fascist agricultural confederation.

Notes

[*Cahiers internationaux de Sociologie*, no. 10 (1951): 70–93, reprinted in *Du rural à l'urbain* (Paris: Anthropos, 1970), 41–62.—Eds.]

1. Setting aside the *aesthetic* analysis of the landscape. In a separate work, I plan to illustrate the relationship between the aesthetic development and social content of the Tuscan countryside. [This work seems never to have been published.—Eds.]

2. Of course, I am referring to capitalist agriculture. I'm leaving aside the general theory of ground rent and the critical analysis of its economic role. [The latter is discussed in chapters 6 and 7 of the current volume.—Eds.]

3. Figures from 1935 (during the Fascist regime). The difference between the statistics and the active population and the farming population has several causes,

but mainly that a given number of *braccianti,* industrial laborers, and artisans possess a small plot of land that is considered to be a "farm."

4. [Francesco Guicciardini (1483–1540) was a Florentine historian and statesman. A friend of Machiavelli, his best-known work is *The History of Italy.* He came from a powerful and well-known aristocratic family and was a supporter of the Medici.—*Trans.*]

5. [The Strozzi were a well-established family of Florentine bankers and, at one time, the richest family in the city. They were bitter rivals of the Medici.—*Trans.*]

6. Managers or personnel who work in the fields as members of the *famiglia colonica.*

7. A scientific evaluation would capitalize (for example, over a period of twenty years) the ground rent. But what is paid by the sharecropper is not a "pure" ground rent, as is the case for the money paid by the capitalist farmer. The benefit with respect to the landholder's contribution in livestock is mixed with the amount paid for the authorization to work the land. It's important to distinguish the elements of the payment, which specifically assumes the "theory of contributions," which must, therefore, start with an empirical calculation.

CHAPTER 4

Perspectives on Rural Sociology

A previous article in *Cahiers internationaux de Sociologie* presented several problems of rural sociology.[1] The time has come to provide an overview of this branch of sociology by presenting—and submitting for discussion—a proposal for a manual or treatise on the subject.

We can speak of a peasant "world," not because that peasant reality would constitute an *isolated* world but rather because of its extraordinary variety and intrinsic characteristics.

Let us again insist on a paradox (only apparent): this reality has been ignored for a long time, especially when it dominated social life quantitatively and qualitatively. For as long as the "urban" reality and its institutions and ideologies, for as long as the successive modes of production, together with their superstructures bathed in a rural milieu and stood on a vast agricultural foundation, the middle and ruling classes paid scant attention to the peasantry. We paid about as much attention to them as we do to our stomach or liver when we are in good health. Peasant life appeared to be one of those familiar realities, which appear natural, and which become objects of scientific study only belatedly. Hegel's aphorism should precede any methodology of the social sciences: "That which is familiar is not necessarily known."[2] A truism that is valid for the gestures of everyday life—such as buying or selling some ordinary object—for labor, for social life as a whole, and even for peasant life.

Peasant realities became objects of science from the moment they introduced *practical* problems.

In France, toward the end of the nineteenth century, the splitting up of inheritances and land, the division of assets, and the rural exodus became a subject of concern to the authorities. The formation of the national market led to a reshaping of agrarian structure: the concentration of ownership and the commercialization and specialization of production. Subsequently, the challenges of the worldwide market and modern technology were added to the first, primarily price protections, profitability, and the introduction of automation. Gradually, familiar and unknown realities were felt to be worthy of interest and scientific study.

Although rural sociology was developed in the United States, it is clear that the peasant problem is the reason for this, and has preoccupied successive governments.[3]

At present, throughout the world, the "peasant problem" has been or is being questioned in multiple forms. We have seen or are going to see *agrarian reforms* in nearly every corner of the earth: in popular democracies, in China, Mexico, Egypt, Italy, Japan, and India, not to mention the great transformations of agriculture in the USSR. Of course, these transformations and reforms have profoundly different characteristics depending on the underlying conditions and political regime. Nonetheless, they imply the vast scope and worldwide actuality of agrarian problems.

Yet sociologists have gone from the study of primitives to the study of urban and industrial settings, skipping this reality, which extends across vast distances of time and space. In France, the study of peasant reality was begun by historians and geographers.[4] But their work must now be resumed, it must be given shape and integrated into a comprehensive schema that can only be provided by sociology, considered to be the study of the totality of the social process and its laws.

We cannot overemphasize the fact that large *entities* (national and worldwide markets, social and political structures) have done a great deal to transform agrarian structures. National and worldwide markets have given rise to specialized markets (for example, on the national level, we have the vineyards of the Midi, and on the world scale, the coffee plantations in Brazil). Social and political organization, the actions of the State, planning—or the lack of planning, or its failure—have acted and affected every corner of the globe. There isn't a peasant today, even in Africa or Asia, who has not been touched by worldwide events.

But there is another aspect of reality, which contradicts the above, that also needs clarification: agriculture drags along with it the remnants and residues of a distant past. This is especially true of countries not subject to large-scale planning efforts, to those that are backward or underdeveloped. These are found primarily in colonial lands but also in "Western" European countries. In a single region of the Pyrenees, we can observe, close by one another, the most archaic culture of the hoe (the "laya" on the Spanish side), the Mediterranean scratch plow, the tractor, remnants of agrarian community life (collective ownership and farming of pasture lands), modern cooperatives, and large, mechanized farms.[5]

Consequently, peasant reality has a twofold complexity:

(a) *Horizontal complexity.* In agrarian formations and structures of the same historical period, especially those determined by contemporary large-scale social and political entities, we find fundamental differences, some of which are contradictory.

Thus, in the United States, we find the limiting case of agrarian capitalism together with very advanced mechanization in working the soil. The "owner" or capitalist farmer, who owns the improved equipment, might spend no less than half the year in town. He leaves for his property when work needs to be done, which is carried out with state-of-the-art technology and seasonal labor. After the harvest and sale of the product, he returns to his urban home.

At the other pole, using equally advanced mechanization and technology but a very different social structure, we find the Soviet *kolkhoz* and *sovkhoz,* and the future "agrocities" (a community within an agglomeration of kolkhoz villages).[6]

Between these two extremes, there are intermediate forms. J. Chombart de Lauwe recently completed an interesting study of the CUMA (Coopératives pour l'Utilisation en commun de Matériel Agricole [Cooperatives for Using Agricultural Equipment]).[7] Production cooperatives, like those of the Emilia region of Italy (near Bologna) or those of the popular democracies, are also intermediate and transitional forms between the above two "poles."

In each case and at each level, a sociological study is possible, which *comparatively* accounts for technical improvements, their relation to the human group and social structure, the productivity of agricultural labor, and population movements: in a word, the aggregate of *conditions*.

(b) *Vertical complexity.* The present rural world offers to observation and analysis the coexistence of formations of *different ages and dates*. As we saw above, this paradoxical juxtaposition—the most archaic next to the most modern—can sometimes be seen across a rather narrow area. For example, in North Africa, pastoral nomadism and seminomadism, where tents (*noualas*) are carried on the backs of members of the community, coexist side by side with the most advanced technology. In the rural world, much more clearly than in the artisanal world, nothing has entirely disappeared. And the fact alone of this preservation of archaic remnants and "sociological fossils"—a relative preservation that does not exclude the influence, deterioration, and more or less successful integration of the archaic into contemporary communities—presents a number of problems.

The two complexities—the horizontal and the vertical, which we could also call the *historical*—intersect, cross, and act upon one another. This results in an interlinking of facts that can only be untangled by some form of solid *methodology*. We must simultaneously identify the objects and goals of rural sociology and define its relationship to the sciences and disciplines that will become its auxiliaries: human geography, political economy, ecology, statistics.

Rural sociology was largely developed in the United States. We know why. Every university has a chair of rural sociology; there are already a large number of studies, manuals, and monographs in existence. Yet one thing is striking about those works—the lack of any reference to a *history*.

For example, there is a large, group work, *Rural Life in the United States*.[8] From the historical perspective, it is limited to a demographic study of the settlement, colonization, and movements of the rural population during the period of industrial development (13–36). The statistical portion (27–29), covering the national origins of immigrant agricultural laborers, is remarkable but it is in no sense a rural history.

Nor do we find in these works an allusion to the essential characteristic of the brief rural history of America: colonization (in the broad sense—the establishment of colonies) and settlement on *open* land. Marxists distinguish colonization of the *Prussian* type (colonization of appropriated land) and colonization of the *American* type. In the latter case, there is no landed property of feudal origin. Until the concentration of capitalist ownership, until the intervention of the banks and trusts, tenant farming is rare. Land assets predominate and the peasant producer does not pay a *rent* to the owner of the land on which he works. As a result, there is no parasitic class to consume a significant portion of national revenue. Feudal restrictions on the growth of productive forces do not exist; the growth of capitalism can be accelerated until its *internal* contradictions paralyze any further development. This explains the extraordinary economic growth of the United States during the nineteenth century. American economists and sociologists are not even capable of seriously studying the conditions of this growth, whose empirical results they present. They fail to follow the formation of the internal market or the intrinsic characteristics of an agriculture that has been massive in scope while remaining largely extensive and of relatively low yield (per acre or hectare cultivated).

Nor have the consequences of the fact that the occupation of the land was carried out from the cities been studied. In Europe, agriculture preceded industry, and the city or town developed in a peasant milieu. The Italian or French peasant [*paysan*] is primitively a "pagan [*païen*]" (*paganus*). Peasant life has its own mores, customs, and traditions. We can, to a certain extent, speak of peasant "culture." But the American countryside received its cultural models from the cities and towns ("patterns"). If a peasant culture exists, it has no originary traditional elements; it represents only a degradation or slow assimilation of urban culture ("acculturation"). There is no conflict between the peasant tradition, its mores and customs on the one hand, and religion on the other. In the absence of an original peasant "culture," and given the slow assimilation by isolated peasants of scientific culture, religion is the only governing ideology in rural areas. So it is not surprising to find rural sociologists in the United States study the church as a social institution in considerable detail (see Lowry Nelson, *Rural Sociology*), identify the distribution of religions among the local population (see Lynn Smith, *The Sociology of Rural Life*), or trace the areas of influence of the church in a given "rural community" alongside the areas visited by the mail carrier or doctor.[9]

It's clear that in the "historical countries," the problems of rural sociology are presented differently than in the United States.

The purely descriptive and empirical method could only arise in a country without history or, more specifically, without significant historical "density." Human reality is placed flat on the ground, so to speak. And sociologists simplify the methodological problem. They arrive at a kind of intrinsic empiricism, a statistical formalism. And, as we've seen, this method is inappropriate, even for a "nonhistorical" country having few historical foundations and sediments in immediately given reality.[10]

Consequently, with respect to France and the greater part of the rural world, we find ourselves faced with a methodological problem, namely, the *connections between sociology and history*. For here we are presented with a reality that has a history and preserves it internally, and that juxtaposes archaic and "modern" formations.

It's a difficult problem in that we wish to avoid allowing history to absorb sociology, or rural sociology to overlook the contributions of history as an *auxiliary* science. Sociology must be based on actual facts, their description. But when those facts have a historical density, how can we ignore it? The difficulty of the problem is further magnified by the situation noted previously.

It is *historians* who have developed and introduced into circulation concepts that, if verified, would dominate rural sociology.

For example, Marc Bloch refers to the *agrarian regime* or *agrarian civilization*. For Bloch, "two major forms of agrarian civilization" come into conflict in France, "which we can, for lack of anything better, call the civilization of the North and the civilization of the South."[11] He characterizes these civilizations or fundamental agrarian structures as shown in the following table.

North	South
Community undertakings	Individualism
Plow	Scratch plow
Aligned fields	Irregular fields
Open fields	Enclosed fields
Three-year crop rotation	Two-year crop rotation

The concept of an agrarian regime corresponds to the concept of "lifestyle" used by geographers. Whether the thinkers of the school of human geography transmitted the concept to historians or historians transmitted it to them (in the case of France) is of little importance here. What is important is that both concepts closely correspond and designate a very ancient reality, one that was stable or, more exactly, *static,* and broke down only under the pressure of mechanization. It reflects a reality that is archaic, or nearly so, and "natural" (unless we attribute it to collective representations inherent in a given race, country, or people).[12]

A more detailed analysis dissolves such fixed oppositions, the static difference between structures. It replaces the contrasts of agrarian "regimes" with a profoundly different model. For example, we find two-year crop rotation in the South of France and three-year crop rotation in the North and East (primarily in Alsace). In the South, we find two-year crop rotation with fallowing and two-year crop rotation and continuous production (without fallowing). Similarly, in the North, we find three-year crop rotation both with and without fallowing. But such continuous production reflects technological progress, better use of the soil, and an increase in productivity. In each region, depending on geography as well as social relationships and political events, we find more or less rapid growth—

held back or accelerated by a variety of conditions—productive forces, occasional stagnation, delays, and regressions.

If agrarian structures were fixed and separate as historians and geographers believed, the sociologist could only describe in detail what the specialists of those sciences would define as a whole.

If there are no agrarian "regimes," or "civilizations," or "lifestyles" but the growth—unequal and subject to complex conditions—of productive forces, sociology would cover a domain, an objective method, and the right to an overview of the facts. Technologists and economists inform the sociologist about such productive forces in agriculture. The historian will tell him which actions, events, and political regimes have accelerated, slowed down, or stopped this development. The sociologist must and may ultimately describe the actual result, seeking to *explain* and *determine* the process as a whole that has contributed to the actual result. Thus, the South of France seems to be characterized far less by individualism or the scratch plow or irregular fields than by a temporal *lag* compared to the agricultural development of northern France. The North almost entirely ignores the sharecropping that tenant farming replaced during the growth in productive forces and capitalist development.[13] The frequency of sharecropping in the southern half of France is worthy of study and deserves an explanation. It would seem that sharecropping has completely disappeared in England, nearly completely in the North of France and northern Italy, persists in the South of France and in parts of Italy. Why? The historian is prepared to inform us. It is clear that the decline of the Mediterranean after the sixteenth century is not unrelated to this finding; that it is associated with the peripheral nature and distance from Paris—the economic and political center—of France's southern provinces; associated as well with unusual remnants of the past such as dialects and patois, and therefore with particular and original forms of life, but not at all with stationary "lifestyles."

It would be preferable to refer to the "gradual, accelerated, interrupted, or delayed development of productive forces." But this model does not imply a kind of poorly differentiated *continuity* in peasant realities.

In light of current phenomena, it is reasonable to assume the existence of radical transformations and ancient upheavals. For example, the eastern Pyrenees (Catalonia, Roussillon) was newly repopulated after the Sarasin invasions. The introduction of sharecropping in Tuscany overturned the previous structure, and so on. We find enormous, long-lasting conflicts, under different forms, such as that between small and large landowners (Gallo-Roman *latifundia,* lordly domains, large capitalist farms).[14]

We know that at least three times in France, large-scale "agrarian reforms" changed the structure of rural life: the invasion of the barbarians, the freeing of the serfs, and the sale of church holdings and the assets of emigrants.

The "agricultural revolution" that began in the eighteenth century laid the groundwork for the physiognomy of contemporary peasant France, especially the economic development of the northern half of the country, and its consequences.

Does this imply the absorption of sociology by history? Of course not. The sociologist must first determine and analyze before explaining. He makes use of history as a subordinate and auxiliary science for studying the social process *as a whole.* Therefore, in the case of rural sociology, we are led to eliminate a number of methods, exploratory techniques, and research procedures.

(a) The *ethnographic method or ethnology* always risks treating as natural developments social facts that have been profoundly affected by history and currently existing overarching structures. These facts appear to be presented with apparent simplicity, wrapped in a form of "primitivity." Ethnography has a fondness for marginal or archaic structures, which evoke this appearance more than others.

(b) The recent theory of "archeo-civilization" suffers from the same criticism. According to this theory, a traditional peasant civilization would have lasted until the recent past (the nineteenth century in France, that is, until the introduction of mechanization) and would have disappeared afterward. Therefore, we could not use the ethnographic method to observe this phenomenon. It would have to be reconstituted or reconstructed in its entirety, having preserved, notwithstanding superficial modifications, an aspect of continuity from its initial appearance on the land up to the time of its disappearance.

The thesis is based on the (false) opposition between the *natural environment* and the *technical environment*. In its social context, at the time of its appearance, the hoe or plow is as "technical" as the turret lathe. And from the historical record we also know about the upheavals brought about in agrarian structure and rural societies by individual private property, by the monetary and market economy, by the consequences in the countryside of the formation of a bourgeoisie (urban and rural), long before the introduction of mechanization.

(c) *Historico-cultural theory* has stimulated research activities but has one significant drawback: it enables the arbitrary construction of "complexes" and substitutes for the study of facts a hypothetical-deductive process based on those complexes, composed of technological and ideological components. (This defect appears in the otherwise remarkable book by Pia Laviosa Zambotti, *Origini e diffusione della civiltà*.[15])

(d) The *monographic method* should be used with considerable caution. A frequently disappointing experiment shows the extent to which good monographs (of a village or country) are rare and how little sociologically useful information is found. Researchers lose themselves in a mass of local details, in descriptions of habitat or crops. The key element, which is immediately apparent to an experienced sociologist, escapes their grasp for lack of proper training, which can only be acquired over time. Unfortunately, the actual conditions of scientific research do not favor the training of experienced sociologists. In any case, the monographic inquiry and the interpretation of documents assumes an overview of the problems at hand. And the proper scientific method always involves focusing on what is essential by distinguishing it from what is accidental, superficial, or aberrant. The monographic method cannot satisfy the requirements of the classification and typology of rural groups. It serves as an auxiliary research technique. And of course, it remains true that any comprehensive study must be based on as large a number of local and regional monographs as possible.

(e) The *technological method* suffers from the general limitations of technology. The invention, adoption, and extension of technologies cannot be developed outside the context of actual social relations. Technology is both a determinant and determined (as shown by the most superficial study of the modern mechanization of agricultural labor). Technological studies are subordinate to an overarching general design: from the vast movement that slowly accrues from the origins of the productivity of agricultural labor and culminates in currently existing structures.

Therefore, I would like to propose a very simple method that makes use of auxiliary techniques and involves several moments:

(a) *Descriptive*. This involves observation informed by experience and a general theory, as well as participatory observation in the field followed by the prudent use of survey methods (interviews, questionnaires, statistics).

(b) *Analytic-regressive*. Analysis of the reality described and an attempt to *date* it exactly (to avoid relying on findings about undated and undifferentiated "archaic phenomena").

(c) *Historical-genetic*. This comprises studies of changes made to a given structure, which has been previously dated, by later developments (internal or external) and by its subordination to general structures. This approach involves attempts at a genetic classification of formations and structures within the context of an overall process. It also involves the attempt to return to the previously described actuality and rediscover the present, but one that is now clarified and comprehended: *explained*.

Take sharecropping, for example. We can provide an exact *description* (ground rent in kind, *colonat partiaire*, servitude associated with the payment of rent, and so on), then *date* it (it coincides with the formation of the urban market and rise of the bourgeoisie, but where capitalism developed, it gave way to tenant farming and, therefore, has a semifeudal origin), then *explain* its transformations and preservation (lack of economic development in sharecropping regions, lack of capital).

As an example, we might examine the village community and its surviving elements, or the peasant family with its own specific characteristics.

These studies operate within a general framework, an idea of a comprehensive process. (I again wish to emphasize that we must always take into account the interaction among structures, the influence of recent structures on older structures that have been subordinated to them or integrated into them.)

(A) Initially we find the *rural community* or *village community*. There is nothing mystical about this term, nothing "prelogical"; it is rather a historical and social fact that is found just about everywhere.[16] Weak in the face of nature, disposing only of simple instruments and technologies, for a long time mankind needed to form tightly knit social groups to carry out the work of agriculture: clearing the land, building embankments, irrigation, crop cultivation (and often the protection of flocks). Consequently, the peasant group remained highly organized, held together by *collective disciplines*. It possessed *collective features,* but following very different modalities.

Over time these peasant communities slowly became differentiated, disassociated. Agricultural progress led to their dissolution. Its modalities were also highly varied but possessed general features (the affirmation of private property, class differentiation, a system of chieftanships, the appearance of exchange and money, subordination to successive modes of production).

In the peasant community, we initially find that bonds of *consanguinity* prevail. When these dissolve, they give way to bonds of *territoriality,* based on residency, wealth, ownership, prestige, and authority. We thus move from the extended family to the limited family (and the predominance of males) and relations of *vicinage.*

But the history of the peasant community is even more complex than this model would lead us to assume. It is subject to the pressure of successive modes of production and administrative, fiscal, legal, and political entities. Sometimes it yields, sometimes it resists. Until it dissolves into individualism (based on competition, the market economy), it manifests enormous vitality.

As I see it, the European Middle Ages and the disappearance of the medieval (feudal) mode of production are incomprehensible if we fail to take into account a resurgence of the peasant community and its deep-seated resistance to the dominance of feudal landowners. Only in this way can we explain the idea of *custom* and *customary law*, which are so important in the study of agrarian life. Every custom implies a form of social support—the community—and a resistance to "demands," that is, anything that acts outside custom.

(B) *Feudal and slave-based modes of production*. It is impossible to study peasant realities in Africa, the Antilles, or the American South without reference to slavery and its survivals and repercussions.

We must first recognize the various forms assumed by the feudal mode of production (Asiatic: based on the ownership of water and the irrigation system; Muslim: based on the domination of urban, artisanal, and commercial centers, a domination that extended to the surrounding countryside; European: based on landed property ownership) if we are to explain existing peasant realities in a large number of countries (including southern Italy, southern France, and elsewhere).

These realities do not reveal their complexity until they are investigated from several different viewpoints. For example, southern France has preserved *Roman* law or was penetrated by it at a very early stage of its reappearance, and yet it is the part of France where *customs* are the best preserved (including local dialects and patois).

(C) *Capitalism* brought about a very advanced agricultural revolution in England but one that was less fully realized in France and Italy. In France there was agrarian reform (leading to the reorganization, extension, or constitution, depending on circumstances, of small and midsize land holdings). Subsequently, it brought about a concentration of ownership of fertile land, situated near markets (yielding the maximum amount of ground rent. It brought about the predominance of tenant farming over sharecropping, individualism, mechanization, and the industrialization of agriculture. How can we study agrarian reality without constant reference to this mode of production?

Slave and feudal modes of production are partly superimposed on earlier agrarian structures (even though they may have tended to the formation of the "latifundia" and domains). That is why the continuation or reconstruction (partial) of these "community" structures has been possible. But the capitalist mode of production from its inception (monetary and market economy) profoundly overturned agrarian structures from within and from without. Capitalist private property has subordinated earlier forms of ownership in hundreds of ways: tribal or clan, communitarian or feudal. This fact becomes obvious when we study the agrarian structure of "underdeveloped" countries—colonial or semicolonial, backward sectors of capitalist countries.

(D) The industrialization of agriculture, the introduction of mechanization, large-scale agricultural production, and increasing productivity are, today, evolving in two opposite directions: capitalism and socialism.

The socialist transformation of agriculture is being carried out in three stages: agrarian reform, cooperation, the creation (barely foreseen) of agricultural towns.

Each of these steps unfolds along different lines, depending on the country. In particular, agricultural cooperation (production cooperatives and *kolkhoz*, which differ fundamentally from production cooperatives) arose around the village structure; that is, they contain what could be described as a renewal—but at a level that has been deeply transformed, and involves new technical means and an equally new structure—of the agrarian community, neighborhood relations, collective disciplines, and so on.

In this way, we arrive at a comprehensive vision of peasant realities. We could compare them to an open fan, presenting and juxtaposing forms from different ages, although the image lacks the continuous interaction of formations and their subordination to ensembles (new structures, the worldwide capitalist and socialist market). This vision of the whole reveals a *lag* in agricultural development compared to industrial development, a lag that only socialist structure overcame, and that requires a particular form of analysis.

This overview comprises *contradictions* (especially the bitter struggle, throughout the course of history, between large and small farms) and *survivals* in the ideological (survival of agrarian myths, folklore, and so on) and structural (village, peasant family) domains. From this general view can be derived the outline of a treatise or manual of *Rural Sociology*.[17]

This would need to begin with a study of existing ensembles, recent structures (capitalist and collective) of the world market (capitalist and collective).

It would include a study of the agrarian community, of its dissolution, its survivals and revivals, insisting on the transition from bonds of consanguinity to bonds of territoriality (along with the associated conflicts and victories); on differentiations, hierarchies, and neighborhood relations, among others.

Based on this comprehensive study, we can produce a typology of *village* types (living communities, communities in the process of dissolution, individualist villages, villages defined or remodeled due to their proximity to a commercial or industrial center, by large-scale land ownership, by cooperation). Important chapters would be devoted to the peasant family, the condition of women, children (oldest or youngest), the elderly, in different types of villages and families. The problem of classes (or stratifications) in rural areas requires a detailed study of methods of land ownership and farming (sharecropping, tenant farming, small or midsize landholders). Finally, we must always situate the peasant group being studied (in general, the village) with respect to larger structures and institutions: market towns and cities, province and nation.

And, finally, peasant "culture" (in the cultural sense) must be defined concretely. To the extent that the peasantry produces a "culture" or a contribution to culture, there is no question of an *ideology*, strictly speaking (although this peasant contribution has an ideological content that can only be isolated by philosophers or theorists coming from a different, more developed, social structure). It is a culture without concepts, transmitted orally, and primarily consisting of anecdotes, stories, interpretations of rites and magic, and examples that are used to orient practice, to preserve or modify customs, and guide emotions and actions by acting directly upon them.

We see then that the peasant contribution to the history of ideologies—confused, diffused, formulated by city dwellers—has been considerable. In particular, the great agrarian myths (Mother Earth) have crisscrossed poetry, art, and philosophy from the origins of mankind to the present day. Even the Christian heresies have had a basis that is in large part agrarian (continuations and memories of the peasant community). From this perspective, rural sociology can provide a non-negligible contribution to the study of ideas, which is to say, to philosophy.

Notes

[*Cahiers internationaux de Sociologie,* no. 14 (1953): 122–40, reprinted in *Du rural à l'urbain* (Paris: Anthropos, 1970), 63–78, and first published in English in Henri Lefebvre, *Key Writings,* ed. Stuart Elden, Elizabeth Lebas, and Eleonore Kofman (London: Continuum, 2002), 111–20.—*Eds.*]

1. "Problèmes de Sociologie rurale—La Communauté paysanne et ses problèmes historico-sociologiques," [*Cahiers internationaux de Sociologie,* no.] 6 (1949) [reprinted here as chapter 2, "Problems of Rural Sociology: The Peasant Community and Its Historical–Sociological Problems."—*Eds.*].

2. [This remark, found in the preface to the *Phenomenology of Spirit,* para. 31, is misquoted by Lefebvre. The original German is "das Bekannte ist darum weil es bekannt ist nicht erkannt." Terry Pinkard translates this as "What is familiar and well known as such is not really known, for the very reason that it *is familiar and well known.*" G.W. F. Hegel, *The Phenomenology of Spirit,* trans. Terry Pinkard (Cambridge: University of Cambridge Press, 2018), 20. Lefebvre similarly misquotes this (in German this time) in *Critique of Everyday Life,* vol. 1, *Introduction,* trans. John Moore (London: Verso, 1991), 15.—*Eds.*]

3. See the recent work by Daniel Guérin as well as the novels of Steinbeck, Caldwell, and others. [Daniel Guérin (1904–98) was an anarchist Marxist. The work Lefebvre is referring to is probably *Où va le peuple americain? (Where are the American People Going?)* (Paris: Julliard, 1950). John Steinbeck (1902–68) and Erskine Caldwell (1903–87) were both U.S. novelists: Steinbeck is particularly known for *The Grapes of Wrath* (1939); Caldwell for *Tobacco Road* (1932).—*Eds.*]

4. By representatives of the School of Human Geography.

5. [A laya is a kind of digging fork with two prongs, particularly used in the Basque region.—*Eds.*]

6. [On *kolkhoz* (a collective farm) and *sovkhoz* (a Soviet or state farm), see note 12 in chapter 2 of the present volume.—*Eds.*]

7. [Jean Chombart de Lauwe (1909–2001) was a writer on agricultural issues. Lefebvre is possibly referring to *Recensements de l'agriculture* (Paris: n.p., 1949) or *La structure agricole de la France* (Paris: P. Dupont, 1946).—*Eds.*]

8. [Carl C. Taylor, Arthur F. Raper, Douglas Ensminger, Margaret Jarman Hagood, T. Wilson Longmore, Walter C. McKain Jr., Louis J. Ducoff, and Edgar A. Schuler, *Rural Life in the United States* (New York: Knopf, 1949). Page numbers in main text are citations to this source.—*Eds.*]

9. [Lowry Nelson, *Rural Sociology: Its Origin and Growth in the United States* (New York: American Book Company, 1948); T. Lynn Smith, *The Sociology of Rural Life* (New York: Harper, 1947), 87.—*Eds.*]

10. Even in the United States, a rural history would be indispensable, especially in the South, where we find, as in Europe, traces of feudalism and sharecropping (a semifeudal form of land ownership), together with the continuation and consequences of slavery. I would again like to point out Paul Landis's *Rural Life in Process*. The author is one of the rare few to have understood the reality of American peasant life in its *becoming* and to have provided a *critical* exposé (up to a certain point) of the actual situation of the American peasant. [See Paul Landis, *Rural Life in Process* (New York: McGraw-Hill, 1948).—*Eds.*]

11. Marc Bloch, *Les caractères originaux de l'histoire rurale française* (A. Colin, 1952). [See Marc Bloch, *French Rural History: An Essay on Its Basic Characteristics*, trans. Janet Sondheimer (Berkeley: University of California Press, 1970). Bloch (1886–1944) was a historian, a cofounder of the journal *Annales d'histoire économique et sociale*.—*Eds.*].

12. To explain the facts, Bloch hesitated between a technological argument (the role of the plow) and an appeal to collective mentality (a community or an individualist point of view). Since then, some sociologists have begun to define an opposition between a "natural" milieu and a technical or "mechanical" milieu, which we find to be as specious as the others.

13. *Colonat partiaire* sharecropping, a form of land tenure in which the sale of products (a specific percentage of a given amount of production) is turned over to the landowner, who owns the land and a portion of the instruments of production.

14. [*Latifundia* refers to large farms constructed from a number of smaller ones. They were originally set up in Rome after Hannibal's invasion. The term was revived in the colonization of the Americas and is used today in Italy, Spain, and Latin America to describe large estates—often with absentee landlords.—*Eds.*]

15. [Pia Laviosa Zambotti, *Origini e diffusione della civiltà* (Milan: Marzorati, 1947). Lefebvre references this with the French title *Grands courants de civilization*, but it does not appear to have been translated.—*Eds.*]

16. See the first fifty pages of the recently translated book by Lord Ernle, *L'Histoire rurale de l'Angleterre* (Paris: Gallimard, 1952). [See Rowland E. Prothero (Baron Ernle), *English Farming: Past and Present* (London: Longmans, Green and Co., 1912).—*Eds.*]. See Denise Paulme, *L'Organisation sociale des Dogon* (Paris: Domat-Montchrestien, 1940), for the numerous studies (not yet systematized) in various languages and various countries.

17. [This is a reference to the "Manual de sociologie rurale," whose manuscript was stolen from a car and consequently never published. See Rémi Hess, "Presentation de la troisième édition," in *Du rural à l'urbain*, 3rd ed. (Paris: Anthropos, 2001), xxii, and the introduction to the present volume.—*Eds.*]

CHAPTER 5

Social Relations, Population Phenomena, and Labor Problems in the Agricultural Sector of Underdeveloped Countries

Before addressing my topic, I want to offer a few preliminary observations.

The subject is even broader in scope when you consider that the so-called underdeveloped countries are themselves predominantly agricultural. Therefore, I can only establish the general outlines of this study, which are applicable to every country, providing the indispensable modifications are made. At most I'll have time to provide a handful of illustrations of general principles. Of course, these are based on a number of facts. But they, in turn, help clarify individual facts. And like any scientific thinker, while I seek not only to generate concepts but to discover laws, I do not operate from a position of sociological empiricism, although I do not, for all that, disdain concrete documentation.

The facts I examine are those that are collectively referred to as "sociological." Therefore, I run a risk, that of returning to questions that have been addressed by other investigators, especially my illustrious colleague Professor Banfi.[1] For this, I apologize in advance.

This risk seems to me inevitable. My subject includes the examination of class relations in the agrarian structures of underdeveloped countries and the transformations of those structures. It also includes the study of what sociologists refer to as *social mobility*, which is considerable in these sectors and encompasses population movements, migrations, the proletarianization of agricultural settlements, partial or complete unemployment. It extends to the examination of relations between underdeveloped countries and the large industrial nations, for I must examine the consequences of the often brutal and externally imposed introduction into traditional agrarian structures, of mechanization, specialized crop growing, commercial and industrial capitalism, as well as the demographic and sociological consequences of their subordination to the needs of colonialism and imperialism.

(1) I would first insist on the essentially relative nature of the fundamental concept of an *underdeveloped* area. A given area is underdeveloped with respect to some other area, a given region with respect to a neighboring region. A well-developed area can rapidly become underdeveloped and vice versa. In other words, the concept encompasses, although not always clearly, the important law of *unequal economic and social development*. This law applies on a worldwide scale as well as among individual nations and regions whenever there is no comprehensive plan or a power capable of applying a plan in a way that allows the underdeveloped sectors to rejoin the advanced sectors (more or less rapidly).

Let's look at an example in France, which passes, and rightly so, for an advanced country, for a well-developed sector of the world economy.

Although in Italy, the south is now, as it has been for many years, considered an underdeveloped zone, this was never the case in France, at least until recently. For we have come to learn that parts of France (the south and west) are rapidly falling into the ranks of the underdeveloped.

In truth, this unequal development of the French economy had not escaped attentive observers. After the Liberation, a regional Economic Committee was established in Toulouse, in which I played a role. We analyzed, in this region, not only the backward nature of agriculture (the lag between agriculture and industry being a very widespread phenomenon and, in fact, an essential aspect of unequal development under capitalism) but the signs of disintegration as well, of a breakdown of social structure. Among those signs I would mention the persistence of sharecropping, with semifeudal characteristics, and even a return to sharecropping among tenant farmers unable to pay their rental costs in cash.

It is only this year that the problem, which has been especially aggravated, has managed to draw the attention of the authorities and official organizations. Two reports, one published by the Inspectors General of the National Economy, the other by the General Confederation of Employers, have shown the situation in the southwest of France for what it is. Compared to the industrial and agricultural enterprises of the Paris region, the north and east of France, the majority of the companies are "marginalized" and, therefore, threatened with disappearance. The problems of restructuring and consolidation in the region are more difficult than elsewhere, even within the framework of capitalist concentration. The decline in wealth is considerable (more than 7 percent in many regions). Unemployment is increasing, although it is decreasing in other regions. A large city like Toulouse, which for decades has experienced extraordinary growth (the population has grown from approximately 70,000 to 310,000 inhabitants), is seeing its industries disappear and the surrounding agricultural lands decay.

Why is this occurring? To answer that, we would need to review the history of France, its economic and social structure. That is not my intent here. I'll simply point to the growing analogy (notwithstanding the many differences) between Italy and France. The northeast of France is becoming a zone surrounded by underdeveloped satellites, almost semicolonies. This presents in a new light the danger of a "Europe" oriented around the industrial centers of the Moselle-Rhine region. A large part of France would fall into the ranks of the underdeveloped, the agricultural counterpart of an industrial zone but with a backward agricultural economy and a decaying social structure.

(2) I would now like to examine these problems on a worldwide scale. Overall, the underdeveloped countries are agricultural, they are a source of raw materials for a few large industrial countries, outlets for their products, investment territories for their capital. The lag in agriculture, its permanent crisis, is an integral part of capitalism. This is so well known that I don't need to belabor the subject.

To actualize the study of these phenomena, we must define the social structures in which the introduction of a capitalist structure does not result from a natural historical process (as in the large countries mentioned) but from an external source, from economic and, often, extra-economic (political) pressure.

I believe we must classify these structures based on modes of production that have been historically superseded in the developed countries and which continue to dominate in underdeveloped countries, or which did until recently.

Thus, we find:

(a) Sectors where very old social structures still exist: relations of consanguinity, whether real or mythical, tribes, so-called natural economies.

In parts of Africa and Asia, the primitive community pursues its slow disintegration, accelerated by the pressure of capitalism. In France, a handful of remarkable ethnographers and sociologists (such as Denise Paulme) have studied several African communities.[2] These are disappearing rapidly, threatened by the cash and market economy, by the need for money to pay taxes, and so on.

(b) Sectors in which semifeudal or feudal structures continue to dominate. We should also mention that there are several kinds of feudalism. Muslim feudalism differs from Asiatic feudalism (India, for example) or European feudalism, which has been brought to other continents, leaving behind several vestiges in South America. European feudalism was based on ownership of the land, whereas Muslim feudalism was based on the political domination of commercial centers, and in Asia the questions of water and irrigation have played a determining role.

(c) Sectors in which capitalism continues to dominate in a historically outmoded form, such as commercial capitalism.

We might ask ourselves, moreover, if there is reason to add to this classification a special category for commercial capitalism; its predominance is not separate from the other survivals of ancient structures: artisanship, primitive agriculture, feudalism. More generally, these survivals often occur together and are superimposed on one another. For example, in Tunisia, which will serve as an illustration for my analysis, we find, side by side, tribes that collectively own the land, remarkable remnants of feudalism, and artisanal production accompanied by an indigenous commercial capitalism, alongside the most modern enterprises (agricultural and industrial), which are closely linked to finance capital.

My goal here is not to supply the frameworks for an analysis of the conditions in which finance capitalism and imperialism can penetrate underdeveloped countries but to identify the laws affecting agrarian structures and populations.

Those laws are as follows:

(i) Capitalist ownership (individual private ownership of the land as means of production) is faced with extremely varied forms of appropriation, possession, and exploitation of the land: collective ownership by tribes, clans, or agrarian communities; feudal ownership with rights held by the vassals of the lord; semifeudal ownership with sharecropping; small peasant landholdings, and so on.

Capitalist ownership subordinates all these ancient forms. It transforms them and reduces them to its own structure using any means available.

(ii) By doing so, it corrodes and destroys traditional social structures, which often broke down slowly but remained compatible with the practices, habits, and needs of the populations. In this way, through actions that are sudden and disruptive, it completes a historical process that was often no more than approximately sketched out.

(iii) In ancient agrarian structures, production was very low. The land fed, but with a very low standard of living, relatively large populations that (aside from periods of bad harvests) enjoyed a degree of security because the essential means of production, the earth, was at their disposal.

Capitalist ownership and its means of production separated the producers from the means of production, in agriculture as in industry.

The greater the mechanization, the greater the number of workers in a given area [*territoire*] who fall below the population living in that area before the introduction of capitalist production and modern technologies.

The disintegration of ancient structures is necessarily accompanied by a considerable freeing up of manual labor that was once integral to production and, therefore, by extensive "social mobility," migration, displacement, and the resettlement of populations.

The growth of productivity and production does not benefit the local population, or very little. They now become a proletariat of wanderers, vagabonds, the undernourished, and the unemployed.

(iv) Yet capitalist ownership doesn't destroy or only partly destroys the old parasitic class of feudal estate owners [*latifondiaires*]. One feudal element continues to live on the ground rent paid by the capitalist entrepreneurs to whom they rent their lands. Another is transformed into capitalists who exploit the lands and enter the bourgeoisie. And yet another, more or less ruined, generally becomes part of the administrative apparatus. But the absenteeism of the former owners is replaced by a new kind of absenteeism, that of the administrators of large capitalist corporations.

We see that, here, there are actual *laws*, that is, objective, necessary, and inevitable phenomena.

These phenomena reproduce, at a larger scale and somewhat aggravated, the historical facts that took place in England and France after the fifteenth and sixteenth centuries, precisely when a rising capitalism was breaking down preexisting social structures. But the actual facts present themselves with greater brutality and gravity. With the power of capitalism established, the action of finance capital, the means at the disposal of imperialism, greatly exceeded the powers of the rising bourgeoisie in the sixteenth century, for example. But there is a deep-seated analogy in the objective process; it does not depend on the good or ill will of individuals, of administrators. It is determined by the nature of things. How many colonial administrators feel overwhelmed, acknowledge being surprised by the results of their most well-meaning initiatives . . .

(3) I said I would use Tunisia as an example. There are several reasons for this. First, because it is close and easy to study. Second, because it is of interest to the Italians as well as the French; because it is in the forefront of current news. And third, because it juxtaposes the mixture, the interaction of all sorts of agrarian structures of very different ages.

In Tunisia we have found, and continue to find, the collective ownership by various groups (tribes, douars, some semi-nomadic and migratory, others sedentary) of what are known as *arch* lands under customary Islamic law.

Alongside *arch* lands we find *melk* lands. This term from customary Islamic law refers to land ownership by large feudal families and small individual and parcellized holdings.

On these feudal lands live sharecroppers. In the north there are the *khammès,* who receive 20 percent of the produce farmed, and in the center and south, the *rebaa,* who receive 25 percent of the produce farmed.

To these two large categories of ownership must be added the *habous,* or inalienable rights, whose revenues are sometimes completely given over to the support of a religious foundation, sometimes partly given to beneficiaries. The inalienability of the *habous* allowed those who feared being stripped of their property to protect themselves and their families against the abuses of power.

Vacant, or "dead," lands remained at the disposal of the public authorities and the prince.

Therefore, in Tunisia, we are presented with a relatively unrestricted range of agrarian structures. Their variety covers the full extent of agrarian history, from the primitive community (tribal) to the large capitalist land holdings of recent date.

We should mention that, at the time when the French protectorate was imposed on Tunisia, this interlocking agrarian structure was already in the process of decomposition, for a variety of reasons. Fees and taxes crushed the peasants, and European products were entering the country, ruining local artisans and local trade.

Let us look now at how capitalist private ownership fostered the disintegration of the social structure by subordinating and absorbing all earlier forms of ownership. Juridically and administratively, this process manifested itself in the negation of customary practices, considered to be poorly defined, and their subordination to the concepts of French civil law and the Napoleonic code. We can imagine how local administrators, whose legal training was in the study of French law and who applied its concepts in good conscience, were shocked at the result.

In the first place, juridical and moral personhood has, for a long time, been denied to the tribes. *Arch* lands, collective lands, therefore, were compared to vacant land, to state-owned lands. Similarly, uncultivated lands belonged to the large feudal families, like the famous "saline" lands around Sfax, formerly uncultivated regions that, today, have given rise to the world's finest olive groves. The Service des Domaines has taken control of vast areas and subdivided them, sometimes benefiting Tunisians but much more often benefiting Europeans, and on much more reasonable terms, in keeping with the "colonization fund" created in 1897.

Second, feudal rights to a fief and its vassals have been assimilated to capitalist private ownership (although every historian knows the immense difference between these two types of ownership). Thus, from the onset of colonization, an investment company would buy from a Tunisian feudal lord the entire territory of the tribe over which he ruled. In this way, the peasants who had paid a small fee to their lord became renters, tenant farmers in the capitalist sense. Additionally, some of these individuals were pushed to the borders of the immense domain thus created and some would become agricultural laborers.

Third, special decrees organized the transfer of the *habous*, in principle inalienable, against a perpetual rent (*enzel*). This process respected—in principle—the inalienability of the *habous*. But the *enzel* soon came to be considered a simple form of capitalizable ground rent that could be purchased in twenty payments. In this way, lands that formerly belonged to religious foundations became capitalist private property.

Fourth, an official policy of record keeping, cadastral registration, land "mobilization," and resettlement in indigenous nations harboring lands suitable for large-scale agriculture recently completed the work undertaken at the end of the nineteenth century by private colonization. I again want to emphasize that, from the point of view of French law, there is no systematic violence in this process, no violent confiscation (although in some cases, where tribes have been resettled outside their territory, we are very close). Here we find the origin of an important misunderstanding. French administrators and civil inspectors have even sometimes defended the local population, for example, by resettling them. *Objectively*, the basis of expropriation is not always found in some extra-economic, extra-legal violence (although this does occur!), in systematic pillaging. It is found, rather, in the application of particular legal norms, specifically bourgeois and capitalist, to the historically earlier social structures that I have briefly described. All the processes, all the contradictions, all the conflicts, all the problems are based on this fundamental conflict of structures, legal concepts, and corresponding practices.

The result? Between 750,000 and 800,000 hectares of the best land was transferred to the European colonists. Whether by resettlement or cantonment, some of the Tunisian peasants have been moved to plots of land that were mediocre or even entirely sterile because they did not possess the technical means to improve them. An increase in the amount of land under cultivation has been accompanied by a drop in the indigenous production of cereal grains intended for immediate consumption. The resettled peasants supply low-cost labor. Their standard of living is low, but some have it worse. The indigenous peasantry was soon divided into distinct social layers: urban or rural proletariat, semi-proletariat, sharecroppers and poor peasants, well-off peasants, and a very small agrarian bourgeoisie. To these layers, which were part of the productive population, should be added vagabonds, quasi vagabonds, and the more or less permanent unemployed of peasant origin who populated the "slums" [*bidonvilles*], especially around Tunis. An entire social structure was destroyed; but it was not replaced by one capable of integrating the former population into the productive economy without a drop in its standard of living or permanent unemployment. It is also worth noting that the migratory patterns of seminomadic peoples were considerably hampered, if not entirely broken, by the colonial farmlands, which were primarily found in central Tunisia and cut the traditional routes taken by their flocks as they traveled between the south and the mountains of the north. The labor needs of capitalist agricultural enterprises were far too limited to absorb the relative population excess. As for industrialization, it was much too slow and, moreover, oriented toward the production of raw materials (phosphates). Some of the hygienic measures taken by the Europeans prevented large-scale epidemics but resulted in population growth and new contradictions. The standard of living of the overall population has continued to drop, and the existence of food shortages has been demonstrated by specialists (there was an investigation by Doctor Burnet in

1937–38).[3] I can provide members of the Congress with data gathered by various investigators and by myself on food supplies, habitation, salaries, and living standards in Tunisia.

The phenomena I have analyzed with the greatest objectivity can be found, notwithstanding the local differences, in all underdeveloped countries. From this perspective, the concept of an underdeveloped country or area encompasses several others that are inherent in it: a decomposing capitalist structure—stagnation, the discontinuation or deviation of possible development—relative overpopulation arising from the formation of a lumpen proletariat, a "reserve industrial army" consisting of the more or less permanent unemployed, a rural proletariat, an urban proletariat, an impoverishment of the strata that do not participate in the transformations brought about by industrial and finance capital, by imperialism.

I've also collected data on Brazil (marked by the predominance of large feudal properties), the Middle East, Indochina, and elsewhere.

(4) What, then, are the remedies or, rather, the solutions to the problems presented? They are easy to determine but difficult to apply. Of course, in their determination as in their application, it is impossible to avoid transitioning from the level of sociology, economics, and demographics to that of *politics*.

Problems and solutions depend on the country, the zone, the region. They differ according to the social structure being directed toward some form of new development.

Yet problems and solutions have common elements everywhere. It is a matter, always, of developing a plan that allows a backward structure or one that is in the process of decomposition to reshape itself coherently, but on a higher level. It is not enough merely to examine the psychological problems presented by individual adaptation to modern technologies. In particular, the example of Tunisia demonstrates how easy it is to recruit highly qualified labor once the objective conditions for that recruitment are favorable.

It also seems quite clear that the inventory of current resources in an underdeveloped country (production, tools, and so on) is necessary but not sufficient. It is a simple element of a plan that cannot be satisfied with recording what has been accomplished or calculating the possibilities immediately available but must be effective in a positive sense and favorably transform the social structure in question.

Such a plan assumes an authority, a government, that is, a political power. The power in question must be independent of the interests that have, until now, weighed upon the area being studied, which have arrested and deflected its development. Meaning that it must be *national*. But it must also consider and even promote the interests of disadvantaged populations, and thus must be *democratic* in nature.

With respect to agrarian structure, it is clear that in the majority of the underdeveloped sectors (excepting those where the natural economy and decomposing primitive community still predominate), *agrarian reform* is essential. Moreover, the problem exists on a worldwide scale, whether it touches South America, Africa, Asia, or parts of Europe. A detailed critical study of the problems, program, plan, and projects of agrarian reform is far beyond the framework of the present survey. I can only insist on the importance of the question, which will certainly be examined by specialists.

But the problems of agrarian reform also lead to the problems of agricultural cooperation. However, these do not in any way impede a freeing up of agricultural labor and its transition to industry. Consequently the steps intended to develop the agricultural sector require development of the industrial sector and vice versa. Here, too, we see the need for a plan.

And here as well Tunisia provides an illustrative example. The objective conditions are ripe for the formation of a national and democratic political power, for economic planning in the direction of future development. Of course, this does not imply that Tunisia will break all its relations with France. On the contrary, it assumes a concretely democratic policy toward Tunisia in France, one that supports, in this underdeveloped country, any and all progressive measures.

Notes

[This was a presentation, published in the conference proceedings, *Atti del Congresso internazionale di studio sul problema delle aree arretrate, Milano, 10–15 ottobre 1954*, 4 vols. (Milan: Dott. A. Giuffrè, 1954–56), vol. 2, 823–33.—Eds.]

1. [This is a reference to the Italian philosopher and Communist senator Antonio Banfi. In 1957 he was to have presented a paper on the relation between theory and praxis at a conference in Warsaw but was too ill to attend; Lefebvre summarized his paper on his behalf, supplementing it with a few comments of his own. Banfi died a few days later. The proceedings were published as *Entretiens philosophiques de Varsovie: Les rapports de la pensée et de l'action, 17–26 juillet 1957* (Wrocław and Warsaw: Ossolineum, 1958). In that volume, see Antonio Banfi, "De l'antinomie theoresis et praxis," 29–42; and the untitled addendum, by Lefebvre, 43–45. Lefebvre also wrote a report, "Les Entretiens philosophiques de Varsovie," *Comprendre: Revue de politique de la culture* 19 (1958): 237–45, which briefly mentions Banfi's illness and death. A commentary on the proceedings is available; see H. L. Van Breda, "Les entretiens de Varsovie (17–20 juillet 1957)," *Revue philosophique de Louvain* 55 (1957): 487–518.—Eds.]

2. [Denise Paulme was best known at the time for *Organisation sociale des Dogon (Soudan français)* (Paris: Domat-Montchrestien, 1940). Her book *Les Gens du riz: Kissi de Haute-Guinée française* (Paris: Plon, 1954) was published the year of this conference.—Eds.]

3. [Étienne Burnet was a medical doctor who was director of the Pasteur Institute in Tunis between 1936 and 1943.—Eds.]

CHAPTER 6

The Village Community

Our friend [Maxime] Rodinson, and our friends [Jean] Varloot, [André-Georges] Haudricourt, Claude Mossé, and Charles Parain, who prepared this wonderful presentation of Engels's work, have raised some very important questions during the conference, and the discussion that follows will be based on their individual expertise. They are our most brilliant specialists on these difficult questions. I wish to speak as a philosopher; that is, my talk corresponds only imperfectly to its title, "the village community." It's true, I have prepared two theses on the study of the village community in the Pyrenees, work that served as a challenge to the specialists. Of course, I want to discuss non-Marxist or anti-Marxist specialists, especially sociologists, historians. This challenge holds considerable risk. For, I can state that I ran up against obstacles and refusals from some of those individuals, for example, on the question of the primitive community, concerning not only questions of vocabulary but fundamental aspects of certain problems as well.

I should add, in passing, that I found the greatest understanding from a sociologist whom we have sometimes criticized, correctly I might add, Monsieur Gurvitch, but it is to his Russian origins that he might owe his understanding of the facts concerning the evolution of the village community.[1]

In this work, I wanted to show that, armed with a good method, the materialist and dialectical method, and a general understanding inseparable from a conception of the Marxist world, the Marxist philosopher could penetrate very specific, very specialized areas of knowledge, study and clarify very specific questions. Moreover, reciprocally, this effort corresponds to a need that is, as I see it, profound for the Marxist philosopher. As such, he cannot limit himself to methodological generalities, to the theory of knowledge. He must penetrate at least into a specialized field, without getting lost, of course, in order to test his method, to test his concepts, and then return to general questions, the methodology and theory of knowledge. I should add that I found great intellectual joy in the study of a very specific region of France, the Pyrenees, through which I traveled, not with a Michelin guide in my hand but with Engels's book in the ancient translation that was published by Costes.[2] It's a region abundant in archaic forms, in sociological fossils, in facts that bear multiple dates, and which are presented to us in space, remainders of the primitive community in electrical power stations!

Consider that ethnographers and sociologists have sought, at great distance, facts and "sociological fossils" that were so close at hand.

I would like to travel with you to those beautiful valleys of the Pyrenees, so rich in things we can learn. But I don't have the time and that is not my objective. Yet I cannot resist the temptation to lead you on a brief excursion. Imagine we are traveling a path that millions of tourists and pilgrims travel each year. We are at Lourdes and, from there, we take the road that leads to Gavarni. When we are two kilometers from Lourdes, we see a small valley on our right, about ten kilometers long, called the Batsouriguère, where the periodic sharing of land is still practiced. Of course, the peasants don't know this. They say: look, the mountains cast shadows and it's not fair that the same people always have the land in shadow because the corn doesn't do as well there. So they switch. They rotate certain parcels without realizing that what they are doing is, for us Marxist sociologists and historians, the periodic exchange of land.

A while later we pass Argelès. I'm sure many of you have traveled this road. Here, we enter a land that is bountiful for ethnography and sociology. In this region the house and courtyard, as Marx and Engels noted, the garden, with a few arable parcels of land, with rights to collectively owned land, still form an indissoluble and inalienable whole: a patrimony. The head of the family possesses, as head of the family and head of the homestead, and as a member of the village community, *neighbors' rights*. That is, the rights of a member of a rural community that has, for a long time, been separated from the bonds of consanguinity and is now linked by bonds of territoriality based on residence and private property. Vicinage relations remain to some extent and are, in a sense, considered kinship relations, although there is no kinship in the legal sense. Every house has a name and the family bears the name of the house. Practically speaking, when a family has died off and another inhabits the house, a house that is not their own, they take the name of the house. In this region, the eldest daughter inherits all the family's assets and, which is quite unusual, even today, her husband and younger brothers are considered to be her "slaves," the servants of this eldest daughter, who is the heir.

Moreover, in this region, as if by accident, collective ownership covers 75 percent of the territory. I could go on telling you about the number of things one can discover in this region.

As for the texts of the old charters of the region, the old notarial documents, what do they reveal? Scandal!

Until the eighteenth century, there were trial marriages, provisional marriages transformed into actual marriages upon the birth of the first child, even legal "common-law marriages," established by a notarial document. And as late as the eighteenth century, there were signs of matrilineal kinship, the remnants of a matriarchy that has been attested in texts by Strabo, the Greek geographer.

Furthermore, the texts illustrate a kind of revival of the primitive community following the invasion of the Visigoths and, as Engels had seen, the diffusion in the region of a law of community, a law that was introduced or, rather, renewed by the Visigothic invasion, and through the long, bitter struggles of the local communities against the feudal lords and against the Muslims.

Here we find the proof of that ardent vitality of peasant communities that Marx speaks of in the texts collected in this book.[3] As I see it, this helped revive a host of problems: the study of civilization in the south of France, which was so brilliant in the twelfth and thirteenth centuries; the problem of the "Reconquista" of Spain by the Christians against the Muslims occupying towns and their outlying areas, from those agropastoral communities, leading their flocks across Spain, and, therefore, from villages high in the Pyrenees, in Castile, in Asturias; and, finally, the problem of heresy, for this is a region of heresies.

Here, I'm abusing my position as a sociologist or historian to introduce philosophy. It is a matter of following, over the course of time, the peasant community in its evolution, its breakdown, its relation to other social formations, to feudalism, and even to the bourgeoisie and capitalism. I believe that this research effort will be extensive and involve, even for us today, a large number of hypotheses. But why should we refrain from such hypotheses? Let me give one example. It seems to me that the split between Rome and Byzantium occurred as a function of the agrarian community. What Rome provided was the part of the Empire in which the latifundia were dominant, whereas what Byzantium provided was the part in which the primitive community persisted. It would be useful to further investigate this point. The Byzantines of the seventh to ninth centuries developed a specific law that accounted for agrarian communities, the long-term lease or leasehold, and it is this law that I find in the law of the Pyrenees of the twelfth and thirteenth centuries, transmitted by the Italian schools of law. It's an idea that would be worth following up.

These assumptions, suggested by Marx, are very broad, too broad perhaps. However, recent studies and important monographs demonstrate the fecundity of such hypotheses. Latin American Marxists have applied to the study of the Inca and Aztec empires the hypotheses that Marx proposed concerning the relation between ancient state formations in Asia and the agrarian community. They tried to show that these empires were fragile state constructions, established by conquering tribes on the basis of a little-known agrarian community structure, along with elements of feudalism or commercial activity. On top of this was erected a structure of great fragility, which collapsed with the first shock of the conquerors.

To return to my Pyrenees. Some may claim that I have sought a simple illustration of the claims of Marx and Engels, others that these are aberrant, intermittent events without any connection to actuality or the great ideological struggles of our time. I disagree. Reactionary sociology and historiography in their entirety are attached to these questions, these facts, and have interpreted them in reactionary fashion. It is not my intention to discuss Fustel de Coulanges alone or polemics about the existence of collective ownership; mostly, I want to discuss the work of Le Play. Frédéric Le Play sought in the Pyrenees the material for his monographs (moreover, they are remarkable as monographs).[4] He established a theory of the family serving any ideology of the right in France, of the classical right of yesterday and, more specifically, of the MRP today.[5] But Le Play made a terrible scientific error. He associated with Roman law and, more specifically, the testamentary freedom of Roman law, the inalienability of family rights in the Pyrenees, whereas it is a customary law having its source in the primitive community. Because of this scientific error, the current reactionary theory of the "stem family" was established. And so, it is through a detailed analysis of the Pyrenean family, used as an example by Le Play, that we can demonstrate his scientific error.

For those who follow the complex path of ideas in our time, we can thus manage, in a somewhat paradoxical and unforeseen way, to clarify certain issues and introduce others concerning our national history, namely, the relation between Roman law and customary law, and the relation between the law of private property and contracts and that of the community.

Here, I ask your permission to jump to an apparently unrelated subject, with the emphasis on "apparently." I wish to discuss the formation of Marxism and an aspect of that formation. It's a very difficult subject and remains controversial. If I say "Hegel," some will immediately refer to neo-Hegelianism. If I say "Ricardo," someone is liable to comment, "Ricardo, a bourgeois savant!" Which happens to be true. Nevertheless, this doesn't prevent him from being one of the sources of Marxism. So, I'm being cautious. If I state that Marx was born in a region where the remains of an agrarian community were considerable, I hope I will not be accused of pushing a theory that uses the survival of the village community to explain Marxism. Clearly, in the region of Trèves, the remaining vestiges of the village community (agrarian) were significant.

But let's address the question seriously. Marx had to respond to all the questions raised by the science of his time, by the ideas of his time. Yet what happened to Marx when, fresh out of the university, he entered active life? Several schools of the philosophy of law claimed priority in Germany at the time: the school of so-called natural law, associating legal rights to abstract human nature; the Hegelian school, associating law with the evolution of the state rationally examined; the reactionary romantic school, known as the school of historical law, associating law with essentially Germanic, medieval, and feudal customs.

Marx was twenty-three years old. He had to confront these problems concretely and he resolved them. Customary law: yes, it is earlier than Roman law. However, the customary law that is earlier than Roman law is not the law of the privileged, the rich, the feudal lords, the landowners. It is the law of the poor, which remained in place from the time when there were no landowners. Roman law is a kind of custom but it is the custom of private ownership of the land and private property, a law initiated by and associated with the State. It is not, therefore, an eternal law. Nor a moral law, nor a law legitimately associated with a higher entity. It's a historical law, but not in the sense that the school of historical law understands it. Marx takes a position about this in an article, one of his first, titled "On the Theft of Wood."[6] It concerns the theft of wood by peasants in the forests of his Rhenish region. The peasants were only exercising their customary right. They did not believe they were stealing. It is this that those who apply increasingly harsh legislation concerning the theft of wood in formerly communal forests fail to understand.

In this way, in a subordinate, minor, but interesting manner, Marx's knowledge of the village community appeared. I note in passing that this question of the relationship between Germanic law and Roman law (the quarrel between Romanists and Germanists) has confused questions concerning the origins and formation of the French nation throughout the nineteenth century.

It would be worth returning to these old polemics to clarify certain problems. Marx, at twenty-three, saw the solution that became an integral part of his entire doctrine. It's easy to see why Marx has always assigned the greatest importance to questions about the agrarian community, as Engels did. Engels's texts should be read in conjunction with those by Marx. I refer to them quickly and in passing. In *Capital*, the new French edition provides [on page 233, volume 2, page 47] a brief description of Hindu communities and arguments about the construction of the State.[7] Later, we find ideas about the subordination of modes of precapitalist ownership to the mode of capitalist production. Lenin would use these facts in his first works on the agrarian question and would later formulate into a law the subordination of older forms of agrarian production and land ownership, whatever they might be, to the capitalist mode of production, and so on.

Here, we get into historical questions and I would again like to move forward. I want to jump to a subject that is, superficially, quite different.

I want to talk about the historical method. It is obvious that the way in which bourgeois historiography discusses problems results in a form of circular thinking. Should we clarify the past by the present or the present by the past? Bourgeois historiography cannot escape this dilemma, this vicious circle. Do we proceed from the historical to the present [*actuel*] or can we illuminate the historical by the present?

There is no obvious way for them to escape this dilemma, especially since they feel obligated to choose between two modes of exploring the past, whereas we, we know that we must employ both methods, that there is a reciprocal movement in history, that we must move from the past to the present and from the present to the past and connect past history to the present, and then shift from the present to the past as we reconstruct it. When they make use of this last method, they use it to factitiously reconstruct the past and then declare that history is impossible!

Bourgeois thought oscillates between what we, Marxist philosophers, call *objectivism* and *subjectivism,* both unilateral, incomplete, and unscientific. Here, there is a real problem and I wish to note in passing that it is through this fissure, this difficulty, that Merleau-Ponty, in his *Adventures of the Dialectic,* lacking a sword attempts to make use of a poison dart.[8] He tries to catch us in a trap: objectivism or subjectivism, although we know that we must not combine these two movements, these two perspectives, these two aspects. Yet are we, Marxists, quite sure of always resolving the problem? I don't know. I use as an example the article, a brilliant one by the way, by François Châtelet in the last issue of *La Nouvelle Critique.*[9] The historian must, he writes, see himself as a historical agent. To demonstrate historical truth means to experience it, and François Châtelet adds that it is because he was engaged in proletarian struggles that Marx was able to understand Greek art.[10]

Is this true? Yes, it's true. Every man and, therefore, every historian, continuously moves to and from an experience. How could this historian know what he's talking about when he talks about money, land, property, class, class struggle, if he lacked some practical experience? The greater and deeper the experience, the better the historian can understand the past. Yet is this experience scientific? I would say no. Science consists of concepts, categories, and not facts or experiences, whatever they might be. History, like the other sciences, is essentially composed of concepts and categories. Marxism, dialectical materialism, is a philosophy of the concept and not of experience or consciousness, even class consciousness.

Thus, starting from a true point of departure, founded, and, moreover, in a way that is quite brilliant, we arrive at empiricism, a latent subjectivism, a certain practicalism, which leads Châtelet to write in this article that the laws of becoming that Marx and Engels formulated do not constitute a vision of the world. Which means that dialectics and dialectical materialism are not laws of becoming. Naturally, we can quibble about the words "vision of the world" or assert that Marxism is a conception of the world and not a "vision." Nevertheless, the laws of becoming constitute a conception of the world at the level of the *concept.* This strikes me as being extremely important for the methodology of history. For us Marxists, then, there is a tendency toward subjectivism, to practicalism for some and objectivism for others.

The response to the problem, I repeat, is that science consists of concepts, of categories. Once established, concepts have an objective and historical content and on that basis a kind of retroactive effect, not through some simple illumination of the past but because those concepts summarize the objective process of history from which they emerge and from which they draw their content. I call this the theory of *deep objectivity* and want to quote a text by Marx that seems to admirably illustrate the theory of deep objectivity, surpassing the opposition of subjectivism and objectivism.

Marx's text is very profound, and I won't draw all its substance from it. It is taken from the *Introduction to a Critique of Political Economy*. I want to read it to you.

> Bourgeois society is the most advanced and complex historical organization of production. The categories which express its relations, and an understanding of its structure, therefore, provide an insight into the structure and the relations of production of all formerly existing social formations the ruins and components of which were used in the creation of bourgeois society. Some of these unassimilated remains are still carried on within bourgeois society, others, however, which previously existed only in rudimentary form have been further developed and have attained their full significance, etc. . . . Bourgeois economy thus provides a key to the economy of antiquity, etc., but it is quite impossible [to gain this insight] in the manner of those economists who obliterate all historical differences and who see in all social phenomena only bourgeois phenomena. If one knows rent, it is possible to understand tribute, tithe, etc., but they do not have to be treated as identical.
>
> Since bourgeois society is, moreover, only a contradictory form of development, it contains relations of earlier societies often merely as very stunted forms or even in the form of travesties, e.g., communal ownership.
> [. . .]

> For example, nothing seems more natural than to begin with rent, i.e., with landed property, since it is associated with the earth, the source of all production in all societies that have attained a measure of stability. But nothing would be more erroneous. There is in every social formation a particular branch of production which determines the position and importance of all the others, and the relations obtaining in this branch accordingly determine the relations of all the other branches as well. [. . .] Agriculture to an increasing extent becomes just a branch of industry and is completely dominated by capital. The same applies to rent. In all forms in which landed property is the decisive factor, natural relations still predominate; in the forms in which the decisive factor is capital, social, historically evolved elements predominate. Rent cannot be understood without capital, but capital can be understood without rent. Capital is the economic power that dominates everything in bourgeois society. It must form both the point of departure and the conclusion and it has to be expounded before landed property. After analyzing capital and landed property separately, their interconnection must be examined.[11]

This text is very important because it shows how Marx formed concepts and categories on the basis of experience, of the critique of contemporary society. I skipped an equally interesting passage that I want to return to here:

> Similarly, only when the self-criticism of bourgeois society had begun, was bourgeois political economy able to understand the feudal, ancient, and oriental economies. In so far as bourgeois political economy did not simply identify itself with the past in a mythological manner, its criticism of earlier economies—especially of the feudal system against which it still had to wage a direct struggle—resembled the criticism that Christianity directed under heathenism, or which Protestantism directed against Catholicism.
>
> . . . Thus the category [of political economy], *even from the scientific standpoint*, by no means begins at the moment when it is discussed *as such*.[12]

It is amusing to note the importance Marx here assigns to bourgeois ethnography, whose critical insight, he claims, resembles Protestantism's critique of Catholicism.

I want to conclude by stating that Marx himself cannot be read without reintegrating him into the historical context, without understanding him historically and critically. In the letters at the end of the recently published volume, Marx assumes that we can make the transition from the agrarian community to socialism. Yet, based on Lenin's teaching and the experience of the Russian Revolution, this would appear to be impossible. I admit to not knowing what is happening in China in this regard, but it seems on the basis of practical experience, of subsequent knowledge, and especially of Lenin's analyses that the transition is impossible and that the shift to socialism assumes the objective dissolution of the agrarian community. The *kolkhoz* does not emerge from the *mir*. In Russia, nationalization of the land was needed, agrarian reform, the formation of completely new relations of production so that the *kolkhoz* could appear. The *kolkhoz*, contrary to a widely held argument, does not emerge from the *mir*. At most, we can associate with the *mir* certain remnants of mutual assistance, certain psychological and moral elements, cultural or superstructural elements, capable of playing a role, but a secondary role. This is important for the theory of the agrarian community.

The theory of the agrarian community is only a fragment of a larger theory, which is the theory of all the agrarian problems in Marxism, itself inseparable from historical materialism as a whole.

Discussion

A MEMBER OF THE AUDIENCE: Concerning the question of the transition from the primitive community to socialism, a distinction would have to be made between the cultural level and the economic level. It seems to me that on the cultural level, there could be a direct transition from the culture of the primitive community to the socialist culture that incorporates primitive elements.

On the economic plane, there must at least be a tentative transition to some form of capitalist economy in order to enable the transition to socialism.

HENRI LEFEBVRE: This seems to me partly accurate and partly questionable. There's a text by Engels that Lenin quotes in his work on the agrarian question in 1917, in Russia, concerning the April theses. The text states that certain ideas that are economically and formally false nonetheless take on a meaning with respect to universal history, and alludes, in this passage, to the ideas of utopian socialism, ideas of justice, for example, which are economically and formally false but, as superstructure, being part of the movement of universal history, play an effective, positive role that we must take into account.[13] There are elements that can arise, not so much from "culture" (and it is this that leads me to criticize your comment) as from the social practice that persists in agrarian communities. For example, the practice of mutual assistance, of shared work. We have a practice that is not based economically on relations of ownership in the strict sense of the word. In the French countryside, these mutual assistance relations help form a population of kulaks, who, within a certain circle of dependence around them, take advantage of such relationships, which they preserve to establish their domination. These practices cut both ways. They are vestiges, which no longer have a direct relationship with the current structure of private property. Conversely, these vestiges can leap over a certain stage, or step, and transition directly into socialism. That's why, in the theory and implementation of agrarian reform in Russia, a distinction was made between the *artel* and the *mir*, the first being preserved and transformed into the *kolkhoz*, the second dissolved in 1917.

MAXIME RODINSON: When I spoke of the transition from a precapitalist form of production to socialism, I wasn't thinking of the direct transition from the *mir* to the *kolkhoz*, but the overall integration of an integrated primitive society into the socialist economy of the Soviet Union.

The Village Community

HENRI LEFEBVRE: I understand the problem better now. There are two questions, superimposed on one another. Can we jump over a historical phase? Yes. Is there a direct transition from the community to socialism? That is a different question. It does not appear that we can superimpose developed, scientific communism, along with its relations of production, on top of primitive communism. That there might be superstructural, moral, literary elements, moving from one to the other is a different question but, objectively, the primitive community has to be dissolved.

JEAN BRUHAT, ASSISTANT AT THE SORBONNE: Lefebvre's discussions always amaze. We don't know what to focus on. I would like to pick up on what he just said about the transition from the primitive community to socialism. Can this transition occur directly? Does it imply a dislocation of the primitive community? The historian must intervene. This is not a conceptual problem but a question of comprehension.

There's one point with which I'm in agreement: the *kolkhoz* is, in no sense, the heir of the *mir* and, obviously, the prior existence of the *mir* was able to ease certain transitions from the psychological point of view.

We need to be more specific about the nature of the rural community in Russia in 1917. It was merely a vestige and already its dislocation had begun, as early as the Stolypin reform of the early nineteenth century. Soviet power didn't have to confront a rural community in the pure state but a rural community in the process of dislocation. We can clarify this problem by comparing, on the one hand, the rural communities as they evolved under the direction of Soviet power and, on the other hand, the rural community dislocated under other regimes. And here a political element is introduced. The historical context is completely different. The transition of the Russian rural community, under the control of Soviet power, toward a transitional phase of peasant democracy that led to the creation of the kolkhoz is a specific, historical path that can be explained by the existence of Soviet power. On the other hand, in the colonial lands dominated by imperialism, we move from the rural community to the formation of large capitalist societies that become owners of the land.

If we wish to go into greater detail, we need to analyze the *kolkhoz* utopias that were supposed to follow liberation movements in countries like Morocco or Madagascar, where some, pointing to the Soviet experience, had believed that, without modifying the relations of production, they could transition, while colonized, from the rural community to the creation of a true *kolkhoz*. The experience showed that we cannot limit ourselves to abstractions when we are discussing historical problems. The problem of class and the State has been presented; we need to know which class the State serves.

HENRI LEFEBVRE: Bruhat's comments are extremely apropos and I would add to his very interesting example that of the *kibbutzim* of Israel, which are fake *kolkhoz* that evolve to the benefit of capitalism, and do so in a way that would also be worth studying critically.

Notes

[*La Pensée*, no. 66 (1956): 29–38. This was a special issue, dedicated to a discussion of Friedrich Engels, *L'origine de la famille, de la propriété privée et de l'État* (Paris: Alfred Costes, 1931).—*Eds.*]

1. [Georges Gurvitch was a Russian-born French sociologist who founded the journal *Cahiers internationaux de Sociologie* and held a chair at the Sorbonne in Paris.—*Eds.*]

2. [Friedrich Engels, *L'origine de la famille, de la propriété et de l'État* (Paris: Alfred Costes, 1931).—*Eds.*]

3. [That is, this issue of *Le Pensée*.—*Trans.*]

4. [See chapter 2, note 4, in the present volume for a discussion of Le Play.— *Eds.*]

5. [Mouvement républicain populaire (MRP, Popular Republican Movement) was a postwar (1944) Christian-Democratic political party active during the Fourth Republic.—*Trans.*]

6. [See Karl Marx, "Debates on the Law on the Theft of Wood" (1842), in Karl Marx and Friedrich Engels, *Collected Works,* vol. 2 (London: Lawrence and Wishart, 1975).—*Eds.*]

7. [Lefebvre is referring to the first volume of *Capital,* which was published in three parts in French. The reference is to Karl Marx, *Le Capital Livre Premier,* vol. 2, trans. Joseph Roy (Paris: Editions Sociales, 1977), 47. The material referred addresses how "possession of the land in common" inheres within certain Indian communities to give rise to a specific division of labor based on subsistence: "Hence production here is independent of that division of labour brought about in Indian society as a whole by the exchange of commodities. It is the surplus alone that becomes a commodity, and a part of the surplus cannot become a commodity until it has reached the hands of the State." See Karl Marx, *Capital: A Critique of Political Economy,* vol. 1, trans. Ben Fowkes (London: Penguin, 1990), 477–78. Subsequently, reference is then made to how developments in bookkeeping impact on communal labor, leading to a "deduction from the common product." Here, it is stated, "Just as with the book-keeper of the Indian community, so the same applies, *mutatis mutandis,* to the capitalist's book-keeper." See Karl Marx, *Capital: A Critique of Political Economy,* vol. 2, trans. David Fernbach (London: Penguin, 1992), 211–12n3.—*Eds.*]

8. [See Maurice Merleau-Ponty, *Adventures of the Dialectic,* trans. Joseph Bien (Evanston, Ill.: Northwestern University Press, 1973). Lefebvre wrote a two-part piece at this time: "M. Merleau-Ponty et la philosophie de l'ambiguité," *La Pensée,* no. 68 (1956): 44–58, and *La Pensée,* no. 73 (1957): 37–52.—*Eds.*]

9. [François Châtelet, "Non, l'histoire n'est pas insaisissable!," *La Nouvelle Critique,* no. 65 (May 1955): 56–72.—*Eds.*]

10. Châtelet, "Non, l'histoire n'est pas insaisissable!," 69.

11. [Karl Marx, "Introduction to a Critique of Political Economy," in *The German Ideology,* ed. C. J. Arthur (New York: International Publishers, 1970), 145–47.—*Trans.*]

12. [Marx, "Introduction to a Critique of Political Economy," 146.—*Trans.*]

13. [As detailed in chapter 7 in the current volume, Lefebvre here is drawing from the dictum "That which is false in a formal and economic sense can be true in a historical and universal sense" that Lenin sourced from Engels. Lenin used this statement to comment: "It is important that Engels's profound thesis must be borne in mind when appraising the present-day Narodnik or Trudovik utopia. . . . Narodnik *democracy,* while fallacious from the formal economic point of view, is correct from the *historical* point of view; *this* democracy, while fallacious as a socialist utopia, is *correct* in terms of the peculiar, historically conditioned democratic struggle of the peasant masses." See V. I. Lenin, "Two Utopias" (1912), in V. I. Lenin, *Collected Works,* vol. 18 (Moscow: Progress Publishers, 1975), 355–59.—*Eds.*]

CHAPTER 7

The Theory of Ground Rent and Rural Sociology

Introduction

In the domain of rural sociology, even slight acquaintance with the facts destroys commonly held opinion.[1]

In terms of time, agriculture came before industry; in terms of space, even today, an ocean of agricultural production surrounds some continents and some small islands of urban life and industrial production. Hence we imagine, in general, that rural life and agricultural structure are simpler than the "modern" life of cities and factories.

But in fact, rural sociology has to deal with extremely complicated realities, especially as it is shaken by contradictory movements. Not only do rural sociologists find themselves confronting structures originating from different historical epochs (for instance, structures historically linked to the Middle Ages), but they confront structures that are disintegrating, mixed with new forms and structures.

There is not much in common between a village in northeastern France (with a strong communal structure, although extensively reorganized through major [*grande*] modern agriculture) and a hamlet [*village individualiste*], although stagnant or declining, from the south. There is not much in common between a typical French village and a village from the south of Italy or Spain, real agricultural towns, from where (every day or at the beginning of every week) thousands of agricultural workers go to work on "latifundia," often very far away from their home [*domicile*].

Today, among the branches of sociology, rural sociology is probably more than others connected to life, to practical action, to efficacy [*à l'efficacité*].[2] The *agrarian reforms* being considered in much of the world cannot be implemented without sociologists, because they pose serious sociological problems. For instance, during attempts (as yet uncompleted, as yet unsatisfactory) to transform the agricultural structure of southern Italy, it was necessary to ask sociologists to study how agricultural workers in large villages could become small-scale farmers with their own individual plots [*exploitation individuelle*]. Another example: in Hungary, on the plain, peasants traditionally spent the winter in agrarian villages (Szeged, etc.), then in the spring they would return to their far-flung farms ("tanyas"). How to put an end to this tradition of seminomadism fixed to the soil and regroup in modernized villages of "tanyas"?[3]

Here we refer only to structures close to us. If we considered Asia (India, China, etc.), it would be much more complicated.

Rural sociology describes complex phenomena. It tries to understand [*pénétrer*] them in depth. But soon it discovers sedimentations, so to speak, which have nothing to do with description but belong to another domain, especially to *history*. The sociologist who wants to understand and know has to double as a historian. How can one understand the agrarian structure of southern Italy without history?

But these historical facts themselves need analysis and explanation. Where can we find them? Or at least in which direction?

The following thesis is held here: rural sociology, by understanding [*en pénétrant*] sociological and historical facts in depth, finds itself confronted with economic facts and laws, and eventually with a theory of political economy: the theory of *ground rent*, the only theory that can explain historical and social facts, namely the structure observed and described above.

II. Development of a Theory

The theory of *ground rent* was born in England. Marx and Engels considered it to be a very important contribution by "classical" English economists to science because "it was only in England that there existed a mode of production under which ground rent had in fact been separated from profit and interest."[4]

Marx took up [*repris*] and developed the theory of ground rent elaborated by James Anderson, Adam Smith, and, most importantly, [David] Ricardo. He modified it profoundly, first of all by criticizing the well-known [*fameuse*] law of decreasing productivity [*loi de la productivite decroissante*] of land (technical progress in modern agriculture confirmed this refutation). Marx showed that the notion of *differential* rent [*rentes differentielle*] introduced by Ricardo must itself be differentiated, in the sense that there are multiple differential rents (rent A comes from natural differences in soils, unequal fertility, diverse situations in relation to markets and communication routes; rent B develops from differences of productivity from successive capital investments in the same soil).

After Marx, then, to *differential* rent must be added the notion of *absolute* rent [*rente absolute*], taken by the owner of the land, even if the land remains fallow (unproductive). This absolute rent does not relate to the price of agricultural products, nor to the profit of the capitalist farmer who invests in the land.

Marx confirmed Ricardo's important viewpoint: the landowner (historically of feudal origin, although in many parts of the world [*globe*] the bourgeoisie displaced and replaced the feudal "latifundium") tends to take all the rent, leaving the exploited with only a minimal part: the average profit for his capital, wage labor for the work accomplished. In this way, Marx answered in a new and thoroughly scientific manner the large problem posed by Ricardo: How do we distribute "revenue" according to the classes of the population?

Curious fact: contemporary economists often ignore the theory of ground rent. Nevertheless, it played a significant role in the formation of "marginalism." But marginalists are content to emphasize the role played by "marginal" enterprises (smallholdings [*petites agriculture*]) in establishing agricultural prices. They leave aside the essential: the source of the "revenues" and their distribution.[5]

Furthermore, the very notion of ground rent becomes obscured. In Italy, where agrarian research institutes are especially active and well equipped, it is officially only a matter of "ground revenue" [*revenu foncière*], and they study its total revenue per land hectare, so that we know neither its origin nor its distribution (what goes to the landlord and what goes to the different categories of farmers [*exploitants*]).

Recently, in France, the study of ground rent has experienced a new revival. Why? Precisely because the problems of the peasantry are raised with increasing acuity. The Sociéte francaise d'économie rurale has published two reports: *Rente foncière et revenu agricole* [Ground rent and agricultural revenue] and *Le problème de la rente du sol* [The problem of land rent].[6] They are rather confused reports referring to Ricardo without considering the Marxist critique. The authors of these studies point out the importance of the problem, but they face a simple fact: strictly speaking, ground rent in France today represents only 2 percent of national revenue. How then can it exercise any influence on the agrarian structure? How does it connect to those problems that trouble the French peasantry?

Meanwhile, the theory of ground rent is investigated and developed, although in more distant countries, especially in China (where the economist and sociologist Chen Po-Ta has just published a remarkable work on this question).[7]

III. The Contribution of Lenin

As we find it in Ricardo and then in Marx, the theory of ground rent is indeed incomplete and unusable. The indispensable complement to this theory and its modern scientific form—that makes it applicable to immense regions [*immenses régions*]—is to be found in Lenin's work.

Marx describes and analyzes how free market capitalism [*capitalisme de la libre concurrence*] was introduced into agriculture. Today, capitalism has changed its structure: it is transformed into monopoly capitalism. Marx, on the other hand, considered (like Ricardo) the agrarian class of feudal origins to be the dominant, but mainly parasitic, class alongside the capitalists. Since then, although it has not completely disappeared in numerous countries (Italy, Spain, Muslim countries, India, etc.), this class of landlords has partially blended into capitalists. Finally, in some places the industrialization of agriculture has become increasingly predominant, even though this has not suppressed some traces of the past such as the "latifundista" type of property, or smallholdings. Nevertheless, increasingly, we have to distinguish here and there but particularly in France (in the Parisian region and in the north) a *new social type: the large capitalist farmer, sometimes owners of land, and sometimes not, but directing industrial businesses and taking land rent from a large number of small- and medium-sized farmers who have abandoned agriculture.*[8]

In his work on the agrarian question [*question agraire*], Lenin[9] considers many new facts and comes to the following conclusions:

(1) *In the agrarian structure of capitalist countries or countries subjected to capitalism, we find the coexistence of different forms belonging to all eras of history, to all successive moments of social development.*[10] Among these formations are counted: rural or archaic communities, more or less disintegrating; the different feudal structures in Western, Muslim, and Asian countries; smallholdings, often dating back to the precapitalist era and sometimes connected to capitalism, for instance in France where the Revolution of 1789 gave part of the land to peasants; and the widespread exploitation of large capitalist estates.

Today, we have to add different forms of cooperation (capitalist, semi-capitalist, semi-socialist, socialist) to this list.

In capitalist countries, whatever the levels of uneven development [*inégalités de développement*], property and exploitation of the capitalist type tends to subordinate all other forms of exploitation and property ownership [*propriété*]. Lenin considered this position as having the value and scope of an *objective law*.

(2) *The introduction of capitalism into agriculture expresses a double monopoly* (this word meaning the predominance of a group, or class, not of a single individual). *The original feudal monopoly is added to the capitalist monopoly.* These two monopolies may fight, combine, or ally themselves, depending on the countries and regions. But despite the variety of combinations, they are almost everywhere and they exercise powerful pressure on the other forms of exploitation and property.

(3) The double monopoly (in its various combinations) simultaneously reorganizes the agrarian structure and the distribution of the "revenue" [*revenu*], or in other words, ground rent.

The large capitalist farmer [agriculteur], *owner* [propriétaire], *or profiteer* [exploitant] *does not simply take an average profit of the invested capital but a considerable part and sometimes all the rent. Moreover, they take the permanent superprofits* [surprofits] *obtained through the low salaries of the agricultural workers, the low cost of production within highly* [puissamment] *mechanized businesses, the manipulation of prices in the market, the application of quotas and custom duties, the credit conditions, etcetera.*[11]

IV. The Situation in France

This theory satisfactorily explains numerous facts observed by economists and sociologists.

It explains why ground rent in the strict sense (rent by the noncapitalist property owner) has fallen in France to 2 percent of the national revenue, while the revenue of those who enjoy the rent in the sense defined above (including therefore the capitalist profiteers) is much higher. We do not have precise figures, because statistics only show the general revenue of the profiteers of all categories. But we can appreciate the efforts of economists who, faced with the facts, fashion new notions, which are very confused and are, in their mind, meant to replace the classic notion of "ground rent" (for instance the notion of "technical rent" [*rente technique*] for the industrialized capitalist farm [*l'exploitation*], which hides the real nature of the revenue, its source and its distribution, and the actual agrarian structure of the country).[12]

For us, a developed Marxist theory applies and is validated across the board. We will be content to mention some facts related to the agrarian structure of France:

(1) In certain regions, such as Brittany, the original feudal monopoly remains powerful and sometimes predominant (although over the last few years it has been challenged by the growth of large capitalist agriculture). In such regions, the agrarian "nobles" and the bourgeois landholders buying feudal estates [*domaines*] still occupy strong positions.

The Theory of Ground Rent and Rural Sociology 111

Nevertheless, this does not prevent the clustering of small-scale landholders and tenant farmers around large estates. The effect of demographic pressure, when aided by ground rent in the strict sense due to the landowner, is strong [*forte*]. Villages are highly populated and dominated by the "castle." An archaic character is preserved, with the strong influence of the Catholic clergy; the excess population emigrates, permanently or not (as sailors and as seasonal workers). Nevertheless, new movements caused by the tendencies of mechanized agriculture and by some level of industrialization fight traditionalism.

(2) In the northern and the eastern part of the Parisian region, the capitalist monopoly dominates. It is here that we can study this *new social type* previously mentioned: the powerful capitalist profiteer [*exploitant*], owner of a "wheat and beetroot factory," often associated with industrial and financial capitalism (fabrication of sugar, alcohol, etc.). Sometimes he is the landlord, sometimes not; but generally he is the leaseholder [*locataire*] of fields owned by several small- and medium-scale landlords. Curious fact: the landlords are then only minor figures [*petites gens*] compared to their tenant [*locataire*]. In this region, the proportion of the exploitation becomes huge and far exceeds the proportion of the property. The multiple farms [*exploitations*] incorporate [*englobent*] the whole village's territory or even spread beyond it. Villages depopulate. Agricultural workers (lodging in or outside the farm) have replaced the older population of peasants and artisans. These workers are often foreigners, badly paid, living in deplorable conditions. Nonetheless, a new "elite" is forming: mechanical technicians and tractor drivers, specialists, technicians of scientific farming, etcetera.

(3) The whole of the south of France is, increasingly, an underdeveloped area, whose agrarian structure is disintegrating. A detailed examination shows, within a general backwardness [*dans le retard général*], great diversity. In certain sectors, the feudal monopoly remains powerful; tenant farming (an outdated and semifeudal mode of cultivation) still persists, for instance in the southwest. In other sectors, inclusive of part of the wine-growing sector, small- and medium-scale property [*propriété*] still exists, although in a lamentable state. Lastly, in sectors of specialized cultivation (vines, fruits, vegetables and early crops [*primeurs*], flowers),

large capitalist farming [*exploitation*] becomes established, although in reduced areas [*surface*]. It is clear that ten hectares of early crops [*primeurs*] or flowers represent a big farm requiring large capital investment (in the statistics, these landholdings are lumped together with the smallholdings of familial [*familiale*] polyculture, which significantly interferes with interpreting the figures).

In any case, the sectors where smallholdings prevail, small property, the familial polyculture is completely declining. Statistics show a decrease of general revenue in the regions considered, as much as 7 percent in twenty years in the southwest.

Villages get depopulated, for many reasons (low birth rate, migration, definite emigration). In this region, which is generally becoming impoverished, wealth gets concentrated in the towns inhabited by landlords owning properties that are held for sharecropping [*métayage*], or in the most important modernized farms [*exploitations*]. These towns are also markets (Toulouse, Perpignan, Montpellier, etc.) and administrative centers. What happens then is a complex and contradictory process that only the theory of ground rent can explain.

IV. Conclusion

The theoretical considerations and the concrete facts noted above therefore seem to scientifically confirm the position indicated at the beginning of this study.

The rural sociologist is confronted with extremely varied phenomena, which they must try to attempt to organize. Beginning with description but soon confronted with problems that exceed simple descriptions, what is required is another tool of investigation distinct from empiricism. By delving deeply into the problems of rural sociology in order to grasp its laws, the process is confronted as simultaneously historical, economical, and social. In order to know the objective process, a theory is needed. In the area of rural sociology, this theory exists: it is the theory of ground rent, developed from classical economics by Marxists.

Translated by Matthew Dennis

Notes

[Contribution to the International Congress of Sociology, Amsterdam, August 1956, originally published as "Théorie de la rente foncière et sociologie rurale," *Transactions of the Third World Congress of Sociology* 2 (1956): 244–50, reprinted in *Du rural à l'urbain* (Paris: Anthropos, 1970), 79–87. Translated by Matthew Dennis and first published in English as Henri Lefebvre, "The Theory of Ground Rent and Rural Sociology," *Antipode* 48, no. 1 (2016): 67–73. The text has been translated into Spanish twice: "La teoría de la Renta de la Tierra y la Sociología Rural," trans. Óscar Uribe Villegas, *Revista Mexicana de Sociología* 27, no. 1 (1965): 7–14, reprinted in *La renta de la tierra: Cinco ensayos*, by Henri Lefebvre, José M. Caballero, Oscar González, and Werner Kamppeter (Mexico City: Editorial Tlaiualli, 1983, 11–18), and as "Teoría de la renta de la tierra y sociología rural," in *De lo rural a lo urbano*, trans. Javier Gonzalez-Pueyo, ed. Mario Gaviria (Barcelona: Ediciones Península, 1971), 77–84. Both Spanish translations have been consulted in producing this version, with the subheadings deriving from the 1983 reprint.—Eds.]

1. [The 1970 French reprint merely says "sociology," not "rural sociology," in this sentence, which appears in the original 1956 French text and the Spanish translations.—Eds.]

2. [It could be argued that the connection made by Lefebvre between rural sociology and practical action, or efficacy, is one that evokes Karl Marx's second of the "Theses on Feuerbach," that "the question whether objective truth can be attributed to human thinking is not a question of theory but is a practical question. Man must prove the truth, i.e., the reality and power, the this-sidedness of his thinking, in practice." See Karl Marx, "Theses on Feuerbach," in Karl Marx and Friedrich Engels, *Collected Works*, vol. 5 (London: Lawrence and Wishart, 1976), 7.—Eds.]

3. [The 1970 French version has this word as *"taïgas."*—Eds.]

4. [Friedrich Engels, *Anti-Dühring: Herr Eugen Dühring's Revolution in Science*, in Karl Marx and Friedrich Engels, *Collected Works*, vol. 25 (London: Lawrence and Wishart, 1987), chapter 9, "Natural Laws of the Economy: Rent of Land," 209. Lefebvre references II, 10; the passage is actually in II, 9. See also Friedrich Engels, *Anti-Dühring: Herr Eugen Dühring's Revolution in Science* (Moscow: Foreign Languages Publishing House, 1954), chapter 9, "Natural Laws of Economics: Ground-Rent," 309.—Eds.]

5. We should note, however, some interesting works published in the United States, in particular Kenneth E. Boulding, "The Concept of Economic Surplus," *American Economic Review* 35, no. 5 (1945): 851–69; G. F. Bloom, "Technical Progress, Costs and Rents," *Económica* 9, no. 33 (1942): 40–52; and H. W. Singer, "An Index of Urban Land Rents and House Rents in England and Wales, 1845–1913," *Econometrica* 9 (1941): 221–30, etcetera. [We have completed and corrected Lefebvre's references.—Eds.]

6. [We have been unable to trace the first publication, but the second is L. Rolland, "Le problème de la rente différentielle du sol," *Économie rurale* 23, no. 23 (1955): 27–33. This journal is published by Sociéte francaise d'économie rurale (SFER, French Society of Rural Economy). We suspect that the first reference is also an article in this journal, but it is not clear which, as there is no piece in it with the cited title.—*Eds.*]

7. [Tchen Po-Ta, "Etude sur la rente foncière en Chine," *Etudes économiques: Cahiers mensuels d'économie socialiste*, nos. 84–85 (1954): 1–67; Chen Po-Ta, *A Study of Land Rent in Pre-Liberation China*, 2nd ed. (Peking: Foreign Languages Press, 1966).—*Eds.*]

8. I have studied this social "type" in numerous villages of Seine-et-Marne, Aisne, Oise (regions north and northeast of Paris). [The 1965 Spanish translation has "new social type" and the description emphasized in italics.—*Eds.*]

9. V. I. Lenin, *Collected Works*, vol. 4, *Capitalism in Agriculture* (Moscow: Progress Publishers, 1960); V. I. Lenin, *Collected Works*, vol. 5, *The Agrarian Question and the "Critics of Marx"* (Moscow: Progress Publishers, 1960); V. I. Lenin, *Collected Works*, vol. 22, *New Data on the Laws Governing the Development of Capitalism in Agriculture* (Moscow: Progress Publishers, 1964). The reader should also be referred to V. I. Lenin, *Collected Works*, vol. 3, *The Development of Capitalism in Russia* (Moscow: Progress Publishers, 1960). [We have completed Lefebvre's references here.—*Eds.*]

10. [Here, and elsewhere, the numbering differs between the 1956 and 1970 French version of the text. We have followed the 1956 version. This section and those below are emphasized in italics in the Spanish translation.—*Eds.*]

11. [As Marx relays on the genesis of capitalist ground rent, "a portion of the surplus labour performed by those peasants working under the least favourable conditions is presented to society for nothing and does not contribute towards governing the price of production of forming value." See Karl Marx, *Capital: A Critique of Political Economy*, vol. 3 trans. David Fernbach (London: Penguin, 1991), 942.—*Eds.*]

12. [In the 1965 Spanish translation, "ground rent" is in quotation marks.—*Eds.*]

CHAPTER 8

The Marxist–Leninist Theory of Ground Rent

The Agrarian Question and the Theory of Ground Rent—From Classical Political Economy to Marxist Science—The Place of Ground Rent Theory in Marx's Capital*—A Brief Summary of the Theory of Ground Rent—Leninist Developments of the Theory of Ground Rent—The Theory of Rent and Monopoly Capitalism.*

1. The Agrarian Question and the Theory of Ground Rent

Let us suppose that we could establish and place in a graph exact data on the current situation of agriculture and the French peasantry.[1] What would we find?[2]

We would certainly come across a great concentration of land ownership [*propiedad*] and industrialized exploitation [*explotación industrializada*], near the big city centers, in the Parisian region and the north, and in the Beauce region.[3] In these regions, we clearly find a large agricultural proletariat. As a result of mechanization, this proletariat is diminishing, quantitatively speaking, in number, and is changing, qualitatively speaking, with an increase in the number of qualified workers, tractor mechanics, etcetera.

Immediately after, we would see stagnation and the subdivision of property [*propiedad*] and exploitation [*explotación*] in other French regions, above all in the western and southern parts of the country.

In this way, the graphs and figures would show that despite technological advancements, the introduction of machinery, and the industrialization of large-scale capitalist production, as a whole, the agricultural sector continues to fall behind when compared with the industrial sector. However, we would also find that in these backward regions there still exists a certain concentration of property, which benefits a small rural bourgeoisie (in particular the "kulaks" who own tractors and other farming machinery, which they lend in exchange for money or services). Therefore, the graphs and figures would clearly show at once overproduction and a generalized state of stagnation, uneven development [*desigualdad de desarrollo*] across different French regions, and differences in class and social strata. These are the characteristics of permanent agricultural crisis, which are themselves located in the overall crisis of capitalism.

Even in the backward regions of France, the graphs would show the development of capitalism and its penetration into the agricultural structure (of precapitalist origin); a development that takes different forms to those of accumulation, all too often considered the only symptom and criterion. This is true of the production of legumes, fruit, milk, specialized crops and of livestock breeding [*cría de ganado*], etcetera. In numerous cases, important capitalist farms [*explotaciones capitalistas*] need no more than a small additional plot of land [*terreno*] (this is the case, for example, in the production of vegetables). It also happens that this aspect of capitalist production is rendered locally in the reduction of areas of farmland destined for cultivation, accompanied by considerable investments into what are relatively small plots of land (as is the case, for example, in the lower valleys of the Durance and Avignon). And yet at the same time we find that a semifeudal mode of production still stubbornly persists and survives (as we can see with the existence of sharecroppers [*medieros*] in the south of France).

Now let us suppose that we could carry out the same study on a worldwide [*mundial*] scale, in reference not only to capitalist countries but also more importantly to those that are underdeveloped. These are predominantly agricultural countries, exploited by imperialism, whose agriculture is generally backward (with the exception of some sectors of single-crop capitalist farming).⁴ We would arrive at results akin to those previously examined: stagnation, inequality, unevenness, and, despite technological advancements, a permanent agricultural crisis located within the framework of an overall crisis.

However, this immense totality of facts cannot be studied, understood, or explained without the Marxist theory of ground rent, which must be used as the point of departure.⁵

Unfortunately, this is a particularly complex and difficult theory and hard to get to grips with. It can be found in the last section of *Capital* (the unfinished section).⁶ Finally, it comes across as abstract and in effect it is abstract, albeit in a way that is scientific and founded in objectivity. Indeed, it is so abstract that it is not at all easy to move from the theory to the given facts. This is especially true when we bear in mind that the facts themselves have changed since Marx wrote his aforementioned work and carried out his analysis of agricultural phenomena in England.

It is for this reason that one still hears, particularly among social democrats, that Marx neglected or ignored the agrarian question and that as a result it eluded Marxism. This allows it to be, at best, treated in an empirical or nonscientific way and, at worst, ignored entirely. This, in turn, has led to a growing acceptance of capitalist and imperialist projects, plans and perspectives within the agricultural sectors of colonial or semicolonial (underdeveloped) countries.

2. From Classical Political Economy to Marxist Science

Let us now recall, as briefly as possible, some of the historical and theoretical elements of our problem.

The study of fixed rent has occupied an important place in the work of bourgeois classical, scientific economists (in particular [Adam] Smith and [David] Ricardo). Their discoveries on this matter are no less important than their other discoveries (most notably their work on the law of value and social labor [*trabajo social*] as the basis for exchange value, etc.). Why? Because despite its claims to objectivism or positivism, the science of political economy has never been put into practice without taking a position. These classical economists criticize feudal society and all its survivals. Among these survivals, ground rent plays an important role. Classical economists have objectively criticized the remaining manifestations of feudalism and this energetic criticism has not harmed the objectivity of their science in the slightest. Quite the contrary!

It was in this way that Ricardo discovered differential rent. Despite the great English economist's serious errors and overall lack of knowledge [*ignorancia*], this was an objective and valuable discovery. The errors: his formulation of the false law [*la falsa ley*] of decreasing fertility of land, which comes from a one-sided interpretation of facts and is a notable example of a false law due to the fact that it is neither dialectical nor historical. The lack of knowledge: his neglect and rejection of absolute rent.

3. The Place of Ground Rent Theory in Marx's *Capital*

In the volumes of *Capital*, Marx responded to the question that had already been introduced by Ricardo (in his *Principles of Political Economy*) but without the latter leaving a scientific solution.

The overall question is as follows: where do profits, that are shared among different classes and strata of bourgeois society (capitalists, landowners [*propietarios de la tierra*], salaried workers [*asalariados*] as well as merchants, landlords, moneylenders, peasant landholders [*comerciantes, rentistas, prestamistas de capitales, campesinos propietarios*], etc.), come from?

This fundamental problem leads to a further problem: how can a capitalist sharecropper [*mediero capitalista*], who receives average profits from his capital, pay, at the same time, rent to a landlord for the land [*suelo*] that he is using (especially as this property is also land [*propiedad del suelo*] that is historically of precapitalist and feudal origin)? And all of this without the law of value disappearing on agricultural products, or in other words, without assuming, as Smith does, that the prices of these products are fixed more or less arbitrarily in the market.

Marx mentions that the distribution of profit between different classes, presented as fair by bourgeois economists as it gives to some, profits from the land, and to others, profits from capital or from work, in fact covers up or hides the distribution of surplus value that is taken from industrial workers and farm workers by the dominant classes and their allies. This fundamental theory, which presents and explains the totality of capitalist society, can be found in the last and unfortunately unfinished part of *Capital*.

This is the part that concludes and crowns the theoretical edifice. And it is in this way that Marx establishes his theory of fixed rent.[7]

4. A Brief Summary of the Theory of Ground Rent

In this study, Marx extends, critiques, and transforms the works of Smith and Ricardo.

(a) He resolutely critiques the fetishism of land, analogous to the fetishism of money and of capital. Land without human labor cannot, any more than money, produce income [*ingresos*] by itself. Current and past expressions in vulgar economy—"ground rent" [*rentas de la tierra*], "fixed rent" [*rentas fijas*], "agrarian rent" [*rentas agrarias*]—have no scientific meaning. Land, in and of itself, has neither a value nor a price; "ground rent, its value," and its price come from society and from social relations, and not from the land itself. In short, the notion of the fertility of land [*fertilidad de la tierra*], frequently understood to be natural and absolute, is in reality relative and historical. It is relative, with regard to the particular state of the technology used, and to the productive forces. It is here that Ricardo made a serious mistake. Land of varying, and increasingly diminished, fertility must be cultivated using a particular technique within a specific level of productive forces. The same work and the same technique, when applied to the same land [*suelo*], becomes each time less productive as the land deteriorates and becomes increasingly exhausted. Changes to technology may, however, modify the natural fertility of the land [*suelo*], and moreover at any given moment, the best plots of land [*tierras*] may not always be the same. The law of decreasing productivity of land, considered to be natural and absolute, is false. Land [*suelo*] must not be considered outside relations of production and property ownership. These are social relations, which are historically determined and which correspond to a specific degree of productive forces.

(b) Once established, Ricardo then correctly demonstrated that the market price of agricultural products is determined by the cost of production of the cultivation of the worst-located and poorest-quality land, which are, regardless, essential to meet demand. The difference between the price of production of the best-situated and highest-quality land, and the least favorable, is what constitutes that which is known as differential rent.

This rent comes from the fact that the productivity of labor (in other words, the performance of living labor) is much greater in better-quality and better-situated land, even though the technology used on them remains the same. In addition to the preexisting differences between different plots of land, there are differences in the instruments and the means of production.

On closer analysis, differential rent can be divided in two, a fact that Ricardo either did not see or did not see clearly. Rent I is derived from differences in fertility between different plots of land (always within the same particular state of agricultural technology), and from its more or less favorable situation regarding markets. Indeed, transport expenses also need to be taken into account.

Furthermore, the capitalist invests capital in the land [*tierra*] that he rents. The productivity of successive capital investments (which is, as a matter of fact, the productivity of labor set in motion by this capital) is uneven and, on the other hand, does not necessarily diminish, although it is limited (for example when the landowner introduces into his already exploited land a new form of technology). These differences constitute the second type, Rent II, or differential rent (which encompasses everything that is derived from technological differences).

(c) Absolute rent, which was neglected or forgotten by Ricardo, should be added to these two kinds of differential rent. Absolute rent is the amount that is handed over to the landowner for the use of his own land [*tierra*], even though this land may be of very poor quality, or might have been left uncultivated or as natural pasture for animals.

(d) Where do these different kinds of rent, which together constitute fixed rent, end up? Essentially with the landowner. Land dividends [*bonificación*], which are the result of investments in that same land (buildings, drainage, irrigation systems, etc.), end up in the hands of the permanent landowner [*propietario fijo*] when the contract comes to an end.

Competition between tenants [*arrendatarios*] always tends to reduce their share and to increase that of the landowner.

In fact, free competition (between capitals and capitalists) reduces the share of the tenant to the average profit of his capital.

But how is he able to pay rent, or rather, "rents," to the landowner? It is here that Marx's theory becomes yet more complex.

Agriculture is not a sector or sphere of social production that is separate from the rest of society. It does not have different or separate laws. It is not a state within a state (reactionary theory). The terms "salary," "value," "surplus value," "price," and "profit" [*salario, valor, plusvalía, precio, ganancia*] all have the same meaning and carry the same objective connotations in both the agricultural sector and the industrial sector. Capitalist society is an all-encompassing whole, and all attempts to present the world of agriculture as a world apart are false, unscientific, and politically reactionary. Nevertheless, the existence of monopoly land ownership grants agriculture specific characteristics, objectively speaking, that must be addressed by scientific study.[8]

In effect, this monopoly, in the hands of one class (landowners of historically feudal origins), has considerable consequences. It plays the role of total monopoly in one field of production. It prevents capital from passing freely from one sphere to another and from being freely invested in the agricultural sector. It also prevents equality in rates of profit. All of this keeps the agricultural sector in a state of backwardness [*una situación retardataria*] when seen alongside the industrial sector, so much so that the landowning class, which is in essence parasitic, is able to extract the majority of its productive investments, if not all its profit.

The result, for agriculture, is a weak organic composition of capital (technological backwardness, and therefore a great proportion of capital and of human labor). Hence, an excess of surplus value, which allows the capitalist of the land [*capitalista de la tierra*] to pay fixed rent and to extract for his benefit the average profit.

So it is that in this way, the prices of agricultural products are determined by their value (which is to say, by the medium of socially necessary labor time). And yet, owing to the specificities of agricultural production within the capitalist regime, the products are sold in the market for more than their social value. This is the most difficult part of the theory: the action of the law of value has destroyed it and yet it is limited by the specific conditions of monopoly.

In this brief synopsis, we must leave out the extension, already drafted by Marx, of the theory of precapitalist forms of ground rent [*la renta del suelo*] (feudal and semifeudal rents, such as those of sharecroppers), along with other forms of agricultural profit such as small-scale peasant landholders, whose situation clearly differs from that of the capitalist on the land.

We must also leave to one side the notable extension of this theory into the rent of water, of forests and of livestock [*ganadería*], of built-up land [*suelo construido*], and of mines. Finally, we must also leave to one side the consequences of the use of land, defined as the capitalization of ground rent.

Let us simply stress, in passing, that ground-rent theory covers an immense sector, both historically and today.

Currently it encompasses not only the agricultural sector but also that sector that is between agriculture and industry in the strict sense, namely the exploitation of so-called natural resources, extractive industries, etcetera.

In temporal terms, it encompasses the entire extension of history; from the dissolution of primitive communities right up until socialism, or specifically, from the days of tithing and tribute up until the theory of production cooperatives [*cooperativas de producción*], by way of systems of slavery, feudalism, and capitalism.

Ground rent is the only theory in *Capital* that goes beyond the study of capitalism and its laws. In this way, it prepares and makes way for the broadening of Marx's methods and historical materialism, later achieved by Engels and Lenin.

5. Leninist Developments of the Theory of Ground Rent

In order to understand the importance, the extent, and the richness of ground-rent theory, we must turn our attention to Lenin.

In fact, the theory of fixed rent, which appears in *Capital,* is limited by the conditions in which Marx wrote his work, and by the fact that this part of the text was never completed.

The method used in the analysis and presentation of capitalist society moves from the abstract to the concrete. Let us be clear: from a scientific abstraction, albeit an objective and well-founded one, to reality in all its complexity.

What's more, Marx arrives at this point by means of an analysis of extremely abstract notions (or categories), which are nevertheless objective: exchange value, commodity, etcetera. From here he carries out an analysis, nevertheless founded in objectivity, of abstract society, which is reduced to the proletariat and bourgeoisie. Paving the way, through the study of history and the formation of capitalism, Marx sees capitalist society in all its complexity. But it is only toward the end of his work and specifically with his theory of fixed rent that he begins an analysis and presentation of a concrete society, with all its various classes and social layers.

And even this last (and unfinished) study continues to be methodologically abstract. Marx took as his hypothesis and point of departure the capitalist landlord [*capitalista arrendador*], completely different from that of the landowner (of feudal origin), hence showing the way in which the capitalist mode of production had already extended itself into agriculture. He only sketches the extent of the theory. On the other hand, he found in England a concrete reality that corresponded almost exactly to this template. He was perfectly aware that in other countries the reality was more complex, and indeed just before his death, he had already begun researching a huge number of documents in reference to Russia.

Let us add that he obviously did not study ground rent in any other way than as part of the conditions of capitalism and free competition.

Lenin picked up the study of agricultural phenomenon where Marx had left off and took as his starting point the particularly interesting and complex events in Tsarist Russia.

He understood the breadth and importance of the theory. He explained its value and completed and developed it. He applied it to the study of countries that were extremely different from England, which is to say, nonindustrialized countries (as well as continuing to apply it to the study of highly industrialized countries such as England and the United States). It is precisely the theory of fixed rent that brought about a step change in Marxism toward the Leninist study of imperialism and the impact of the agrarian question in the entire world. It is an essential part of Marxism–Leninism.

At last Lenin could triumphantly respond to all the criticisms of bourgeois, liberal, and Menshevik economists ([Pyotr] Struvé, [Sergei] Bulgakov, [Pyotr] Maslov, etc.).[9]

Lenin discovers laws (that are implicit in Marx's text but that he did not formulate explicitly) and introduces new notions. For example, Lenin shows that the capitalist form of production, with its corresponding relationships to property and exploitation, following an encounter with the most varied and different forms of land ownership, finds itself necessarily subordinated to them. Examples of these varied and different forms include the collective property of a community, of a clan, of a tribe, large feudal or semifeudal property, small farm, etcetera. The forms of this subordination must be studied in each case, in each country, and in each concrete situation. The phenomena that emerge in colonial or semicolonial countries reproduce, but in a much more accelerated fashion, those that accompany the formation of capitalism and its penetration into agriculture.

This law is extremely important in order to objectively study what is happening in colonial or semicolonial countries such as North Africa, where different forms of property ownership coexist (tribal collective property, feudal property, the property of religious foundations, small-scale peasant property, etc.).[10]

Lenin introduced at the same time the very important notion and well-developed theory of double monopoly.

The monopoly of land ownership by virtue of the right to property (a monopoly of feudal origin), and the monopoly of the capitalist exploitation of land, are logically and historically speaking two different things.

Capitalist tenants [*arrendatarios capitalistas*], as part of the capitalist class, can have a true monopoly without ever needing to be a landowner.[11] Indeed, what is characteristic of the capitalist exploitation of land [*suelo*] is the investment of capital in the land and not land ownership [*propiedad de la tierra*] itself.

The fact that the extension of arable and good land [*tierra*] (in a particular state of agricultural technology) is limited presupposes and conditions, in the capitalist system, the monopolization of the exploitation of land as a means of production: as the object of the economy and not as the object of the right to property.

The thesis that says that competition completely eliminates monopoly is false. Let us imagine an extreme hypothesis: even if the capitalists had already occupied all the land available, this would not eliminate among them a certain amount of competition in the market and in investments of capital. Once again it must be said that there should be no confusion between the question of exploitation and that of property.

It goes without saying that if a monopoly exists, competition is eradicated. It also goes without saying that if there is free competition, to make any monopoly impossible, it must not suffer any restriction. There has never existed, in any place, absolute free competition, and nor can it be said that where there is a monopoly it is all over for competition; an absolute monopoly has also never existed. Competition and monopoly are mutually defined and limited and the relationship between the two must be studied in every concrete situation.

Limitations to the extension of land (and of good land) are different from the question of ownership of those same lands. The latter is created within a capitalist system and under conditions of competition between those in possession of capital, which establishes a particular kind of monopoly. The only thing that this means is that all the land available is used, or could be used, by capitalist entrepreneurs [*los empresarios capitalistas*] who work for the market, and it is this market that brings together products from different plots of land because the products from good plots of land are not enough. These differences are inevitable, given that they depend on the natural fertility of the land [*suelo*], of the situation of businesses in relation to transport networks and places of sale and consumption, and of the productivity of investments in the land. As long as we do not forget that these differences have various causes, they can all be summed up as differences between good land and mediocre land. Taking this into account, the price of products is established according to the price of production of the worst plots of land (or according to the cost of production of the least productive investments). The fact that land is finite in these conditions prevents the formation of an average calculation. In order to establish an "average output" that determines price, such as occurs in industry, not only would it be necessary that every capitalist invested his capital in agriculture (something that is theoretically possible, as long as in agriculture there exists a certain freedom of competition), but it would also be necessary that every capitalist, in agriculture just as in industry, created a new agricultural company. And it does not happen in this way because of the existing use of the land [*suelo*] and because the extension of land [*tierras*] is finite. Besides, if there were any difference between agriculture and industry, it would disappear.

In this way, then, the exact relationship between free competition and capitalist monopoly is analyzed in the agricultural sector. Consequently, the question of land [*suelo*] ownership has nothing to do with differential rent. This kind of rent is necessary in the capitalist system even though the land might belong to a nation, to a state, to no one, or even to the Almighty himself (this ironic remark comes from Lenin).

So far in this analysis we have left completely to one side the question of land [*suelo*] ownership. Lenin insists on many occasions that this abstraction is justified for both methodological and historical reasons. Regarding the law, exploitation (capitalist) is distinguished from ownership and the sole fact of its localization (fixation) [*localización (fijación)*]; it only needs to be proved. As a matter of fact, historically speaking, land [*suelo*] ownership preceded capitalism. Here and now, our analysis introduces a new element: that of land [*tierra*] ownership. The order of the presentation will now disrupt the historical order so that it can be understood better. Let us now suppose that all exploitable land [*tierra*] is private property at the moment in which capitalists want to invest. What impact might this have on rent? Taking as a starting point their legal right to property, the landowner will take from the farmer [*cultivador*] the differential rent. If we take into account that differential rent and surplus profits [*superprovecho*], average profit and competition (in the sense of the competition of capitals as part of the investment in agriculture), have all been simultaneously created by the development of capitalism, the landowner will look for a capitalist who is happy to settle for the average profit, and who will leave to the landowner the surplus profits (differential rent). In this way, private property does not create differential rent but instead transfers it from the hands of the capitalist entrepreneur to those of the landowner. The conditions that create differential rent are the same ones that enable its transference. But, in order for this transference to be realized, a monopoly of land ownership, with historically precapitalist origin, must already exist. In this way, the two monopolies are combined. They are closely tied and joined together and at the same time oppose one another, as the interests of the capitalist oppose those of the landowner. And the transfer of the rent into the hands of the landowner can only take place to the extent that, in the capitalist monopoly of the exploitation of land, there is free competition of capitals. Therefore, it cannot be fulfilled completely except in very limited cases. As a matter of fact, because competition is limited by the reasons already examined and by the monopoly of property, the transference can never be fully realized. One part of the differential rent, which varies according to the circumstances and relationships of power, always remains in the hands of the capitalist entrepreneur.

In this way, have the consequences of land ownership been exhausted? No. As already demonstrated by Marx and by Lenin, who insist again at length on this. Is it possible to imagine that the landowner might allow the capitalist entrepreneur to use for free any plot of land, even if it is barren, or to cultivate for free a mediocre plot of land from which this entrepreneur might only extract the average profit [*provecho medio*] of his capital? Surely not. Given that there is a monopoly of landed property, the landowner will demand rent even for the most mediocre plot of land

and even when it has been left barren. This amount constitutes absolute rent. It has no relation whatsoever to the investment of capital and its differences in productivity or output. It is a result of the second monopoly. Ground rent, just like differential rent, comes from the competition within the frameworks and limits of the capitalist monopoly of exploitation. Absolute rent also comes from the monopoly of land ownership.

On the other hand, it is clear that in practice, ground rent does not present itself to us as spontaneously or naturally divided into two well-defined parts. It will never be possible to know for certain that which is derived from absolute rent and that which comes from differential rent. And this difficulty allows bourgeois theorists to brush away the theory of ground rent and to lump everything together either with products from the land or with fixed products.

It is unusual that a landowner spends nothing on his land even if it is only on buildings [*construcciones*], etcetera. Therefore, the interest of this capital is in practice mixed up with the rents. When the landowner is at the same time the one who exploits the land, the rent is no more than one part of the profit [*ganancias*] and superprofit [*superganancias*]. If he is at once a profiteer from landowning [*propietario explotador*] and a worker [*trabajador*] (as often happens with the small- and medium-scale peasant farmer), he can, in favorable conditions, attain rent. This is added to a salary that he pays himself for his labor, and to the average profit, which he attains as a result of his small capital [*pequeño capital*]. Nevertheless, as this peasant land holder [*ejidatario*] finds himself very often in the poorest conditions (mediocre plots of land, far from transport networks and markets, lacking in both capital and farming equipment, etc.), in the majority of cases he receives neither rent nor the average profit from his capital, which anyway is at best very meager and at worst nonexistent. In the extreme, he receives nothing more than a salary for his labor and that of his family, a salary that he pays himself after having sold, that is if he is able to, his products in the market. His situation can be worse than that of a salaried worker.[12]

Let us now consider Lenin's perspective on the situation of the capitalist farmer [*agricultor capitalista*]. On this point, Lenin improves Marx's theory, and deepens and completely modifies Ricardo's, in the sense that he examines in detail this concrete situation and does not only limit himself to the extreme case in which the landowner succeeds in filling his pockets with all the ground rent. Until his rental agreement expires, the capitalist farmer can always appropriate a part of the rent, and effectively this is what he does, from the very moment in which he invests new capital in the land. Throughout the entire duration of the rental agreement, the question of private land ownership disappears for this farmer. When he invests capital in the land, he obtains new profit and new rents, which, instead of ending up in the hands of the landowner, remain in his possession. As stated by Marx, this farmer does not receive rent that was recently created except when he terminates the rental agreement and following the signing of a new contract. Through what mechanism does this rent pass from the pockets of capitalist famers to those of the landowner? As we already know, it is only through competition.

The successful business [*empresa ventajosa*], which gives to the capitalist not only an average profit but also a superprofit equal to created rent, will attract more capital. If competitors appear, the old tenant is eliminated, but the new land capitalist will lose a part or all the rent created by the previous investment. If seen in this way, as long as all the other variables stay the same, then the losses are profitable for the capitalist farmer in the long term, and profitable for the landowner in the short term. The same can be applied to the constant changes in exploitation. There is therefore a constant struggle between the two monopolies: between landowners and capitalist farmers, over competition, for which the latter fight between themselves. In this struggle, there are victories and defeats for each of the adversaries. But then a question emerges: what type of rent is it that reaches the capitalist throughout the duration of the contract? Is it differential rent or absolute rent? It is impossible to say, as the two rents are mixed up: absolute rent, as we have already seen, intervenes in the fixing of the prices of agricultural products and is included in these prices; differential rent comes at once from the diversity of cultivated land [*tierras*] and from differences in the productivity of capital used in that same land [*suelo*]. On the other hand, cultivated land offers an advantage, as capital can be successively invested in it without causing damage to previously invested capital (this is one of the principal arguments by Marx and Lenin against the false law of decreasing productivity). The most that we can say here is that the part of the rent that goes to the capitalist comes from that which this analyst characterizes as Rent II.

If in practice these rents become mixed up, distinguishing one from the other is not in the least important. Only analysis enables us to respond to problems regarding nationalization, socialization, or municipalization of land (communization in the precise and local meaning of the word "commune"). As is already known, Menshevik law denied the nationalizsation of land as it was considered an extremist revolutionary measure. The revolutionary socialists (popularists), deeming the denial of private land ownership as the denial of capitalism, proposed socialization and assigned land [*suelo*] to the commune.

First Marx and then [Karl] Kautsky (*Agrarfrage*, 79–80) proved that nationalization could do no more than abolish absolute rent by transferring it to the state.[13]

As regards differential rent, nationalization can modify it by establishing the practice of land concessions to those who work it. It does not abolish it. In particular it does not modify Rent II; and it leads to all the rent being passed to the agrarian capitalist [*capitalista explotador*] without leaving anything to the landowner.

Even if at first the greatest and most complete equality and freedom prevails among small-scale farmers, on land that belongs to the nation, they still form part of a regime of market production. They are tied to the market and subordinated by it. Exchange is composed of the power of money and the transformation into money, which intrinsically implies the transformation of labor into money, the conversion of money into capital.

In this way, the idea of the nationalization of land, when seen at the economic level and considered according to the economic base, is a category of bourgeois and capitalist society. Its content is neither that which the leftist socialists believed in nor was it that that was imagined by Russian peasants at the time in which Lenin was writing. Nationalization of the land? This is the logical term of the bourgeois democratic revolution, reclaimed by radicals, partially realized in some countries and particularly useful for a young bourgeois society, which has not yet developed its own internal contradictions.

The nationalization of land abolishes absolute rent but allows differential rent to remain, since it is born not of land ownership but of its capitalist and mercantile exploitation [*explotación mercantil*]. Furthermore, in abolishing one monopoly, that of property, and allowing the other monopoly, that of exploitation, to live on, it breaks the ties of the development of this latter monopoly. Which is to say that it creates the conditions for the accelerated development of capitalism, of its "theoretically pure" development (very far from having power to accompany it, as it has been thought by some, a high development of capitalism and the segregation created by it among land workers). In this way, the theoretical concept of nationalization cannot be examined outside the theory of ground rent.

Nevertheless, nationalization of land is still a measure that must be taken into account, in concrete and defined conditions, with regard to the proletariat.[14] Why? Obviously, because when absolute rent is abolished, the price of agricultural products in which this rent is included is reduced proportionately. It reduces the exploitation of the agricultural proletariat [*proletariado agrícola*], as well as the rent in general, with the part of surplus that remains after having paid the average profit of capital. Lastly, and above all in Tsarist Russia, it corresponded to the aspirations of peasants. Objectively speaking, it put an end to feudal and semifeudal relations, to any remaining communality used by the state and by big landowners, and to the separation of the classes, which themselves were divided and separated from the peasantry. This was a terrible blow to private property in general as the means of production. "The dialectics of history is such that the Narodniks and the Trudoviks propose and promote, as an anti-capitalist remedy, a highly consistent and thoroughgoing capitalist measure with regard to the agrarian question in Russia" (Lenin).[15] Nationalization, accompanied by agrarian reform and equal distribution (as opposed to communalization, which would have made the *kulaks,* the owners of capital, goods, and socialized farms), was then, for Russia, the most urgent progressive economic measure. Let us not forget, Lenin continues, the remarkable words of Engels: "That which is false in a formal and economic sense, can be true in a historical and universal sense." Engels formulated this profoundly important thesis in relation to utopian socialism and the concept of justice. "It is important," Lenin adds, that "Engels's profound thesis must be borne in mind when appraising the present-day Narodnik or Trudovik utopia . . . Narodnik *democracy,* while fallacious from the formal economic point of view, is correct from the *historical* point of view; *this* democracy, while fallacious as a socialist utopia, is *correct* in terms of the peculiar, historically conditioned democratic struggle of the peasant masses . . ."[16]

However, nationalization and agrarian reform, which are both measures that must be taken in specific conditions, do not resolve the peasant question. On the contrary, they present it in clear terms, stripping it of its continuing feudal and communal remains. Why? Because they abolish absolute rent and leave differential rent to remain, and by doing this they pave the way to agrarian capitalism, to capitalism in general, to the *kulaks,* and to the second capitalist monopoly (which is, let us not forget, that of exploitation). So it is that the problem of putting an end to this kind of development and its transformation immediately presents itself—a difficult problem.

The failure to distinguish between rents has, then, the most serious consequences. Some theorists who oppose Lenin have denied the distinction that he makes between them: they have denied absolute rent. Where then can the formal question, "to whom does the rent go and how?" be found? Truly profound questions only emerge when the nature or essence of rent is considered. Bearing this knowledge in mind, how to guide political action, which will have an impact on the development of the agricultural sector? Lenin again insists that Marxists have not always been quick to understand that their job is to introduce the historical element into the study of the agrarian question, and to substitute the point of view of the petit bourgeois (the abstract idea of equality and of justice) with that of the proletariat, founded on the real principles of the fight to transform society and to change it, in an objectively favorable way, broadening perspectives, the development of capitalist society itself. In other words, on the one hand, Lenin considers ideas as transformative forces and, on the other, he calls for the abandonment of a point of view founded on abstract ideas, adopting instead an objective knowledge of the future, which is scientific and which fits with the interests of the proletariat.

Lenin analyzed the spontaneous aspirations of the peasantry, which are essentially contradictory. Peasants want to bring an end to the wrongs caused by the penetration of capitalism into agriculture but through measures that enhance this penetration. They wish to secure their ownership over the land [*suelo*], but such ownership cannot be conceived of without the existence of the free sale and purchase of land [*tierra*]. How might this freedom be limited without limiting the right to property and without abolishing it? (On the other hand, as noted by Marx, peasant ideology forgets that the need to spend capital on the purchase of land [*tierra*] has been the great obstacle to the economic development of medium- and small-scale peasantry.) Capital has employed mortgage and usury to overcome the obstacle of small-scale ownership and to succeed in its free penetration of agriculture. Regardless of the form that the credit institution takes, credit, which is so often required by peasants, is precisely the path to capitalism.

Let us now come back to one last aspect of ground-rent theory, made more precise, extended, and developed by Lenin.

Differential rent does not have a direct or immediate influence over the prices of agricultural products, as it finds itself tied to its own determination. By contrast, on joining itself directly to the price of these products in the market, absolute rent has an influence over them. These prices are determined by the expenses of production of the least fertile land (which does not produce differential rent), increased by the average profit of invested capital and absolute rent.

Absolute rent comes from private land ownership. It does not necessarily exist in capitalist agriculture, although it is conditioned by private land ownership and therefore tied to the backward character of agriculture, which is the result of a historical process and preserved by the monopoly.

As we have already indicated, this monopoly of precapitalist origin creates and tries to conserve its own conditions via a kind of vicious circle, which is, above all, particularly evident in backward countries or regions.

Although private land ownership benefits from the arrival of capital and from its rivalry, it also prevents this free competition, paralyzing the movement of capital, impeding the leveling of profits and the formation of an average profit. The technology of agricultural production is inferior to that of industrial technology, and the organic composition of capital invested in agriculture can be distinguished from industrial labor by a greater proportion of variable capital, related to constant capital. It is therefore different from the social context and the productivity of weaker agricultural labor; by preventing the free leveling of profits, private land ownership allows the sale of products no longer according to the highest cost of production but instead to an even higher individual cost, to which paid rent is also incorporated. The price of production is determined by the average profit of capital, and as absolute rent does not enable the formation of this average profit, it establishes a cost or price of individual production upon the foundation of the monopoly.

It is in this way that the theory of distinction between different types of rent is specified. Differential rent, derived from the price of production (of its determination), and absolute rent, derived from the surplus of market price on top of the price of production. The first one is derived from surplus value, under the form of superprofit, either momentarily or over a longer period of time, and is provided by more productive labor and carried out in better or better-situated land [*tierra*]. The second has as its origin in the additional output or the excess labor of all types of agricultural labor, and cannot be obtained except as preprofit [*preganancia*] on top of the amount of existing values, to the benefit of a parasitic class of landowners.

As such, the value of agricultural products is in general greater than their price of production—bearing in mind the work that they imply—and surplus value is greater than profit (average). The monopoly of land ownership prevents this excess from falling into the hands of the masses, with the preexistence of the rate of profit. It is for this reason that absolute rent is collected strictly from this surplus. But this surplus value is nothing more than the equivalent, in money, of a superprofit that is made up of a particular amount from this or that commodity. Lenin shows that the idea of self-determination cannot be understood as science might understand it but in the ways in which objective, and more or less known conditions, determine its dimensions. The material form of superprofit in agriculture is otherwise of little importance. The landowner does not consume more wheat or sugar than other men; he does not consume the wheat or sugar that his own land produces. What matters is that superprofit is realized in commodities and money in order to be more substantial in relation to capital, in agriculture, as in other areas, and that this surplus does not fall into the hands of the masses. Absolute rent does not emerge from the organic composition that is specific to agricultural capital; this organic composition allows only for the previous collection of absolute rent, which comes from private land ownership; this is the element of monopoly.

The agricultural superproduct [*superproducto*], like all superproducts, is made in the market (exchanged for industrial products, etc.) so that it can convert itself effectively into surplus value. And it is within society as a whole that the landowner presents a quality, which although he denies it, he lends to society, in the name of the sacred principle of property. This is the way in which absolute rent, by lowering capitalist gains, increases the price of food products and burdens the working class, which leads to increased exploitation.

This analysis, which is taken further by Lenin, holds an even greater interest for us. It shows that absolute rent only depends on the generalized backward character of agriculture and the weak organic composition of agricultural capital, of the limits that it imposes on land ownership, and the investment of capital, etcetera.

This is largely, though not exclusively, applied to so-called backward or underdeveloped countries and regions, in which feudal and semifeudal structures persist (*latifundia* of precapitalist origin with extensive agriculture) or continue to survive, such as in the case of sharecropping.

If we imagine that agriculture mechanizes itself, that the organic composition of capital increases but that the difference between agriculture and industry diminishes in a country or region, the questions related to differential rent remain intact. Conversely, questions regarding absolute rent acquire great importance, even when it diminishes as such. In effect, under these conditions (there is another monopoly), after the monopoly with precapitalist origin, appears another, that of the monopoly of capitalist exploitation, which takes center stage (along with the forms of competition, which are at once set and limited by this monopoly).

On the other hand, as long as there is private land ownership and the right (legal) to land ownership as a means of production, absolute rent cannot disappear.

Whether or not the landowner is of feudal origin, whether he is different from the capitalist exploiter [*explotador capitalista*] and in conflict with him, or whether he colludes and is mixed up with him, as long as he is still the landowner, he nevertheless continues to offer to society a quality that he is obliged to pay for according to his own principles (his own legal superstructures).

The Leninist theory of double monopoly directly enables an analysis of today's agricultural phenomena, both in France and in the rest of the world.

By way of example, we will limit ourselves here to a brief examination of the current French reality.

6. The Theory of Rent and Monopoly Capitalism

To begin with, we will examine recent events, contemporary to monopoly capitalism, that have emerged as part of the agrarian question in France and which emerged after Lenin wrote his works on ground rent and its problems.

(a) Firstly, the most notable fact is the introduction of mechanization into agriculture (close to 250,000 tractors in France in 1954), the increase in productivity of agricultural labor (average production of wheat increased from 16 to 22 quintals [*quintales*] per hectare).[17] The decrease in the agricultural population is equally undeniable: from 1900 to 1950 the active working French population [*la población activa francesa*] fell from 48% to 32% (figures from INSEE).[18]

It is possible that what might have happened was a decrease in absolute rent. Although this is not the prevailing opinion. Indeed, we must remember that absolute rent does not come from the organic composition of agricultural capital; this organic composition only allows the aforementioned rent to be paid. Besides, what counts is the difference in the organic composition, between the industrial sphere and the agricultural sector. The organic composition of industrial capital has increased considerably and the difference persists.

On the other hand, the game of capitalist economic laws does not completely define absolute rent (this is simply derived from that which, historically speaking, is earlier than capitalism). Power relations are therefore of considerable importance, and it is with the political program that economic determination is progressively achieved. The weight, the political importance of landowners, then plays a role. Land ownership, which is to say, absolute rent, has in France been dealt some fierce blows: from the bourgeois democratic revolution, up until decisions taken in favor of landlords [*arrendadores*] and sharecroppers following the liberation. But what has happened after each defeat is that the landowners have managed to rise up again and to more or less slow down the progressive measures that have been made against them. Therefore, the problem of absolute rent in France demands a detailed examination, which at this moment is difficult to undertake.

Even if we take into account the development of agricultural mechanization, the general backwardness of agriculture, a specific characteristic of this sector, has not disappeared, and this is particularly true in France. The agricultural population of France continues to be greater than those of other large capitalist countries (6% in England), and the productivity of agricultural labor, even taking into account improvements in mechanization, is less than that of industrial labor (50–70% according to assessments that are, incidentally, very approximate). This backwardness has adopted the concrete form of great unevenness in capitalist development between different French regions, uneven agricultural development, which corresponds to the unevenness of industrial development. Stagnant French regions, from an industrial point of view, are also backward from an agricultural point of view.

It is true that the landowning class of feudal origin, which is different from that of exploiters of land (capitalist landlords), is diminishing in importance in France even though it has not completely disappeared. And yet something very different is happening in nearby countries such as Italy, Spain, etcetera, and above all in many underdeveloped countries.

Moreover, this class has partially fused with the capitalist bourgeoisie (which is something that has always prevented the application of radical measures against land ownership).

Recently, other fusions have taken place in France. For example, between agrarian capitalism [*capitalismo agrario*] and industrial and financial capitalism [*capitalismo industrial y financiero*] (we can think of the sugar industry, directly tied to the production of sugar beet, to the factories, which sometimes take their raw materials directly from the land that surrounds them and that belongs to the same landowner or to the same capitalist society).

In any case, private ownership of land does not stop functioning. Landowners perpetually transform themselves, either as an extension, or not, of the feudal class, which demands absolute rent and part of differential rent. However, in other cases, these fusions have resulted in the mixing up of absolute rent with differential rent, profit and in the category of a maximum profit, capitalist superprofits [*superganancias capitalistas*].

In cases in which the capitalist landlord constitutes an independent force, when he opposes landowners and, above all, when these landowners are small and medium in scale, the result is a decrease in absolute rent, accompanied by an increase in differential rent, from which the capitalist entrepreneur benefits.

(b) But this only takes us back to the matter of our fundamental problem. After having studied Marx's theory of ground rent and its laws of free capitalist competition, what remains of monopoly capitalism?

We have already seen the role that average profit and competition, among those who possess capital, plays in the formation of ground rent.

The law of the formation of average profit (via the competition of capitals and its decline) is replaced, in monopoly capitalism, by the pursuit of maximum profit and its corresponding law. Therefore, should we abandon ground-rent theory and simply substitute it for the analysis of maximum profit in agriculture and industry?

No, this cannot be. This theory would mean that agriculture could take over industry, something that is, as we already know, false. It would mean the complete fusion between land ownership and capitalism, something that is not precise enough, and even when this fusion is allowed, the theory would prevent us from analyzing the political and economic activity of capitalism, as landowner and agricultural entrepreneur, and as industrialist and monopolist.

Let us examine things more closely: it is not that the law of maximum profit says that average profit has disappeared. It simply claims that the tendency to form a rate of average profit is no longer the internal regulating law of capitalism. The great capitalist [*gran capitalista*] no longer calculates his production expenditure by adding it to his expenses (in variable and constant capital), salaries paid, repayments [*amortizaciones*], raw materials, interest from invested capital, etcetera, the rate of average profit.[19] He desires, and cannot stop desiring, maximum profit. And yet it is not that the average profit has ceased to exist. Objectively speaking, an average is formed between capitalist profits. But monopoly capitalism cannot be fulfilled with the average rate alone (Stalin). The average profit becomes the bottom line [*el límite inferior*] under which capitalist production is made impossible (Stalin).

And why doesn't the competition of capitals carry the capitalist's profit back to the limits of average profit? Because monopolies prevent the free circulation and investment of capital. They keep areas of investment to themselves and practice self-funding. These obstacles to the competition of capitals (not of commodities) are accompanied by new forms of competition, which, far from abolishing monopoly capitalism, give it its law and actual forms. This law is no longer regulated internally but is instead one of disequilibrium: a development at once stagnant, uneven, and unstable.[20]

Now then, what have we seen in agriculture? At the exact same moment in which free trade capitalism was being developed (of commodities and capital), agriculture was already being presented as an element of monopoly. And even, as Lenin demonstrates, of double monopoly. The monopoly of land ownership was already preventing the development of productive forces and aggravating the contradictions of capitalist society, thereby increasing stagnation in a sector of production and general overexploitation [*sobreexplotación*] of workers, in particular those from the aforementioned sector. And all of this limited the competition of capitals, hindering its free movement from one sphere to another and its free investment in agriculture.

For the capitalist entrepreneur, the average profit was already the bottom line under which production was made impossible.

The law of the formation of rates of average profit acted only in a limited way on the agricultural sector and was not its internal regulator. On the contrary, the specific character of this sector had a tendency to consolidate superprofits, in the form of rents. And this particularly benefited a parasitic class, who played no active role in production.

In summary, we have arrived at the following conclusions:

Agriculture, insofar as it displayed elements of monopoly, preceded in some respects monopoly capitalism, which is to say, current capitalism.

We must ensure that this does not lead us to forget that in traditional agriculture, the obstacles to the development of productive forces came above all from the survivals of feudalism [*supervivencias feudales*], which is to say, from relations of production and of property prior to capitalism, within which relations of production, properly speaking, were developed. The monopoly (historically capitalist) of land ownership presented in this way a contradiction that was found at the core of capitalism, within its own foundations, which is to say, not only within the legal superstructures and foundations but also between relations of production and productive forces.

The monopoly of capitalist exploitation, different from the monopoly of land ownership, can be opposed to it, and in the extent to which it embraced and allowed the competition of capitals; it stimulated the development of productive forces. It was also able to join with the previous monopoly (in the historical sense) and to more or less fuse completely with it. In each of these cases, obstacles to the development of productive forces, which are born from historical conditions from which they had to grow, and from the capitalist character of development according to its internal laws, have been overcome.

This is how the agricultural sector, within the decaying capitalist economy, was able to integrate itself with monopoly capitalism.

And all this, without ground rent (with its own characteristics and specificities) disappearing. And without the specific character of agricultural production disappearing (a certain kind of backwardness, etc.).

There may be a fight between the monopoly of land ownership and that of exploitation to keep, to increase, or to lower absolute rent.

There may be a fight for the distribution of differential rent.

Finally, there may be integration of absolute rent, differential rent, and permanent superprofits, with the pursuit of maximum profit, with the latter an economic category and its law.

The struggles and conflicts are far from meaningless. In some cases, they lead to antagonisms and their effects are added to the existing struggles of agricultural and industrial workers,[21] and in colonial and semicolonial countries, to the national aspirations of the industrial bourgeoisie. But for now let us put aside those questions that exceed our problem. What is essential here, for us, is that monopoly capitalism and the law of maximum profit have eliminated neither ground rent nor its laws. Regarding conflicts, they take place within a monopolizing capitalism [*capitalismo monopolizador*], more than in capitalism and the remains of previous historical periods (although when referring to backward countries, one should be cautious in this affirmation, so that with scientific prudence, we avoid taking it as absolute).

The move by the bourgeois state in France and its capitalist leaders, which opens the scissors to the detriment of agricultural prices, does not destroy this theory. It is true that in moments of acute crisis, industrial capitalism tries to throw all the problems at the agricultural sector and at the working-class masses (peasants and others), and with the same blow, in part, at whatever is left of the landowning class.

But as we will see further on, the "targeted" fixing of agricultural prices makes room for absolute rent, for differential rent, and for the pursuit of maximum profit on behalf of agrarian capitalism, above all with regard to capitalists tied to industrial and financial monopolies.

The fact that economic questions are increasingly intervening in the planning of the political state, as well as in the relationships of power between monopolies, does not invalidate the laws of the monopolistic capitalist economy. On the contrary: the state intervenes to protect the functioning of these laws or at most to limit the damages. The state class, as an expression of the bourgeoisie and of monopolies under the appearance (not to be underestimated and even important, as such) of democracy, decides the conflicts in the interior of society as a whole. It serves the stronger monopolies and when necessary puts a limit to their ambitions, when these are exaggerated and put at risk the whole of society.

> (c) According to this theoretical analysis, we can now examine the numerical data.

First, we observe that the facts are in essence complex and contradictory, so we must be careful to establish a single and absolute criterion. The concentration of property is an important element in the study, but it is far from being the only element. We have seen the degree to which the concentration of exploitation differs from that of the concentration of property. This is reflected in the first monopoly, while the concentration of exploitation reflects the movement of the second monopoly. Furthermore, the investment of capital, the main objective criterion for the development of capitalism in agriculture, can be carried out without a concentration of property and exploitation.

With regard to ground rent, the official figures are as follows:[22]

Years	Agricultural profit	Profit of landowners	Profit of salaried workers	Profit of agrarian capitalists
1950–51	1,200	120	175	905
1951–52	1,370	155	205	1,010
1952–53	1,500	160	215	1,125
1953–54	1,545	150	225	1,170

We already know that these numbers are approximate, and founded on a previous study, on the "rental value" [*valor locativo*] of land.

Besides that, we should note that even within this study, the ground rent of landowners is scarce in comparison to the national general income, and is strong in relation to agricultural income. Significant fact: it decreased a great deal following the liberation (in 1945–46 it went from 15 billion as part of an agriculture income of 395 billion; to 40 billion in 1946–47, as part of an agricultural income of 690 billion). After this it stabilized and stayed at about 10% of agricultural income.

But these numbers do not give us a very clear image of reality. The rental value of this land, even when we take into account the amount that goes to landowning farmers [*propietarios explotadores*] as part of their income (see *Études et conjoncture*, Oct. 1954, 909), is nothing more than a fraction of total ground rent [*la renta de la tierra global*].[23] The study does not take into account differential rent that goes to the capitalist exploiters.

It does not consider, then, anything except absolute rent and the part of differential rent that goes to the traditional owner [*propietario tradicional*]. It is careless about that which some bourgeois economists know very well under the name of "technical rent" [*renta técnica*].

An analysis of agricultural income should try to establish the average profit of the capital invested, superprofits (or maximum profits), and rents that have been mixed together in order to distinguish them from traditional rent. But this analysis is difficult, or perhaps we should say impossible, due to lack of documentation. We have no more than a very imprecise idea of the capital that is invested in agriculture.[24]

As a matter of fact, the "state-directed" fixing of prices has increasingly officialized the mechanism for determining the prices of agricultural products, thereby warranting absolute rent and differential rent.

Under the guise of democracy, the protection of small-scale agriculture, of the small-scale peasant worker, landowner, landlord, or sharecropper [*pequeña agricultura, del pequeño campesino trabajador, propietario arrendador o mediero*], in fact, is all about protecting the income of capitalist agriculture [*agricultura capitalista*]. Indeed, the very development of agricultural production threatens it.[25] The growth of general productivity and production, the transformation of expanses of land into fields, brings with it the abandonment of poor-quality land, left barren, even when it still has the potential to be cultivated. These abandonments threaten to lower differential rent. Differential rent is also preserved with the fixing of prices, destined in principle, to save a "vital minimum" for the small-scale peasant, who works poor or badly located plots of land.

On the other hand, in the current situation, agricultural prices can be at once too high for society as a whole and too low for small-scale peasants to survive. But when dealing with the preservation of rent, profit, and superprofit, the current situation reveals itself very enthusiastically, for example in the stubborn rejection of a differential price, the absence of advantages received by society as a whole (and most importantly in workers, via increasing productivity and agricultural production, etc.).

Rental value (which is nothing more than an element of rent that is in effect realized) varies considerably from region to region. It is dependent on factors that we have already analyzed: the intensity of competition, power relations between monopolies, etcetera.

In the Sena and in the Marne (and in Paris), capitalist monopoly largely dominates. The capitalist landlords are powerful, well organized. The competition is weak and landowners—almost always small and medium in size—cannot defend themselves against their landlord. The rent, paid to the landowner, includes absolute rent and differential rent and is fixed *in natura* at around 4 to 5 quintals of wheat per hectare. In these regions (Beauce, Sena and Marne, Oise Aisne, etc.), the amount of differential rent, elegantly called technical rent, that goes into the hands of the capitalist landlords is enormous. It exceeds by far the effects of the relative depreciation of agricultural products, with relation to industrial products.[26] On the other hand, in this region, agriculture is tied to industry (production of sugar beet and therefore of alcohol, etc.). It is the region of maximum profit. These kinds of agriculture carry out self-funding and furthermore receive subsidies either in a disguised form or more or less directly (for example, in order to cultivate sugar beet and transform it into alcohol).

By contrast, in other regions, which also have substantial farms [*explotaciones*], such as Pays de Caux, a region in the north, the potential of capitalist monopoly has yet to reach the same level of refinement and organization. The rent that goes to the landowner is also higher (6 to 8 quintals per hectare and sometimes even more).

In Brittany, in various districts [*cantones*], the monopoly of feudal origin still dominates. And owing to its large population, the competition is strong, the rent high. On the other hand, in the backward regions of southern France, although the land ownership has frequently occupied a strong position, the population is weak and therefore so is the competition. Although overwhelming for the small-scale landlord [*pequeño arrendador*], the rent lowers to 2 quintals per hectare and sometimes even less.

It lowers almost to the point of absolute rent, which could be estimated provisionally and in a very approximate way, at about 4,000 francs per hectare in France.

Let us repeat that in order for this study to be strengthened, it is necessary to carry out new scientific investigations.

But for now, it is enough that we have proved that the current configuration of French agriculture can be explained by the Marxist–Leninist theory of ground rent and by it alone. Therefore, consequently, this theory—scientific, objective—has been proven and there it remains, according to the facts, which allow this prediction.

Translated by Sîan Rosa Hunter Dodsworth

Notes

["La teoría Marxista-Leninista de la renta de la tierra," trans. Sîan Rosa Hunter Dodsworth, in *Estudios sociológicos sobre la Reforma Agraria* (Mexico City: Universidad Nacional Autónoma de México, 1965), 129–54. This publication is composed of papers delivered at the Fifteenth National Sociology Congress of Mexico, held in Tepic/Nayarit, October 19–24, 1964.—*Eds.*]

1. [Throughout, the text talks of "Problemas agrarios," which we have translated as "the agrarian question," the more common formulation in English.—*Eds.*]

2. This data and these graphs have not been established nor can they be at this time, except in an incomplete way. Some of this data and some facts are found dispersed among numerous publications. Perhaps the forthcoming agricultural census might enable us to complete this information, although until new official orders are passed, the statistics will continue to *shine,* if one can put it that way, due to their incomplete, superficial, and often tendentious nature. There is no excuse for the lack of documents about the agrarian structure of France; the statistics confuse exploitation [*explotación*] with land ownership [*propiedad*], and do not consider the structure of these in any way. If we turn our attention to simpler and less rocky terrain, the figures on milk production and cattle breeding vary surprisingly in their proportions. Officially, ground rent is calculated from the "rent value" of the land in question, which in 1938 was estimated to be approximately 10 billion francs. It is impossible for us at present to realize, in France, studies as ground-breaking as those carried out in Germany and the United States by Lenin on agriculture during Russia's Tsarist period. This is due to a lack of documents. New kinds of research and teamwork would be indispensable and at the moment, we do not appear to have the means . . . We cannot even attempt an investigation like that carried out by Tohen Po-ta in China. [Although the name is misspelled, this is a reference to Tchen Po-Ta, "Etude sur la rente foncière en Chine," *Etudes économiques: Cahiers mensuels d'économie socialiste* 84/85 (1954): 1–67; and Chen Po-Ta, *A Study of Land Rent in Pre-Liberation China,* 2nd ed. (Peking: Foreign Languages Press, 1966).—*Eds.*]

3. Let us define "land ownership" and "exploitation" with precision. In these regions, the agrarian capitalist is frequently both owner and landlord. However, whether he personally possesses land or not, he often leases out small- or medium-sized plots of land to other owners, which altogether make up a single substantial system of exploitation. The concentration of exploitation is therefore greater than that of land ownership. And yet this process is nowhere to be found in the statistics. It is in this way that the same agrarian capitalist gets, at once, profit or superprofits, and maximum profit and rent. It is important to emphasize this point because, at least in one part of France, the traditional figure of the landlord, as a small-scale farmer and not as an owner, does not correspond to reality.

In regions where there are small- and medium-sized properties, various forms of exploitation can relate to the same property owner. In regions of widespread exploitation, several properties can fall under the long-lasting dependency of the same large capitalist exploiter [*explotador capitalista*]. From this comes the complex, and up until now poorly researched, new phenomena regarding accumulation and rent. [Beauce is a region in northern France.—*Eds.*]

4. Only incomplete and fragmentary data is available to us: the results of the International Congress of Milan (October 1954) for the study of underdeveloped regions, carried out by different national institutions and scientific and statistic research organizations. This data was provided by the FAO (Food and Agriculture Organization of the United Nations), which has its headquarters in Rome. It is yet to be systematically organized. In Italy, these types of studies have been better developed, and it is here that better documentation can be found. This is not so much due to the official institutions but to the services of the General Confederation of Labour (CGT), of the Federterra (Federation of Agricultural Laborers), and of the agricultural section of the Italian Communist Party (PCI). [Lefebvre is referring to *Atti del Congresso internazionale di studio sul problema delle aree arretrate, Milano, 10–15 ottobre 1954*, 4 vols. (Milan: Dott. A. Giuffrè, 1954–56).—*Eds.*]

5. Is it merely a coincidence that French society (in a rural economy) has suddenly taken an interest in this issue? Two studies are already in circulation on the topic: *Ground Rent and Agricultural Income* and *The Problem of Ground Rent*; these are brief, convoluted, and incomplete studies that are closer to Ricardo than to Marx but that partially acknowledge the existence of the issue. They are, furthermore, unsuccessful as, numerically speaking, in France, when ground rent appears in the statistics, it represents no more than 2% of the national income, a fact that seems to contradict Ricardo's theory regarding the rise in land rent. Later on, in this text, we will identify the mistake made in this analysis, derived from another mistake, which is regularly made about the notion of ground rent. To fully understand the importance of this, we must define the notions and place them in relation to the agrarian structure and its transformation. The work by Jacques Servant (CERES, April 1953), titled *French Agricultural Trends* [*Tendencias de la agricultura francesca*], contains serious information and is a remarkable attempt to interpret numerical data. Nevertheless, it lacks a theoretical framework and simplifies the issues of accumulation; capitalist development in agriculture; the reduction of areas for cereal cultivation; productivity in agriculture, etcetera. [As indicated in chapter 5, one of Lefebvre's references is to L. Rolland, "Le problème de la rente différentielle du sol," *Économie rurale* 23 (1955): 27–33.—*Eds.*]

6. [See Karl Marx, *Capital: A Critique of Political Economy*, vol. 3, trans. David Fernbach (London: Penguin, 1991), especially part 6, "The Transformation of Surplus Profit into Ground-Rent," 751–950.—*Eds.*]

7. Now available to French readers but only in the translation by [Jacques] Molitor, volumes XIII and XIV. [This is a reference to *Oeuvres complètes de Karl Marx*. Volumes 13 and 14 include the later parts of *Capital*, vol. 3.—*Eds.*]

There are plenty of texts on ground rent in the works of Marx and Engels; let us mention here the most important ones: *The Poverty of Philosophy,* Chapter II.4; the introduction to *A Contribution to the Critique of Political Economy,* translated by Fiard, 342–45; *Anti-Dühring,* Part 2, Chapter IX, and above the collection of works published with the title *A History of Economic Doctrines,* edited by [Alfred] Costes. [See Karl Marx, *The Poverty of Philosophy,* in Karl Marx and Friedrich Engels, *Collected Works,* vol. 6 (London: Lawrence and Wishart, 1976); Karl Marx, "Preface to 'A Contribution to the Critique of Political Economy,'" in Karl Marx and Friedrich Engels, *Collected Works,* vol. 29 (London: Lawrence and Wishart, 1987), 261–66; and Friedrich Engels, *Anti-Dühring: Herr Eugen Dühring's Revolution in Science* (Moscow: Foreign Languages Publishing House, 1954), part 2, "Political Economy," chapter 9, "Natural Laws of Economics: Ground-Rent," 305–13. The citation to *A History of Economic Doctrines* is a reference to Karl Marx, *Histoire des doctrines économique,* 8 vols., trans. J. Molitor (Paris: Alfred Costes, 1924). This is the collection in English known as *Theories of Surplus Value,* the "fourth" book of *Capital,* which is now usefully available in one volume; see Karl Marx, *Theories of Surplus Value,* Books I, II, and III (Amherst: Prometheus Books, 2000). Lefebvre's mention of Fiard is unclear, but this is likely to be a mistake for "Giard." For example, see Karl Marx, *Contribution á la critique de l'économie politique,* trans. L. Lafargue (Paris: Giard and Brière, 1909).—Eds.]

8. Let us not forget that the term "monopoly" does not mean ownership or control by a single individual but by an entire class or class fraction.

9. Lenin's main texts on the question that currently occupies us are as follows: *Collected Works,* 3rd ed., Moscow-Leningrad, T. II, 427–71 (*Bulgakov's Criticisms of Kausky* [Stuttgart: Agrafrage, 1899], IV, 175–263, about the law of growing fertility, etc. . . . VIII, 219, 224; XI, 310, 328: XI, 391 and ss.: XIV, four important articles, etc. . . .). Here a summary of Leninist theses on ground rent can be found spread across several articles. [See inter alia V. I. Lenin, *The Development of Capitalism in Russia* (Moscow: Progress Publishers, 1974); and V. I. Lenin, "The Tasks of the Proletariat in the Present Revolution ('April Theses')," in *Revolution at the Gates: A Selection of Writings from February to October 1917,* by V. I. Lenin, ed. Slavoj Žižek (London: Verso, 2002), 56–61.—Eds.]

10. Besides going over my report for the International Congress on the study of undeveloped areas (Milan, October 1954), in which a study on the aforementioned theme in Tunisia can be found, there is not much more I can do. This report can be found in the Congress minutes. It would be necessary to carry out the same research on a broader scale so that all African and Asian countries might be included. [See Henri Lefebvre, "Les relations sociales, les phénomènes de population et les problems du travail dans les pays sous-développés, secteur de l'agriculture," *Atti del Congresso internazionale di studio sul problema delle aree*

arretrate, Milano, 10–15 ottobre 1954, 4 vols. (Milan: Dott. A. Giuffrè, 1954–56), 2:823–33; it is included in the present volume as chapter 5.—*Eds.*]

11. Is it really necessary to stress the profundity of these ideas formulated by Lenin more than fifty years ago and which might be admirably applied to all that is happening now in northern France? (See above, part 1.)

12. Current estimations for various small farms [*explotaciones*] in the south of France are as follows: 30 to 50 francs per hour of work for the farmer and his family. Surely these small-scale peasant workers are not fully aware of their own situation as they keep no financial records and practice self-consumption [*autoconsumo*].

13. [Karl Kautsky, *Die Agrarfrage: Eine Uebersicht über die Tendenzen der modernen Landwirthschaft und die Agrarpolitik der Sozialdemokratie* (Stuttgart: J. H. W. Dietz, 1899), 79–80; Karl Kautsky, *The Agrarian Question*, 2 vols. trans. Pete Burgess (Winchester, Mass.: Zwan, 1988), 1:82.—*Eds.*]

14. It is known that popular democracies [*democracias populares*] have not nationalized the land. They have implemented radical agrarian reforms, thereby abolishing feudal remains. They have also limited the right to own property, the right to rent [*arrendamiento*], to sell, etcetera, and in this way have limited capitalist exploitation and the second monopoly, the development of *kulaks*. But in reference to production cooperatives, differential rent persists and sometimes even in the form of absolute rent.

15. [See V. I. Lenin, "Two Utopias," in V. I. Lenin, *Collected Works*, vol. 18 (Moscow: Progress Publishers, 1975), 355–59. The Narodniks were a middle-income movement in Russia of the nineteenth century, also translated as "populists," who had among their theoreticians V. P. Vorontsov and N. F. Danielson. Trudoviks were a socialist workers' party in Russia, representing agrarian workers as well as industrial ones, and held seats in the Duma in the early twentieth century. After the 1917 revolution, they opposed the Bolsheviks.—*Eds.*]

16. We quote this text at length, translated in *Selected Works*, L, 664–65, as it is, of course, fundamental to the theory of Agrarian Reform in general, and of the measures taken by the government of the Soviets and, furthermore, for the dialectical and objectively extensive theory of superstructures. [See Lenin, "Two Utopias,'" 355–59.—*Eds.*]

17. As everyone knows, this increase in productivity has hardly benefited the consumer at all.

18. [Institut national de la statistique et des études économiques (INSEE, National Institute of Statistics and Economic Studies).—*Eds.*]

19. [We have corrected a typo in the original text that reads "rasa," taste, rather than "rata," rate.—*Eds.*]

20. [Three interpretative injunctions have been made here: (1) to translate *disequilibrio* literally as disequilibrium, (2) to stick with translating *desigual* as

uneven, and (3) to translate *convulso* as unstable rather than tumultuous. The focus on disequilibrium—unevenness—unstable resonates more directly with wider Marxist scholarship on crisis theory.—*Eds.*]

21. For more on the antagonisms between capitalist landlords and landowners in Italy, particular in the Po valley, see the collection of articles in *Rinascita* by Duccio Tabet, 1954–55. [Duccio Tabet, "La lotta contadina nella valle Padana e la riforma agraria," *Rinascita* 11, no. 7 (July 1954): 450–52; Duccio Tabet, "La giusta causa e la mezzadria," *Rinascita* 12, no. 2 (February 1955): 84–85; Duccio Tabet, "Imposta sul sale, imposta sui poveri," *Rinascita* 12, no. 10 (October 1955): 601–2. *Rinascita* (Rebirth) was one of the main journals of the Italian Communist Party.—*Eds.*]

22. Taken from *Estudios y situaciones*, Oct. 1954, 909, and Dec. 1954, 1081. [The pieces mentioned are "L'évolution des revenus agricoles en France depuis l'avant-guerre," *Études et conjoncture* 9, no. 10 (October 1954): 899–917; and "Le revenue de l'agriculture en France en 1953–54," *Études et conjoncture* 9, no 12 (December 1954): 1059–87. These articles clarify that the amounts are "billions of francs." The French franc was revalued in 1960, with 100 old francs becoming one new franc. In the mid-1950s, 1,000 francs were equivalent to about 1 British pound, or about 3 U.S. dollars.—*Eds.*]

23. [See previous note. We have corrected the misspelling of the journal title.—*Eds.*]

24. This is what permits a Monsieur Rolland, chief engineer in agricultural services, in the previously cited tract, "Le problème de la rente différentielle du sol," to declare the fragility of rent theory, only known to him through Ricardo. We have already seen how we might differentiate Marx from Ricardo and how Lenin developed Marx's theory.

25. A form of development that does not block the phenomena of degradation and disaggregation. Let us not forget the contradictory character of these processes. With regard to milk, it seems that according to official texts, the state has subsidized mountainous regions and fixed the price of milk at a slightly higher rate. It is up to the reader to reflect on this claim.

26. This was noted by J. Servant in the previously cited study [note 5—*Eds.*]. Although he did not see that the change in land value [*valor de las tierras*] only shows the phenomena in an imperfect way. The great exploiter [*explotador*] feels no need to buy the land that he cultivates. By doing so he would freeze capital. This is a new fact and one of great importance.

CHAPTER 9

Introduction to the Psychosociology of Everyday Life

How can we define everyday life? It surrounds and assails us; in time and space it is in us and we are in it and also outside it, endlessly attempting to banish it so we can launch ourselves into fiction and the imaginary; we are never certain we can escape it even in the delirium of dream. All of us are familiar with it (and only with it) and all of us ignore it. Doesn't the history of ideas reveal that men and peoples, ages and civilizations achieve what they are and have been since their origin only at the last moment? For them to clearly express what they are, they must see it from without, comparing it with other ways of life. Some go so far as to claim that a culture can only define itself and achieve awareness by exhausting itself, so that awareness, clarity, might also bear the black mark of destiny. Without going to such extremes, doesn't the same apply to our everyday life, at least to some extent? And if we do achieve a heightened awareness of everydayness, isn't it already overwhelmed by the human adventure? If we can conceive of the human world, the world of mankind and everyday practice, isn't it because mankind and technology, and our possibilities, already surpass what we are even though we don't know where they will lead?

What then is everydayness? We won't risk much or get very far by claiming that it's the best and the worst of things, like language and speech according to Aesop. The best would be found if, in everyday life, each of us entered into contact with an already realized human world, with the innumerable objects produced in distant places or hidden from view (workshops, factories) and which become goods. Taken together, all these goods are available to our wants and stimulate our desires; some of them are withheld and remain inaccessible. The science of social reality cannot confuse this field of experience with production and distribution, aspects of political economy. An advertising specialist is more familiar with the relationship between "goods" and desires than the economist or statistician. Neither sociology, which focuses on groups, or psychology, which focuses on the individual, not even social psychology, which is mostly concerned with opinions and attitudes, can comprehend this immense field in its entirety, a field that a single word can define: appropriation (by humans, of life in general, and of their own life in particular).

In everyday life, a privileged sector of practice, needs become desires. They take shape there, and biological needs (animal and vital needs) become human needs. This metamorphosis faces considerable adversity: self-control and the sometimes unlimited postponement of legitimate satisfactions, the inevitable choices and options between the possible objects of desire. Need passes through the filters of language, of external prohibitions and permissions, of inhibition and arousal, labor and gain. Needs are part of the general human condition: sex, food, habitation and clothing, amusement and activity. Desires are individual and based on the group we are part of. The socialization and humanization of need goes hand in hand with the individualization of desire. However, this does not occur without conflict, without sometimes irreparable harm. Each man and each woman resembles a tree, some of whose branches are twisted, dead, and broken, while others remain stubbornly full of sap.

There is a richness to everydayness. In it the most authentic creations are outlined, styles and ways of living that blend contemporary words and gestures with culture. The incessant renewal of humankind takes place within it as well: the birth and education of children, the growth of generations. An art, an image, a myth that is not part of everydayness ("lived life [*le vécu*]") remains abstract or dies. Conversely, the deepest desires and the most legitimate aspirations take root and abide there.

Misery and poverty. Everyday life is also the repetition of the same gestures—getting up in the morning, preparing coffee, leaving, following the same streets every morning, crossing the same squares, taking the subway, getting lost in the crowd, reading the paper, entering by the same door into the same workshop or office. It is pointless to continue.[1] Women, more than men, bear the weight of the everyday, they more ardently seek to emerge from this gray world; they readily follow the ambiguities of daydreams, half practical, half fiction, supplied by what are known as women's magazines or sentimental publications.

Misery. In everyday life, the young man who fulfills himself, who succeeds or fails, loses his youth, matures, and grows old. He realizes no more than a portion of his potential. From childhood he has before him the image of the man who is only one of many possible men, having lost the others: his father.

In everydayness we come face to face, at the very core of our existence, with what the enormous resources of modern technology have not managed to control and may do so only through their destruction: spontaneity, physiological rhythms, unlimited hopes. Thus, the everyday is revealed to be the domain of fortune and misfortune, of accident and destiny and their surprising combinations. The fictional and extraordinary mingle with the trivial. It is the extraordinary aspect of the ordinary. It is also worth noting that, recently, modern technology (the "household arts") has been applied to the everyday and has pushed back the limits of the sector dominated by humankind. Thousands of instruments, improved traditional tools, and "gadgets" have changed the everyday. They haven't destroyed its repetitive nature, however. The vacuum cleaner accelerates housework; the woman who "does the housework" continues to repeat, on a daily basis, the same familiar gestures, although she has more free time. For what? Sometimes to read vapid or frivolous gossip, sometimes to grow bored. Technology invades everydayness and changes it, but there is no metamorphosis.

Nor is there any understanding of everyday life without critical analysis. It combines privation and frustration with the enjoyment of goods, needs that have become desires, and the constant capacity for pleasure or joy. Everydayness brings together accomplishments and what some philosophers refer to as the "alienation" of the human being. In it the possible and the impossible, joy and pain and boredom come face to face. In this sense it contains the thing that makes us human. Even exceptional activities, such as art, science, and politics, or the destiny of exceptional individuals, or moments of sublimity, fail to provide this degree of human fulfillment.

So where can everydayness be captured? To this question, my response is again apparently ambiguous. "It is found everywhere and nowhere." It is found not in our work life, not in business or at the office; not in our home life and its environment and relationships, not in distractions, or leisure and its many activities. And yet, it is all of this—the life of the human being who moves from one to the other, who is realized and loses himself as easily at work as at home or at leisure. For it is the same man and the same woman who works, marries, raises children, goes to the movies, goes on vacation. And yet, not exactly the same. The "person," as we say, diversifies while retaining a certain unity.

If we insist upon a precise definition of the everyday, I would define it negatively at first. We can eliminate distinct, specialized activities: technology, part-time work, culture, ethics, and accepted values. In which case, what remains? Positivists and scientists would say nothing. Philosophers and metaphysicians would say everything—the profound being, essence, existence. I would say "Something: the substance of humankind, human material, that which enables him to live, simultaneously residue and totality, desires, capacities, possibilities, essential relationships with goods and other humans, the rhythms through which he moves from one distinct activity to another, his time and his space, or his spaces, his conflicts . . ."

It goes without saying that social science cannot satisfy itself with a negative definition. Note, however, that a confrontational movement, such as that which transforms need into desire, contains a form of evidence that is unique to it. It clarifies while also requiring further clarification, providing we approach it through analysis and then expose it in its totality while penetrating beneath its surface.[2]

To take this a step further, I would like to quickly point out the scientific findings about everydayness.

Signs and signals populate space and time. Signals are simple, precise, reduced to a minimum (green and red, long and short lines, and so on) and, therefore, often to binary systems. They control and condition behavior. Signs are more ambiguous, more complex; they form open systems. A word is a sign, but so is a door, a window, a necktie, a dress, a hat, a gesture such as shaking someone's hand in greeting. The door signifies an entrance, a passage closed to some and open to others—the inhabitants of the home and their relations.

My apartment is populated with objects that have a use and, at the same time, are signs, arranged in a certain order that the "logistics" of everydayness studies. Dishes and saucepans in the kitchen signify my alimentary tastes. The street, too, is filled with signs; one woman's dress signifies that she is going to go for a walk and another's that she is going to work. In everyday life, we know (more or less) how to translate into our everyday language these interlocking systems of signs. If we are unable to translate them, we miss something; we are then thought to be peculiar, or a foreigner, or stupid.

But that is not all. Consider, for a moment, our monuments (Notre-Dame, the Arc de Triomphe, the Louvre) or, simply, a face, known or unknown. We cannot compare them to systems of signals such as those that govern circulation, nor to systems of signs, enigmatic but rigorous, such as those used by mathematicians. They do not tell us everything they have to say; they tell it slowly and have yet to finish. For that reason, we compare them to symbols, endowed with an inexhaustible meaning. We judge them to be expressive as well as significant. Thus, Notre-Dame symbolizes the continuity of Paris as well as the grandeur of a former age and the faith of its builders; it encapsulates a view of the world along with centuries of history. Faces and monuments, all symbols introduce depth into everydayness: the presence of the past, individual or collective actions and dramas, weakly determined yet more cogent possibilities, beauty and grandeur. With the spectacle of the everyday and the participation of the individual in life, we have the kernel, the center, the point of penetration in something that is more profound than repetitive banality and nonetheless cannot be separated from it. Paris is its streets, its people, the countless signs and signals, as well as the symbols, without which the presence of the city, its people, and its history would be absent. Without symbols the banality of signals, the triviality of known and repetitive signs, would reign over a space and time deprived of the unknown, deprived of meaning. We could say the same of Marseille or Lille, of a village, or a landscape.

I can now offer a few scientific definitions.

1. Sign and signal systems are intertwined in everydayness, together with symbols, which are not system forming. These all become part of a system that is both partial and privileged: language. Critical understanding of everyday life is defined as an important part of a science we refer to as general semantics.

2. We define the total semantic field as the largest ensemble of significations that language (which is only one part of it) strives to explore and seeks to equal. Knowledge of everydayness, therefore, is found in this field. It is exposed to various partial sectors that are distinct from it. (For example, Mr. X finds his job boring, or disappointing, or fascinating. Given this appreciation, motivated or not, coherent or not, he becomes part of the general field. The household of Mr. and Mrs. Y may be good or bad, a success or failure, which give it meaning, and so on.)

3. Contrary to what some "semanticians" believe, signification does not exhaust the semantic field; it is incapable of doing so and cannot act alone. We don't have the right to overlook the expressive to the benefit of the significative. There is no expression, of course, without signs and significations, through which it is expressed and, therefore, exhausted; but there is no signification without an expressive function, which it translates by stabilizing it, by making it commonplace. Between these two terms, there is unity and conflict (dialectic). Meaning results from this fluid relationship between expression and signification. Unlike signals, symbols are obscure and inexhaustible; signs wander between the clarity of signals and the fascinating obscurity of symbols, sometimes approaching an empty clarity, at other times an uncertain depth.

The total semantic field unites (in variable proportions depending on the place and time) symbolic depth and the clarity of signals. Signs (and language most of all) enable us to express meaning.

4. In more precise terms, signals, which imperatively command yet teach us nothing, which are repetitious and always identical, are socially redundant. But symbols always bring surprises, novelty, the unexpected, until their reappearance; they surprise us; they have an aesthetic character. Both numerous and too rich, they overwhelm us and become unintelligible. Signs, however, are informative.

5. In this way, we can define the social text. It is the result of the combination, in infinitely varied proportions, of the aspects and elements described above. Overloaded with symbols, it ceases to be legible because it is too rich. Reduced to a collection of signals, it becomes banal; because too obvious, we find it boring (redundant), repetitious. A good social text is legible and informative; it surprises us but not too much; it teaches without overwhelming us. It is easily understood, without an excess of triviality.

The richness of the social text can be measured by its accessible variations: by the wealth of possibilities it offers to individuals (we decipher it while also being a part of it). These possibilities require options, which are as numerous as the openings of the possible; for the possible and the impossible go hand in hand; we must choose, and the unchosen possible becomes impossible. Thus, the large city offers many more choices than the small town or village. These are referred to as its "seductions," its "temptations," its "appeal," whether it's a question of goods we desire, skills we learn, friends we visit, or lovers we win over. The choices and the abundance of choice are found side by side with the multiplicity of possibles that can be read in the social text. There is, consequently, an inherent uneasiness in the richness of the everyday, an uneasiness that is itself proportional to the growing number of entreaties, to the demands for the decision that engages, realizes a possible, that is precluded from going backward.

And how can these theoretical notions be used for the description, analysis, and unmasking of concrete life?

I want to introduce here, without further examination, a proposition that could be discussed and analyzed at length but which would exceed the boundaries for discussion in this essay. It can be formulated as follows: "In the society to which we belong and which we can observe, intermediaries have privileges, sometimes exorbitant, to the detriment of that which has greater reality." Doesn't the truth of the statement rely on the simplest form of practical experience and the presence of everyday commonsense? It means that everywhere around us, the places where we meet and interact with one another—the street, the café, the train station, the stadium—have greater importance and hold greater interest in the everyday than what they connect. It is a paradoxical situation that familiarity forces us to acknowledge. But this wasn't always the case. At one time, the house or the workshop had as much reality as the street. Means of communication and their intermediaries were subordinate to mankind.

Let us begin with language.

Its poverty and wealth, its connection with everydayness, can be understood by analogy with the social text. We can proceed by doing the reverse of what the majority of "semanticians" do, who study that which exceeds language, of which language is only a part. Such theorists do not always seem to realize that they are, in their own way, "translating" a crisis, even a serious disease of spoken language. They fetishize it; they have developed a philosophy of discourse and language, but that is only because speech—everyday or specialized—has already revealed its inadequacies. Is it because modern man already suspects language? Fetishization of the means of communication reveals the absence of communication, an uncertainty about communication—we fail to understand how it operates or in what way or at what level.

Poverty, misery. Speech can be used for trivial purposes, for banalities. We speak of the rain and the sunshine, our neighbors and friends, our children and the cost of living, of sex and the intrigues of the ambitious, of hierarchies and salaries. The same words are repeated in pointless exchanges. However, these exchanges are significant. They bear witness to the most general concerns and a certain need—timid, clumsy, too modest or too vulgar—for communication. We experience, here, the full "redundancy" of the social text. Banal discourse holds sway there.

Often, an unforeseen impulse orients such an exchange of trivialities. We tell someone our life story. We share confidences (only a few, except for the foolish among us, who provide the switch with which they can be beaten; sometimes to create a connection, or to draw out other confidences; sometimes offering too many, while bluffing, a bit like poker). The conversation grows heated and becomes a serious game; there is one partner, then another, a challenge, a mix of defiance and confidence, a risk, vague or specific. In such cases, words cease to be reduced to signals, becoming signs and taking on meaning. They allow us to catch sight of the novel of a person's life. Well-known idioms, though commonplace, appear, but are charged with meaning: with metaphors and images. Keywords, often symbolic, appear: love, hate, father, mother, childhood, old age, home and away, family and relatives. Big words follow, big themes, figures and values, generally unspoken, which play the role in discourse that monuments play in a city: proverbs rich with references, proper names that provide surprising bits of information, dramatizations, rhetorical figures, principles, family and social folklore, often arising in a distant past. And in this way the conversation, overloaded, tedious, stops. It becomes a pointless dialogue, one of extreme triviality, but in the opposite sense, because it is too rich and abandons the middle regions of communication.

The study of language in everyday life is not limited to this relation between "expression and signification" from which meaning arises. But there are things that language doesn't say, which it avoids saying, which cannot and must not be said. On the one hand, discourse is full of gaps and holes; on the other, it possesses a harsh reality, a solid "structure." Words and their sequences, "reflections" of actions and objects, are also, in their own way, things. Language acts as a filter, or a net, or a cage. It captures desires and imposes a suitable form on them, whereas symbols obscurely stimulate desire (although also producing a "crystallization" that is frequently disturbing because of its fixation). When needs and desires are unable to find the words to make themselves known and attempt their realization through communication, they wither—or they rebel.

As a result, out of everyday life new words are born, turns of speech (often marginal when compared with official speech: slang, common idioms). Repressed desires cut a path by means of indirect expression. They seek a social existence. The changes in language and speech arise out of everyday life.

Take the street as an example. We can speak of the streets of a large city, of a busy street, one that has been completely urbanized and is without any relationship to the countryside and nature other than the surprising reminder provided by trees or a few scattered flowers, or the sky and the clouds scudding over the city. A highly privileged intermediary between the sectors of the everyday—the workplace, the home, places of amusement—the street represents everyday life in our society. It is the almost complete representation, the "digest," although it is outside individual and social existences, or because it is outside. The street is nothing other than a place of passage, interference, circulation, and communication. Therefore, it is everything, or nearly so: the microcosm of modernity. An unstable presence, it offers publicly that which is otherwise hidden. And it makes this happen on the stage of a theater that is nearly spontaneous.

The street repeats itself and changes, like everydayness: it repeats itself in the incessant alteration of people, appearances, objects, and times of day. The street offers a spectacle and is only spectacle; the man who hurries by, rushing to get to work or to a meeting, fails to see this spectacle; he is part of it. But isn't "modernity" itself essentially a spectacle and spectacular, in the street as well as on television or the movies, on the radio, and in any number of ceremonies and demonstrations? The spectacle of the street, changing and identical, offers only limited surprises, other than accidentally (that is, aside from the occasional accident, which provokes considerable emotion and multiplies interest). Rarely does the sensational disrupt the driver's monotony of the street. It places before our eyes a good "social text." All kinds of people are found there. The appreciable or ostentatious differences of class and social layers have disappeared, differences that might increase the picturesqueness of the street but would soon make the crowd circulating around the Champs-Elysées or the large boulevards unbearably garish. Social layers and classes continue to reveal themselves by multiple signs that are imperceptible to the casual viewer. The spectacle of the street shapes the gaze and stimulates the spirit of observation. Many women are able to classify another woman at a glance, by evaluating her shoes, her stockings, her hairdo, her hands, her walk, her dress, or her coat. Far more than men and far better than men are able. They also know how to classify men into suitable categories: handsome or ugly, agreeable or antipathetic, rich, intelligent, refined or vulgar. In short, in the street, any number of interesting moments pierce the indifference of the permanent spectacle in which each of us becomes a spectator.

When on the street, I am a participant. I'm also a spectacle for others. For better or worse, I am part of the social text, a small, familiar, but possibly slightly irritating sign because enigmatic, expressive. I am present, with a good conscience or bad, passively or aggressively, depending on my mood, my objective, my situation, content simply to wander around if I have some time ahead of me, if I'm well dressed (and if the passersby appear to notice), if the weather is nice. I proceed, satisfied or dissatisfied, bored or amused, preoccupied or distracted, and my situation is more clearly revealed to me as soon as I leave the office, the factory floor, or my home. I am again available, or I head to work, or I hurry because someone is waiting for me. A thousand small psychodramas and sociodramas unfold in the street, especially my own.

An overpopulated desert, the street fascinates and, yet, is never static enough to be disappointing. It encompasses possibilities: spectacle of the possible, possibilities reduced to a spectacle, beautiful, charming women the flâneur will never know, ugly or visibly stupid women, disgraceful or seductive men, foreigners who are strange simply because of their foreignness, occupations or preoccupations whose traces they bear. The most distant human rubs shoulders with us here in a nearly inexhaustible diversity that commits us to nothing (except, in the limiting case of a parade, fight, or political demonstration). When overcrowded, the street becomes the home of the crowd in which we lose ourselves, unless we avoid it entirely. When deserted, or empty, the street fascinates by this emptiness.

It offers, as well, the spectacle of all the goods of the earth, laid out before our gaze and our covetousness, objects of desire, exciting to the point of frenzy, exciting because inaccessible, our desire heightened by this inaccessibility. Behind the display windows, objects lead a sovereign life. They achieve the fullness of their existence as commodities and as exchange value; in their path between production and consumption, they rule the street, an intermediary among men. They are fetishized, and this fetishism is metamorphosed into a kind of splendor that turns some streets (rue Saint-Honoré in Paris, for example) into museums and large department stores into cathedrals. Here the circuit is completed that changes merchandise into a desirable and desired object: into a good. Through objects and their beauty, what they offer and what they withhold, the street becomes the site of dreams closest to the imaginary, and the site as well of the harshest reality, that of money and frustration. Men, and women especially, court these things: queenly things, fairy things that their worshippers change from behind the display windows into ghostly things. Through these objects and pleasures, both possible and impossible, money proclaims itself king above all these other royal presences.

But humans will have their revenge. Whether in dream or in thought, they chase these objects, judge them. They choose among them, whether in imagination or in practice. The number of possible choices is a measure of the interest of the spectacle (we mustn't forget that this measurement—oh, the irony—can take a mathematical form and has its own laws, the laws of information, generally).

Space and time stamped with the seal of abundance, of envy, and therefore of poverty and deprivation, the street, shopping, window shopping, all dramatize individual lives without disturbing them much. The street harbors the unknown, in boutiques, at the end of hallways, at intersections. This unknown carries minimum risk. Almost as if it were reduced (although not completely) to the known. It defamiliarizes but does not disorient. Adventure awaits us at the street corner, mostly inoffensive, except for those exceptions that confirm the rule or change its meaning: it exposes the most unsettling possible. It wasn't always like this. The medieval street contained brutal dangers and temptations; it tore the bourgeois, the artisan, the workman from the tranquility of the home and patriarchal life. God and the devil fought for control over and in the street. Malodorous, prey to prostitutes and criminals, it displayed its truculence in its sordid reality. Restif de la Bretonne has left us a picture of the streets of Paris at the height and at the end of this now distant scene, whose echo we find in Naples or the cities of the East that have remained Asiatic.[3]

The village street remains immersed in nature. A passageway for man and beast, traveling from house and stable to the fields, it is subject to the rhythms of the world, which dominate social life and continue to govern mankind: hours and days, weeks and months, youth, marriage, old age, burials, all ruled by the master of time more than of space: the temple or church, the bell and clock tower.

The café. Rather than investigating the history of coffee and cafés, I'll simply point out its value to explain certain forms of sociability in everyday life and understand the formation of certain social groups. Cafés played a considerable role in the appearance of the "intelligentsia" as a group, or "youth" in the eighteenth and nineteenth centuries. It is enough to read Diderot or Balzac to understand this. Is the importance of the café unique to France, though? It seems that in other countries (Vienna and Austria in general, among others), we find analogous phenomena; but in France, would social spontaneity, driven from public life by State bureaucracy and from private life by traditional moralism, have found a refuge there?

The café, a place of often promiscuous encounters, where fantasy is grafted onto day-to-day repetitiveness, is also the place for games and speech for the sake of speech. It bears the mark of its destination: derisively sumptuous decoration, mirrors that multiply presences that are far from illusory, corners and nooks in which fleeting intrigues are planned, labyrinths that are pallid imitations of life and consciousness. The unusual [*l'insolite*] (a term fashionable in 1960) becomes banal, and the banal unusual.[4] But aren't the old cafés more interesting, more attractive than recent arrivals? Modernity, with its harsh lighting and improved technologies and devices, has not enhanced the charm of such places. Harshly lit, functional, but without the shadowy corners and worn velour banquettes, the site of young loves and guilty love affairs, the modern café no longer symbolizes. But what does it signify? Restlessness, disturbance, uncertainty, the unease of modernity beneath the stolid gaze of machines and robotic humans.

Specific cafés for intellectuals, for artists, for billiard players, chess or card players, did not dispel their attraction, and were accessible to everyone. They ranged from the "small café" for neighborhood regulars to the "grand café," where crowds gathered. They still run the gamut between these two poles of attraction. The stable elements—décor, waiters, cashiers, customers—give value to those who pass through their doors; from such elements they receive a tonality that changes them, so that stability is not reduced (to a certain extent) to boredom or the unusual to uncertainty.

"Women." We can discuss the exact meaning of this term and its validity endlessly. Some authors claim it has no meaning at all. For them, "women" do not constitute a social group; they belong to groups and classes; they are an integral part of society; sexual differences belong to the realm of biology more than to an understanding of human reality. The word, "women," is said to harbor a false and pejorative intention from the outset by situating them outside society, and reflects a prejudice espoused by "men." Others, on the contrary, feel that the physiological differences cannot but affect social life: the characteristics of the feminine sex and its specific functions (maternity, a function simultaneously social and physiological) affect humanity as a whole. Women, according to this belief, have shared concerns, making them part of an informal but nonetheless real group. Through social differences, natural or conventional, they come together, recognize one another; intrigue, innuendo, even complicity unite them, especially against "men." The battle of the sexes, which predates, historically and sociologically, the great struggles among peoples and classes, and has been relegated to the background by those struggles, has not, for all that, disappeared.

Only critical awareness of everydayness affords a relatively precise content to these terms (I want to insist on the importance of relativism—the content changes with the society; it is not the same in capitalist society and socialist society, and it is pointless to discuss the matter further). Everydayness weighs upon every woman individually and on all women with all its weight. They experience the heaviest, most burdensome, dullest, and most repetitive aspects of everyday life both in the form of housework and the efforts required to raise children, and in the generally inferior forms of social work reserved for them. In almost all categories and social classes, the woman bears this load (except for the upper layers of the bourgeoisie and the aristocracy, but even this distinction requires further refinement). Consequently, woman's work does not entirely resolve the old conflicts, as was believed in an overly optimistic period of evolutionism. Nor does culture. It so happens that woman's work, or culture, that is, the individualization of the feminine personality, aggravate conflict situations.

I don't want to dramatize or darken this view of things. Overwhelmed by everydayness, women have always experienced renewal through maternity, children, and childhood. Today, household appliances relieve them of a share of their burden, although presenting them with one of the significant problems of "modernity"—boredom. Industrial labor and work in general, having become as repetitive as the everyday drudgery of housework, the difference has shrunk. Moreover, the diversity of their responsibilities spares women some of the consequences of the extreme division of labor that men endure. Having entered production, women govern consumption; it is they who choose, and the fact of their choosing has almost become a social function.

The analysis of everydayness helps us understand one of the great contemporary phenomena: the ambiguity of the situation of women (the "female condition," as it is sometimes referred to). The most obvious aspect is the great push by women toward an improved status, one that would extract them from this ambiguous blend of subjection and superiority in which they have been struggling. But what status would this be? It's not exactly clear, and many men feel that this unsettling push harbors the possibility of a new matriarchy, whose symptoms could be seen in the most advanced industrial societies. On the other hand, this massive effort to escape ambiguity assumes ambiguous forms, as witnessed by the press and by literature, both of which strangely struggle to unite a heightened awareness with day-to-day practice. Singular dialectical movements (astonishing contradictions) intersect this ambiguity. Don't women, the most natural elements of everyday life, also exhibit the greatest artificiality: fashion, affectation, the most artificial aestheticism? Don't they often willingly accept these contradictions?

We could say the same about youth and "the young." Everyone is part of a group, itself part of a class and society as a whole (together with the tensions and conflicts that oppose the group and the class to other groups and classes within that society). And yet "the young" have their own needs and desires, their specific problems, their demands and hopes. They form a large group, one that is open, formless, and without a well-defined structure but nonetheless real. In this sense they are found in every sector of the everyday (work, family, entertainment, and leisure activities) just as they are in the working class, among "intellectuals" considered as a group, and so on.

To conclude this "digest" of everyday life, I want to offer some comments on networks and conduits. These form the weft on which the everyday is woven, which it embroiders and covers with ornamentation whether brilliant or dull, new or outdated. These networks and conduits remotely connect small groups, superficially closed or attached to a particular physical location: families, villages, neighborhoods of cities, professional associations, local associations.

Networks and conduits do not overlap with larger entities whose analysis goes beyond that of everydayness: classes, nations, labor unions, parties. Yet they are an element and an aspect of it; they situate larger groups within everydayness and vice versa. Along network paths, news and commentary are transmitted by word of mouth, sometimes with surprising speed but never without deformation and filtering. Broadcast news parallels the written press and official information, but networks do not exclude written channels: we move from newspapers, leaflets, programs, and pamphlets to rumors, stories, tales, and interpretations. Sociologically, the major political parties—through their "organizational system," local leaders, militants, members, sympathizers—and churches (priests and the faithful), and large, structured groups (freemasons, labor unions) make use of networks, as do some professional groups (sales representatives, booksellers) and even some "informal" groups (art lovers and bibliophiles). And there are other, stranger "networks" as well, such as those among homosexuals. But "the young," "children," and even "women" also have networks. These are sometimes easy, sometimes difficult to identify, and their links or knots are found in a given store, or a given "leader," or in a given place that is more or less accessible to the profane. At times a communications or information group can become a pressure group without, however, losing its connection with everydayness and its linking function between the everyday and the non-everyday.

Conduits differ from networks in that they transmit people and not only "noise," information, and gossip. Through these conduits, the young find jobs, start a career, move from the countryside to the city. With their help, we discover the artisan who can repair an object, the bookseller who has a given title, the physician or lawyer who is right for us. Social advancement moves through these conduits; they open the path to success or failure. In terms of everydayness, they support formal relationships and represent formal institutions: the bureaucracy, economic organizations, the application of regulations and laws, the connection between city and country, between Paris and rural France, between home and abroad. They play an important role in "social mobility." In terms of everyday "lived" experience, they introduce broader perspectives. It is rare that an individual, no matter how isolated he may appear, isn't a member of a network or conduit, often without realizing it. Most people participate in several of these "informal" groups.

In this brief inventory of everydayness, I have made use of a concept both well known and obscure—alienation. Alienation applies to any vital and conscious activity that is lost, dissipated, torn from itself, and, consequently, turns away from its plenitude. The study of everyday life obligates philosophers to soften and concretize this concept. Alienation and disalienation, far from being exclusive, are interrelated. That which frees and "disalienates" an already alienated activity may turn out to be "alienating" and, therefore, require other forms of disalienation. This can continue in the form of a dialectical movement, composed of continuously resolved and continuously recurring contradictions.

In this sense, leisure activities release and "disalienate" us with respect to fragmented and backbreaking labor but harbor their own kind of alienation, such as passivity and nonparticipation in the spectacle (television, movies), or the contrivances of the "leisure industry," vacation clubs and villages that claim to rediscover nature. Thus, the signal systems that accumulate around us facilitate day-to-day practice and expansion; at the same time, they condition behavior, subject it to overwhelming discipline, and change humans into robots; they "cyberneticize" everyday life, already packed with redundant and repetitive significations; they authorize activities that are more varied than ever before, promote intermediary activities, traffic, mass communication; they alienate life, and the desire to escape the tyranny of abstract signals no doubt plays a significant role in the aestheticism (also abstract) that runs wild in the modern world. The more profound symbols produce abstraction; they attract, fascinate, alienate.

In the everydayness of the family, the father represents life at its most expansive, the most fully realized, the most deeply embedded in social practice. The child imitates him. In this way, he overcomes childhood and frees himself. Of all the possibles, the father has realized only one. Along with the image of life, he provides that of mutilation; with disalienation he brings alienation, and conversely.

Notes

[*Encyclopédie de la psychologie* (Paris: Fernand Nathan, 1962), 102–7, reprinted in *Du rural à l'urbain* (Paris: Anthropos, 1970), 89–107.—Eds.]

1. A novelist had the original idea of providing, as a background to his adventure tales, the dull calm of everyday life. His possibly brilliant idea assumed that the bustling and dramatic "world" of crime is less interesting than the

monotonous blandness of day-to-day experience. And so, being an admirable authority of the everyday, he reversed the customary novelistic viewpoint. His success, which was certainly deserved, nonetheless implies the gentrification and subjugation of the crime novel. Every reader will have recognized the author to be Simenon. [Continuing his ongoing focus on literary space, Lefebvre here has in his sights the novelist Georges Simenon, the creator of the fictional detective Jules Maigret. Note, though, that in drawing attention to literary space, or the space of literature, Lefebvre's interest is not reduced to a particular writer's or artist's "world," because "signifying processes (a signifying practice) occur in a space which cannot be reduced either to an everyday discourse or to a literary language of texts." See Henri Lefebvre, *The Production of Space*, trans. Donald Nicholson-Smith (London: Blackwell, 1991), 8, 136.—*Eds.*]

2. For example, take the "need" to smoke. There is no connection with a physiological need, other than the very general need for stimulants and excitants that keeps the organism in a state of "vigilance." Most likely, the use of tobacco leads to organic disorders. Therefore, we can say that this need is "factitious" or "anti-natural." Yet it becomes an intense and constant desire that assumes the characteristics of a vital need in spite of the warnings, dangers, and expense.

3. [Nicolas Restif de la Bretonne (1734–1806) was a French novelist whose works included *La Pied de Franchette* (1769), translated as *Franchette's Pretty Little Foot*, about shoe-fetishism. Restif is also attributed with coining the term "pornographer" in a separate novel. —*Eds.*]

4. [*L'insolite* was used by the surrealists and symbolists to translate the German term *das Unheimlich,* uncanny, unfamiliar, or unusual, famously used by Sigmund Freud. Lefebvre may also have been thinking of Jean-Paul Clébert, *Paris insolite*, with photographs by Patrice Molinard (Paris: Denoël, 1952), translated by Donald Nicolson-Smith as *Paris Vagabond* (New York: New York Review of Books, 2016). Clébert's book was a prototype of the *dérive* of the Situationists.—*Eds.*]

CHAPTER 10

The New Urban Complex
Lacq-Mourenx and the Urban Problems of the New Working Class

Economic changes and the transformations of production technologies go hand in hand with large population movements: movement to or away from cities, concentration and decentralization, consolidation, new urban centers. This presents the practical and theoretical problem of the *optimal formula.*

A problem such as this assumes that (sociological) research becomes or can become efficient, practical, "operational." It tends to actualize working hypotheses, to confront them with requirements and possibilities. At the same time, it implies the notion of *value* and tends toward an option, toward a preferential judgment that entails an objective decision. Aren't we thereby escaping the realm of scientific understanding?

This is an old discussion, one that has already given rise to a number of considerations, some of them byzantine, others profound. Acting in the name of a philosophy of science, which is often presented as nonphilosophical (strictly positive), some thinkers will always protest the judgments that detect values in facts. Moreover, these scientific types are right to affirm the need for rigor. However, taken literally, this rigor eliminates problems and the problematic. It accepts only faits accomplis, acknowledges problems only when they have been resolved and alternatives when they are overcome.

Boredom, to take just one example, is an observable human phenomenon, which comprises, as a "positive" fact, the protest against one's existence, the rejection of one's condition, and, therefore, also an element of negation. Dissatisfaction is a fact, like satisfaction. For now, there's no point in expanding these concepts and their dialectical associations. We can accept their relativity and, to put it somewhat differently, their ambiguity as well. It is easy to establish that "satisfaction" corresponds, in human phenomena and in the humanities and social sciences, to the very general idea of (relative) equilibrium, a concept accepted in all the sciences and by the most prudent or the most rigorous of positivists. When "satisfaction" predominates in a group, is more prevalent than "dissatisfaction," that group tends toward a degree of stability. "Dissatisfaction," whether collective or individual, entails conflicts in social relations; it harbors multiple forms of disequilibrium. Unless we are willing to reduce human phenomena to numerical elements, quantitative, static and statistical, how can we do without such concepts?

There are consequences to this. The aforementioned research, which purports to be operational, acts on a *virtual object,* addresses a *possibility*: the satisfactory (optimal) whole, assuming it can be conceptualized, anticipated, realized. Understanding avoids, to the extent possible, the verb "to be" and the indicative. Its preference is for the conditional.

Large modern cities get bad press. They are almost always referred to with a pejorative or defamatory epithet: monstrous, tentacular, *cités-molochs*. On this point, many sociologists and urbanists agree with the technicians of circulation, with those who study air pollution in such cities. We can more prudently refer to them as "historical cities" or "spontaneous cities," withholding for the moment the meaning of these labels and their implied relationships. But we should not overlook the fact that such large cities possess a powerful collective individuality, a historical originality (Paris). They harbor, for individuals and small groups, a maximum of information, of possibilities (practical or "spiritual" and cultural), of the unforeseen, of surprise. The functionalism of new cities cannot avoid the confrontation with the scope and pulsing life of spontaneous cities.

Researchers have written scathingly about those cities consisting of individual houses and suburbs of small homes on individual lots. Paternalistic ideology doesn't atomize societies into individuals, as individualism does; it represents it as a collection of entities—a collection of families. This ideology turns out to be even more harmful and destructive of social life when the people gathered there have fewer collective traditions, urban or otherwise. In the mining villages of the north, an intense social life has its source in the conditions of mining; that life is maintained outside the mine, in everyday life and leisure. This social activity withers or disappears when workers, in more recent industries, without traditions, are gathered in bedroom communities or ghettos (or *"clapiers"* [a rabbit hutch], to use the energetic expression coined by the sociologists who studied Le Péage-de-Roussillon, the cities of the Moselle, and so on).[1] Such cities lack collective and even individual resources (heating facilities, for example) because of cost. Even the idea of expanding the markets for durable consumer goods would be sufficient to eliminate them.

Some Suggested Solutions

For new developments, either under construction or planned, what solutions have been proposed?

Solution one: *the neighborhood unit,* adjoining a preexisting spontaneous unit (village, market town, city).

Objections. This proposal immediately raises several a priori objections associated with the general problem, even before an examination of the facts. We are justifiably concerned with embodying in time and (historical) space the new development, with transferring onto it and in it an already active spontaneous sociability. Can we be certain that spontaneous sociability will be preserved, rediscovered, invested in the new development? There is no certainty that neighborhood relations (good and satisfying relationships) will be established between those who are now close neighbors, purely by chance, accidental members of a housing unit, without the existence of a historical background that would play a role in "lived experience [*vécus*]." The created unit becomes the artificial and mechanical appendage of an organic collectivity (a term borrowed from Durkheim), which it risks disturbing and dissociating even while receiving its positive influence, unless both collectivities simply remain foreign to one another. We will shortly have a clear idea of how this works out by looking at the case of Bagnols near Marcoule.[2] The new unit can literally capture and condense what is most lacking in the old unit. It then becomes a kind of ghetto. What's more, the infrastructure appropriate to this much larger development cannot be employed for a smaller unit. Either the costs are enormous or the use of collective infrastructure becomes simply inconceivable. Finally, in this context, we fall back on the problem of housing and large buildings, already planned, developed, and partially resolved (primarily by Le Corbusier, whose projects embody what is most vital and stimulating in this field).

Solution two: *the communitarian city*. A number of researchers, sociologists, and urbanists lean toward the collectivity "on a human scale." They start, apparently, from an in-depth critique of large cities, from a study of neighborhoods and neighbor relations. In a grouping of individuals and families that is neither too narrow nor too broad, the members may know and like one another; the immediate, simple, direct nature of relationships would ensure the ethical nature (moral value) of those relationships. Spontaneity would be restored at a much higher level. Once mechanical, the group would again become organic. Thus would be born a genuine human community. The optimal number of members for such a group would be approximately five thousand.

Objections. No matter how honorable the concerns of the researchers in question, no matter how worthwhile and serious their work, I have a number of reservations about this solution. More than any other, it harbors unspoken assumptions. Without having any goal other than that of clarifying the problem through a discussion of a "highly scientific" nature, it might be useful to formulate certain objections and explicate the underlying assumptions. Wouldn't a development in which everyone knows one another present as many drawbacks as advantages on a human level? Such a development would be a village, a market town, at best the county seat in a canton. Are we going to "cantonalize" new constructions at a time when worldliness has become widespread, along with its uncertainties and opportunities? The oppressive atmosphere of smaller market towns and small cities can also be found in the communitarian city. Doesn't a closed community inevitably become a closed circle—a vicious circle—

from which we desire only to escape? Is it anything other than an abstract utopia? Would this community have a genuine social life? How would it achieve the level of cultural life that assumes, at least, a theater, an orchestra, middle schools, a university, a large library? Would inhabitants willingly allow themselves to fetishize a form of community life accompanied by a kind of cultural asceticism? Don't we risk establishing a particularly oppressive moral order, a risk heightened by the fact that it would be freely chosen according to the norms of collective life?

It appears that certain intellects, although well informed, operate on two planes, which they distinguish only to confuse them all the more: the precise determination of material facts and data, and the ideal construction. Some of them even appear to transpose an existing form into the general sociological model, that of the religious community (parish). Perhaps they would reply that this community has nothing fixed about it, that, on the contrary, it is open to the "transcendent." To this act of faith, the sociologist would reply that in doing so we are leaving the field of knowledge.

Solution three: *the functional city.* This solution could be called the technical or even technocratic solution. It would claim to be the only scientific solution. Unquestionably, it has the merit of not backing away from a consideration of large-scale housing developments [*Grands Ensembles*].

Following this path, specialists would carefully study (primarily in existing cities) all the *functions* assumed and provided by the urban collectivity. Proceeding analytically, they would distinguish these functions by determining their connections and their structures. Then, working more theoretically toward a final synthesis and practically toward an on-site "projection," their project would include the total functional ensemble.

Finally—with respect to needs and to modern life in general—these projects would provide the necessary public and collective services, from commercial equipment to cultural equipment. The technicians of urbanism claim to be participants in an organization that seeks to be unified (or "total").

Objections. By what criteria do we determine that the expert of social and urban realities has exhausted the city's "functions," discovered their hierarchy of urgency and their connections in time and space? Will the spontaneous allow itself to be defined, reduced to analysis, enclosed in an operational synthesis? It has not been demonstrated that aspirations and needs (individual and social, inseparably) coincide with the "functions" formally overseen by the urban group, which does not comprise the social totality, not even the cultural totality. These are the implicit postulates of this puerile functionalism; it assumes that the expert can plan and arrange everything. But no one can anticipate everything. And must we even anticipate everything? To the extent that the sociologist can study the work carried out in existing developments (none of which, in France, has yet to achieve the size of a "large-scale development"), they project a kind of positivist or, rather, "zoo-technical" conception of man onto the landscape. The consequence and corollary of integral functionalism is boredom, the profound boredom of the being who promptly carries out his functions. The more he is pushed, the kinder he becomes, the more he plans, the more this project refines the discomfort of an unsatisfied satisfaction without an opening toward the possible. With new and more powerful, more intelligent means at his disposal, the zoo-technocrat develops an attitude of paternalism. Although this effort has unquestionable benefits (the first of which being its scientific seriousness), it remains within narrow limits. With this approach, the home and everyday life (public and private) remain secondary to the technical organization of work.[3]

Solution four: *dialectical humanism*. This is a virtual solution that has not had the opportunity to be applied and which, as a result, assumes a doubly hypothetical, almost speculative aspect. It can provide only a direction for further research. The sociologist would very seriously study functionality while criticizing the analysis that separates the elements ("variables") and breaks their unity. The nonfunctional, supra- or transfunctional (certainly not "transcendence") in social relations would have to be addressed. These would not be exhausted by the concept of a functional reality. If, for example, someone claims that *games* have a social function, he is making a somewhat empty proposition. Wouldn't going beyond all function be the function of games? They provide gratuitousness. The ludic restores, within structured social reality, the abundance of pure spontaneity, the unexpected, and the unpredictable, emotion and surprise. "Spontaneous" life has functions, fulfills them, exceeds them, delights in itself and tends toward plenitude (satisfaction). Could those functions be anything other than means? Could the goal of social life be determinable in advance, or economic or ethical? In their own specific way, art, culture, play are inseparable. Couldn't the same be said of social facts and significant human phenomena?

Whenever the sociologist acknowledges the elimination, by the experts, of the customary places of spontaneous sociability (cafés, small places of business), whenever he assists in the functionalization of meetings and the destruction of the ludic element that is so alive in our "monstrous" cities, he grows concerned. But he is not surprised to find the manifestations of deep-seated and growing dissatisfaction and its consequences: a counterfeit and distorted sociability, the need for evasion at any price.

Some Facts

The starting point and reference for the investigation previously outlined is Mourenx, an entirely new city under construction around a vast industrial complex, which is now being built (near Lacq and the surrounding areas).

The research considers the new city as a social laboratory (not in the sense understood by Kurt Lewin but, nonetheless, quite precisely: like a crucible in which well-defined social forces are manifest and where the tangible results of macro-decisions appear).[4] It also considers the life of the new city as sociodrama (not exactly as understood by Moreno but accurately enough: barely constructed, the new city has a history, not lacking in dramatic character, a history that the investigation follows from the start).[5]

Mourenx, a new city, may become a large-scale housing development, given the rapid growth of the complex and increasing number of industries nearby. Lacq-Mourenx serves as a "growth center," relatively small but real, to use the terminology of François Perroux.[6] It was sited in a traditional rural environment. The investigation, a part of the study of the rural environment, has monitored the consequences of the shock produced by this development.

Using this development as a theoretical frame of reference, the investigation will eventually become comparative. The elements gathered so far are only touchstones that will lead to an investigation that could extend to other new towns in France, underdeveloped countries, socialist countries, or those newly introduced to modern life (Israel, for example).

Because of its well-determined features (completely new city, created on the basis of a block plan determined by existing government agencies in a large industrial country, established in the heart of the countryside in a region that is almost completely underdeveloped), Mourenx represents a kind of especially interesting and possibly typical *limit case*.

To clarify my ideas and formulate this typical character, I want to proceed comparatively. We can quickly compare Mourenx, an entirely new city, to the new areas of a very old city, particularly rich in spontaneity: Aix-en-Provence. The reasons for the comparison between two limit cases, two poles, will soon become apparent and give rise to explicit formulations.

Aix-en-Provence, a former university, legal, and administrative center, has grown, in a few short years, from a city with a population of 27,000 to one of 70,000. It has experienced the influx of a very mixed active population, partly from neighboring regions (Basses-Alpes, etc.), while preserving its ties with its physical origins. The ancient city had to be joined to the newly developed neighborhoods, some of which have a local existence and others of which are merely dormitories for Berre, Marignane, and neighboring towns.

These new quarters illustrate the diversity of administrative and legal solutions provided to developers of urban developments. Among them we find large construction companies, who sell or rent high-priced housing—various forms of co-ownership—as well as different types of municipal or departmental control, sometimes in partnership with private companies or subsidiaries of the Caisse des Dépôts et Consignations.[7]

This administrative and legal aspect is not our concern here, however. Of sociological importance is the fact that the new habitat reveals a highly advanced and highly differentiated form of stratification, distributed in "neighborhoods" that are not very far from one another but do not constitute a uniform whole.

Starting from the "bottom" (and, in fact, on the site, this development is called "Pinède d'en bas"), we have the homes of the *lumpen-proletariat*. The so-called emergency development, built "to last" but built very quickly, houses people and professions from all walks of life: scavengers, night watchmen, seasonal construction workers, North Africans, and so on. Proletarians down on their luck mix with social misfits. The specific characteristics of the lumpen-proletariat thus isolated are dangerously delineated and dominate other social traits. Each family becomes a "case" and is only too aware of its being a "case." Relations with the outside world increasingly take the form of assistance. And the role of professional social workers is reduced to that of a public writer. The same is true of the political militants who tried to work with the "emergency housing development" and its "cases." According to one of them:

> In this population in which the character of the lumpen-proletariat predominates, people know how to read but don't know how to use the act of reading. They can no longer rely on themselves, not even to read or write the simplest document, whether it's an official document or something else. Their social isolation has an impact on the simplest activities. There is nothing left to stimulate them. In Pinède d'en bas, there is no longer hope or despair. And yet, they are not lacking for televisions.[8]

At a somewhat higher level, we find Pinède d'en haut, where a number of families have been housed who have been evicted or whose homes have been dispossessed (who have, in general, left their dilapidated homes for relatively modern housing). Proletarian elements seem to predominate, but very mixed with low-level civil servants, sales representatives, employees.

Above this subsidized housing and its low rents, we have a layer of more comfortable subsidized housing, with slightly higher rents (500 apartments), housing primarily young households who were previously housed in cheap quarters or living with their parents. The mixing between the layers of populations and classes is here complete.

It should be pointed out that the public facilities available to families in this development, notwithstanding its size, are limited, where they exist at all.

Finally, we have co-owned properties, of various degrees of comfort, from average (whose occupants are tradesmen, midlevel civil servants, technicians) to very good (college professors, doctors, business executives, owners of large retail businesses).

The dilution of the proletariat (as a class) in the new development is striking. It is greater, according to this spectral analysis of urban reality, than it is in the "spontaneous" city, where the working class mixes with traditional craftsmen. It is even greater than what is suggested by this brief description. Workers, whose numbers are difficult to determine but sufficiently large, have rented or purchased apartments better in quality and price than what they might ordinarily be able to afford. They have assets, land, or homes, in their place of origin. Construction workers are quoted as having built homes while on vacation and then sold them so they could purchase a comfortable apartment.

The analysis of "lived experience" in these new homes in an old town reveals curious conflicts between two forms of practical reality and awareness: life and class consciousness, of historical origin—life and consciousness based on strata.

In the new town of Mourenx, something completely different is at work. Among the stationary population, the *lumpen-proletariat* does not exist, no more than artisans, small shopkeepers, etcetera. The proletariat or, rather, the "new working class," subject to automation, with its specific characteristics, occupies the housing blocks that have been assigned to it. Skilled workers (generally) inhabit the towers that dominate the town, tall buildings whose block plan was intended to break the monotony of horizontal lines. As for administrative personnel and high-level executives, they have large homes on the hillsides.

We can now formulate our findings; these do not claim to express laws but at most trends.

The New Urban Complex

In the first limiting case (Aix), we find the local projection, in now distinct elements, of the social structure of an existing (spontaneous) city. The projection is the result of a series of unconnected microdecisions seeking to resolve local problems. Social segregation yields disturbing results. It is restricted by other phenomena, notably the dilution of the working class as such in the differentiated strata. This gives rise to unique tensions and conflicts.

In the second limiting case (Mourenx), the sociologist finds the local projection of the technical structure (hierarchical, professional) of the enterprises involved. This projection is the result of macrodecisions made at the national level. Social segregation results in cohabitation in the same housing blocks and under identical conditions of the same socio-professional categories. Inevitably, this results in the reconstruction, on a new foundation, of the reality and consciousness of class. This reconstruction is intensified by the suppression of intermediaries (artisans, small shopkeepers) and slowed by the general isolation, monotony, and boredom.

I would like to add a few comments, from notes made in 1959, when the new town of Mourenx was then two years old and had approximately 4,500 inhabitants in residence (the size of the considerable floating population being difficult to determine). Approximately 100 households arrived each month.

The sociodramatic aspect, previously indicated, became visible in the "lived experiences" whose importance was more than literary and anecdotal.

Here is an excerpt from my field notebook [*carnet de route*] dated November 8, 1959.

> Arrived at 11 a.m. at the Mourenx city hall. Unable to interview the people I had planned because of some considerable commotion among the local dignitaries and leaders of organizations (unions, etc.). They had decided on holding a lavish ceremony on November 11 (plus a ball in the evening). Obviously, the local authorities wished to use the occasion to unite this newly established community, to publicly acknowledge its existence, to emphasize the action of the recently elected municipality. The mayor, a clever

and active man, somewhat overwhelmed by the magnitude of his job and its responsibilities, didn't hide this fact. However, it became apparent that one essential ingredient was missing: the dead. There were no dead in the radiant city, no monuments in the new town; personified in its representatives, it hesitates and begins to question itself; it needs the dead, it needs a past. The police commissioner, very important, arrived, and then what? I don't recall the name of the individuals. . . . A decision was made, the ceremony will take place in the old village. It seems that the handful of people from the new town who have died, including those who died from an occupational injury, have been buried in the old village.

Commentary (the commentaries may exceed the immediate content). The above notes may appear to be literary to sectarian "quantitativists" (Sorokin would write: "quantophrenics").[9]

The above requires a two-pronged commentary. First, such an odd (and also symbolic) bit of information would not have exceeded the narrow framework of the new town and its personalities if a sociologist hadn't passed by there quite by chance. As information, the human phenomenon would have been stillborn. On the other hand, the presence alone of this sociologist has loosened tongues. The new town, which is seeking to make its own way, which strives to be a collectivity or a community, also wants to make itself known. It releases bits of information as if they were calls for help; it welcomes (under these circumstances) anyone who will listen.

Second, this fact signifies the overall social pressure on the new town, which obeys or rejects. In this case, it obeys, which requires it to seek a past and the dead, wherever they are found: in this old village, which the new one dissociates and denies by its very existence. The two polarities meet here. The culture of society as a whole, which seeks to become a part of the new town—not without difficulty and not without conflict—is itself complex. Not only is it based on a historicity and a history, but it is connected with a religious attitude. It's a Christian culture in which the dead hold an important place, a culture built on tragic foundations.

Concerning the "social laboratory" aspect of the new town, I would now like to offer a few observations on "lived experience" together with a commentary, which also intentionally exceeds a strict analysis of the contents.

Observation 1. (Comments are excerpts from "in-depth" interviews.) "Why would we go to the neighbors? We know what's going on. No need to change rooms, no need to move."

Commentary. Throughout the interview, the subject (34 years old, control console operator) complains bitterly about the noise in the apartments, above, below, and on either side (closets, floors, ceilings). He can't get to sleep during the weeks when he works nights. The children bother him; so do conversations, shouts, radios. We would need to be able to monitor him closely to determine if there's a link between his attitude at work (where he monitors a console) and his attitude in daily life. The interviews reveal a constant theme, the connection between "the lack of privacy and isolation." The lack of privacy, far from promoting relations among neighbors and sociability, destroys it. This cannot be understood without taking into account a range of habits and attitudes, because, in other countries, with other "mores," a lack of privacy and, even, overcrowding—and the accompanying shouting and noisy scenes—does not interfere with the spontaneity of relationships. Children, who can facilitate relationships and anchor sociability, here, under these conditions, tend to inhibit them.

Observation 2. "You can hear a pin drop. I'm telling you, I can hear the cat running around in the apartment upstairs."

Commentary. The interviewee (teacher, 38 years old) strongly supports the impression summarized above. From her statements it appears that, at least for a number of individuals sensitized by their job, their attention is focused literally on the surrounding sounds and noises. Such individuals can't separate from the surrounding neighbors; they follow activities and actions; they monitor it with an attitude of annoyance or growing irritation, which can lead them toward neurosis. Of course, to reach these specific conclusions, we would need to share the everyday life of the subjects, which presents considerable difficulties. Except for rare cases, it seems that the sociopsychiatry of new towns doesn't escape the context of the minor neuroses—headaches and behavioral disturbances—which are more than enough to make their lives miserable. This diagnosis could change over time.

Observation 3. "Saturday is for boating."

Commentary. The interview subject, recently discharged from the Navy (Loire-Atlantic region), assimilates the Saturday excursion by car to the seashore or the mountains to the conclusion of his military service. He complains of the boredom he experiences in the "radiant city" and sharply criticizes a Parisian weekly that published a piece on Mourenx with that title. He claims that the photos accompanying the text were taken elsewhere. Without using any academic language, he attacks the myth. His words reveal the impossibility of completely functionalizing leisure activities. Aren't there functional leisure activities that are or could be integrated into everyday life—relaxing, reading the paper, and so on—and nonfunctional leisure activities—playing, seeking the unexpected, breaking with the everyday?

Observation 4. "We would be better off living in a town where there are slums."

Commentary. This is a strange thing to say. The interview subject must certainly have experienced terrible living conditions (although she doesn't admit it). She doesn't anticipate returning to a slum, her and her family. The slum would be for other people. She expresses, although poorly, the idea that a "spontaneous town," even with its defects, provides greater variety than a new town.

Observation 5. "It's not a town [*ville*], it's a housing complex [*cité*]."[10]

Commentary. This statement surprised and shocked the observer, who was careful to write it down. The term "housing complex [*cité*]," in certain milieu, refers to something noble and beautiful (because of its associations with the classical city or perhaps with Saint Augustine and the "City of God"). Here, it has a clearly pejorative resonance (probably because of the association with housing estates for workers). The interview subject also spoke the word with a degree of emphasis, which indicates both that the term is not part of his everyday vocabulary and that he wishes to emphasize it by giving it a certain weight.

Observation 6. "It's not a town. There's nothing here, no church, no cemetery. Not even a place to go for a walk. We thought we were coming to the Midi [Southern France]."

Commentary. These comments confirm the previous impressions. The rational function of a cemetery is to house the dead. For the members of the group (and, in a traditional culture, very deep seated), it has a symbolic value. It expresses continuity, a connection with history, time, and space. Its absence might go unnoticed in a large modern city; at least, it would be less of a loss. Here, given the size of the town, its absence is extremely obvious. It is as obvious as the lack of a place for pointless and unexpected encounters: the promenade (similar to shops, malls, or large avenues in many cities, in the south of France or elsewhere). The subject (40 years old, graphic designer, originally from northern France) correctly expresses a lack: the absence of the "suprafunctional" element that makes it worthwhile to have lived one's life in a city. Without managing to express himself, he circles around aesthetic and ethical problems.

In this sense, we note that the experience of new towns, especially Lacq-Mourenx, enables us to perceive *needs* in their spontaneous, native, and raw state. They are not yet hidden behind motivations, artificiality, ideologies, and justifications. They are expressed. Their paradoxical order of emergence continues to astonish us. In spite of the lack of complicated motivations and ideologies, aspirations and needs of a "cultural" nature (in the broad sense) emerge in these interviews along with the most urgent demands for heating, services, small shops, and so on.

Here, a question of method arises. How can we observe this birth (emergence) of needs? How can we measure them? Their order goes hand in hand with disorder, or conversely. They are expressed tumultuously. They change or seem to change. What quantitative analytical method could be applied here? Can we accept the concept of "latent structure" and [Paul] Lazarsfeld's techniques?[11] How would we identify a "continuum" here and discriminant variables? Could hierarchical methods of analysis

([Louis] Guttman) address this intense mobility?[12] Doesn't the identification of variables risk breaking the unity of the total human phenomenon and its effervescence? It seems clear that quantitative methods (the mathematics of quantity, which should be clearly distinguished from the mathematics of quality) can only grasp evident realities, invariant or considered to be invariant. When we speak of statistics, we also speak of statics rather than a moving generality or totality, which is manifest in the smallest details and the most elementary concepts.

Demographic Questions

The overpopulation of children in new towns has already been pointed out and numerically established by specialists, so I don't want to dwell on the issue. In Lacq-Mourenx, the age pyramid differs sharply from the average general configuration in France. The majority of child-bearing couples (from 28 to 45 years of age) have a large number of children under 10 years old. As of June 1959, out of 4,500 inhabitants and approximately 920 families (approximate numbers because of the constant influx of newcomers and several departures), there were 1,120 children. This already greatly exceeds the forecasts about the need for schools.

This proliferation in the new town does not appear to be slowing down. As of the above date, more than three hundred women were pregnant. This figure is greater than the averages and seems to correlate with the "struggle against boredom" that will be discussed.

Another aspect of the demographic situation has been less studied in its consequences, aside from its numerical expression: the absence of adolescents and the young (also the absence of the elderly). *The young town lacks youth*. The distribution of layers and classes of age is missing certain elements. One element is clearly lacking: the one that most intensely introduces turbulence, the unforeseen, or play into a collectivity. It is not solely this absence, of course, but it is because of it, among other things, that the observer comes away with the impression of impeccable and implacable order, enormous boredom, and complete predictability that the new town gives off.

Along with the element of uncertainty and disturbance, of a threat to the established order, youth and adolescence provide another irreplaceable element. The lack of an older population cannot overcome this lack; it aggravates it. Women who do not have parents to take care of the children or to help with the housework must stay at home, although household appliances help shorten the time needed for housework. Additionally, there are few job opportunities for women among the local businesses.

When necessary, the (moral and social) order solidifies against youth, assuming for itself a consciousness both more lucid and more assured. Observers, obsessed by "gangs" and "delinquents," and by moral and social order, risk not seeing these phenomena as a whole. How can the "ludic function" (although I use the expression cautiously) be fulfilled? It is accomplished not so much spontaneously, even though the need for it remains profoundly spontaneous. Rather, it is organized. It is the associations of adults (groups, clubs) that take up the challenge.

Does the absence of adolescents and the young have an effect on children (of about 7)? Most likely it contributes to their withdrawal from groups; they lack "models" for activities that are intermediate between adults and themselves. Groups and gangs, mostly invisible, take refuge in obscure locations (the upper or lower landings of tall buildings, the entrance to basements, or the basements themselves). Their numbers alone make social life difficult for them. They are literally hunted, caught between parents and guardians. Under the pretext of keeping order and limiting damages (some of which do not appear to have been the fault of children alone), local block guardians—employees of the Société Immobilière de Crédit, a subsidiary of the Caisse des Dépôts et Consignations—can hand out tickets. A rather sinister order seeks to impose itself on the radiant city.

The "New Working Class" and Urban Democracy

Recently, sociologists have pointed out the problems that can arise from new conditions of working life, both at work (technical changes, increasing automation) and outside work (everyday life and the family, leisure).

There is an inherent "problematic"[13] in the very general investigation of the fate of *the* industrial society (or industrial *societies*).

Observation of the new town provides some elements of a response and enables us to put forward several hypotheses.

In Lacq-Mourenx, during the last municipal elections, a ballot claiming to be "apolitical" won out over one that was much more highly politicized and clearly right leaning. The ballot claiming to be "apolitical" was, in fact, one by the left, put together in a rather interesting way by a local alliance between union members (the three main unions with "representatives," but not assigned and not designated as such), peasants wishing to defend their interests against government agencies, and intellectuals, teachers and professors at the new lycée. The "new working class," far from being isolated, broke through its isolation (at the local scale) and put an end to the plan to divide it.

The use of the term "apolitical" was not a ploy. It was backed up by a program: the reestablishment of commercial freedom—against a veritable monopoly held by a "supermarket"—and the reestablishment of local freedoms, with the new municipality demanding autonomy and its attributes: budgeting and property, buildings and offices, public gathering places, markets, streets. And this was done against the omnipotent and bureaucratic possessor (if not the "owner," although this was not private property) of the buildings and land, namely, the SCIC.[14]

The "apolitical" label therefore conceals a remarkable and profound aspiration for democracy in urban life, the active self-management of the community, and a form of socialization—directed against government control and a centralized bureaucracy—that includes concrete liberties.

Elected by a sizable majority (increased in the second round), the new municipality has initiated a difficult and multifaceted program of activity. It is fighting on every level, even the cultural. Spontaneity, sometimes clumsy but always passionate, helps sustain it. There has been a growth in the number of local organizations as well as expressions of community involvement: art, sports (tournaments), exhibitions, and so on.

These phenomena suggest several hypotheses that need to be verified and altered if there is reason to do so during an expansion of the research (and which surveys confirm).

(a) The "new working class," those employed by technologically advanced companies (fully automated like the SNPA, Lacq) tends to assume responsibility for the life of the "development."[15] Its interest never wavers and it refuses to yield to higher authorities—state, bureaucratic, or even purely political.

(b) Therefore, the "new working class" has none of the characteristics of the old "workers aristocracy": passivity, indifference, corruption. Established on new foundations (mastery of production processes, whose unity is created by the "continuous flow" of comprehensive automation) and in spite of contradictory factors (the passive nature of a large part of the "work," which consists in inspecting and monitoring equipment, and a strict technical and professional hierarchy, which has repercussions outside the workplace), a practice and a consciousness are formed that have a class character. The "local projection" of the technical hierarchy in the new town does not result in a dilution of the working class among shapeless and undivided strata.

(c) Until a fairly recent date, the "work environment" (or, preferably, the production process) resulted in complex human (social) relations that were content rich mainly because of the contact of workers themselves with tools and "matter."

The situation is changing today and is even showing signs of a reversal. The production process, at the cutting edge of technical progress, breaks the contact with "matter" and even with tools. It becomes monotonous, work changes into "non-work" (inspection and monitoring, as typified by the operator's console). Yet the unity of the process (continuous flow) stands out all the more clearly. The new working class, endowed by its role in production with a strong sense of social cohesion, seeks to create, "outside work," in the housing development, complex social relations that encompass cultural creativity. It reinvests in work a portion of this content, acquired outside work, in order to enrich it. Seen from this perspective, the new town offers many more possibilities than local spectral refraction in the new residences of the population of "spontaneous" cities (Aix-en-Provence, for example).

(a) In its own way and with its (modest) means, the "new working class" is initiating a struggle of immense importance against the wound of the modern world: boredom, the monotony of labor, the order of the functionalized, bureaucratized city.

How can we restore, by various means (theater, sport, organized games), the active ludic element? This phenomenon alone deserves a study of its own.

The struggle against boredom has begun. We don't know if this public enemy will be overcome. Yet the stakes [*enjeu*] and the fate of "modernity" depend—up to a certain point—on the outcome of this struggle.

Notes

[*Revue Française de Sociologie* 1, no. 2 (1960): 186–201, reprinted in *Du rural à l'urbain* (Paris: Anthropos, 1970), 109–28.—*Eds.*]

1. Robert Caillot, *L'usine, la terre et la cité* (Paris: Éditions Ouvrières, 1958).

2. A study on this subject has been carried out by I. Chiva. [Lefebvre is referring to Isac Chiva, and probably to his report *Les Communautés rurales: Problèmes, méthodes et exemples de la recherche* (Paris, UNESCO, 1958).—*Eds.*]

3. [Lefebvre would develop these claims in his book *Position: Contre les technocrats en finir avec l'humanitié-fiction* (Paris: Gonthier, 1967).—*Eds.*]

4. [Kurt Lewin (1890–1947) is often heralded as a founder of social psychology, with his major publications including *A Dynamic Theory of Personality*, trans. Donald K. Adams and Karl E. Zener (New York: McGraw-Hill, 1935).—*Eds.*].

5. [Jacob L. Moreno (1889–1974) was one of the leading social scientists of the twentieth century, founder of psychodrama and pioneer of group psychotherapy.—*Trans.*]

6. [François Perroux (1903–87) was a French economist and professor at the Collège de France. As well as his notion of *poles de croissance,* he was also known for his support of corporatism and criticism of Western programs for the developing world.—*Eds.*]

7. [Founded in 1816, Caisse des Dépôts et Consignations is a French public-sector financial institution responsible for a range of long-term economic development activities and management of public pension funds. Activities include investment in housing developments, business, the energy sector, and conservation. Its activities are local, national, and international in scope.—*Trans.*]

8. [Unfortunately, we have been unable to source this quotation. Since Lefebvre does not provide a reference, it is possible it was simply said to him.—*Eds.*]

9. [The reference is to Pitirim Sorokin (1889–1968), the Russian-born sociologist, and his reflections on excessive use of facts and figures derived from statistical or mathematical procedures and their inappropriate application in anthropology

and sociology. See Pitirim Sorokin, *Social and Cultural Dynamics*, 4 vols. (Cincinnati: American Book Company, 1937–41).—*Eds.*]

10. [The word *cité* in French can refer to a city proper, to the city core, or to a housing development or complex.—*Trans.*]

11. [Referring to the sociologist Paul Lazarsfeld (1901–76), a founding figure of twentieth-century empirical sociology.—*Eds.*]

12. [Referring to the sociologist Louis Guttman (1916–87) on social statistics, scale, and factor analysis.—*Eds.*]

13. Placed in quotes to indicate the risks of incautious use of the concept.

14. [The Société Coopérative d'Intérêt Collectif (SCIC, Cooperative Society of Collective Interest) is a multistakeholder legal entity structured as a cooperative and intended to serve local community interests. Its activities are generally socially relevant and pursued on a nonprofit basis.—*Trans.*]

15. [The Société nationale des petrôles d'Aquitaine (SNPA, National Petroleum Company of Aquitaine) was founded in 1941 to promote petroleum exploration in southwest France.—*Trans.*]

CHAPTER 11

Experimental Utopia
For a New Urbanism

"Even if it were possible for the individual to compensate, through energy and luck, for the initial mediocrity, it is essential that a people as a whole and with all its energy engage in this adventure between history and legend, between sun and ice, between metals and wave, between work and play, between necessity and fantasy, which can become its life on the threshold of this new age." These poetic lines, which evoke and provoke creativity, conclude the preface written by [Jean] Giraudoux for the Athens Charter.[1] They presage a programmatic approach compatible with the size of the modern world. They could serve as an epigraph to *Die neue Stadt* [The New City], the collection recently published in Zurich by a team of architects and sociologists, including Professors [Ernst] Egli, [Ernst] Winkler, and the architects [Werner] Aebli, [Eduard] Brühlmann, and [Rico] Christ.[2]

This magnificently illustrated volume summarizes the preparatory work for the construction of a new urban development: a city of approximately thirty thousand inhabitants in Furttal, not far from Zurich. The authors' project is specific, responding as it does to a set of known requirements. Nearly all fields of knowledge and scientific practice were used for earlier studies. Specialists carefully studied the soil and water of the Furttal valley, its microclimates, local production, and the social structure and history of existing villages. Other technicians, architects primarily, sought a comprehensive understanding of the problems of the new town. To that end, they made use of sociology. The enormous theoretical effort resulted in the detailed plans contained in this volume.

Its originality lies in the fact that its authors exceeded the scope of an estimate. They refused to be bound by the narrow standards of purely technical research, which architects and urbanists generally do when they prepare a block plan. The Zurich team addressed much larger problems. They sought to provide a methodology, a sociology, almost a philosophy of the New Town. Although they may not have achieved this, and although certain postulates and conclusions of this vast undertaking are questionable, as a whole it is of considerable merit.

Consciously or spontaneously, the authors of the project used the investigative procedures of programmatic thinking, which operates on virtual (possible) objects and compares them to experience, because it seeks to introduce the imagined object into practice, in short, to realize it. This approach also seeks to invent forms, but concrete forms. It does not disdain appeals to the imagination, but an imagination solicited and controlled by practical data. The method is one of *imaginary variations* around themes and requirements defined by the real in the broadest sense of the term: by problems presented by reality and the virtualities it contains. This manages to avoid two possible risks, two dead ends. On the one hand, it avoids a purely empirical finding (or one that claims to be), which is limited to recording and then extrapolating from what it has found in its attempt to conceive the possible. On the other hand, it avoids a priori constructions; in the present case, the abstract utopia that describes the ideal city, without any relation to specific situations. The method meanders between pure practice and pure theorization. To refer to these operations of rational thought, to employ them coherently, don't we require a vocabulary, concepts, and a methodology? We could use the term "transduction" to refer to a reasoning process that is neither deductive nor inductive, one that constructs a virtual object on the basis of information about reality and a specific problematic (it is in an analogous sense that the well-known theoretician of information, Benoît Mandelbrot, uses this term).[3] We could also call "experimental utopia" the exploration of the human possible, with the help of the image and the imaginary, together with an ongoing critique and ongoing reference to the problematic found in the "real." Experimental utopia exceeds the customary use of hypothetical reasoning in the social sciences.

The reader of *Die neue Stadt* eagerly scans the summary of projects for new or ideal cities from the sixteenth century to the present day (pages 51 and 59: figures and plates 94 to 117). He will learn that [Albrecht] Dürer drew plans for cities that were harmonious, rational, and functional based on the ideas and needs of the time. He will discover or rediscover the originality of somewhat forgotten works, those of [Claude-Nicolas] Ledoux, or the great utopian socialists, [Robert] Owen and [Charles] Fourier.[4] Professor Egli, the author of this chapter, demonstrates the determined historical nature of projects that were intended to be or assumed they were timeless and final. He also shows the growing importance of sociology in bringing together and organizing the data for the problems raised, data that is both local and general.

Several project variants are prepared and compared from different points of view: use of surfaces, reciprocal relations between clusters and the interior centers of the city, relation between the city and its surroundings and the rest of the countryside. Before the finalization and comparison of variants, several projects that scattered the planned development across the Furttal or that included a second development were eliminated. An initial set of choices resulted in identifying the contours of a model. A second set of choices subjected the variants of the model to already experimental criteria. The "prospective" consideration of a final development of the city, the valley, and the region (Zürich) played a large part in the process. The final variant responded—or, at least, is claimed to respond—to a totality of actual or potential imperatives. On the one hand, it becomes part of a strategy, that of regional and national growth. On the other hand, it represents—or, at least, is said to represent—the desirable optimum.

Under the title "Planung des Wohnens [Housing Plan]," the working group prepared a grid of needs that the development had to satisfy. In this double-entry table, the rows present and rank the sociological levels or degrees in question: individual, family, neighborhood, quarter. The columns establish and rank needs, from food to culture and leisure. Based on this first grid, Egli and Winkler prepared a carefully designed and quantified infrastructure grid: occupied surface area, essential services at different stages or degrees (pages 33 to 41).[5]

It should also be pointed out that the execution of the project was supposed to unfold dynamically. At each phase of the operation, on site, the completed section would comprise both habitations and infrastructure. But in doing so, does it avoid the scandals of those "large-scale developments" in which the inhabitants flowed in without providing them with schools, stores, or group services, other than those hastily improvised in cheap sheds? One can only hope. In any event, the Zürich team provides a model of serious, honest, and intelligent effort. During the metamorphosis to rationally programmed stages of the new city, the old village, partly preserved and incorporated, plays an important role. It serves as the core and center for services and infrastructure during construction.

A central theme draws the reader's attention. The project escapes the limits of empiricism, practicalism, and pure technicity. Its main concern is mankind. In fact, it offers human beings a program of everyday life. It does not limit itself to providing future inhabitants with a framework and a décor, a relatively rigid or flexible framework, a somewhat successful décor. It seeks to offer them multiple, rationally ordered means for accessing the growth of the individual and small groups within the community. It offers harmony. On the basis of this program, it assumes a moral responsibility. In this sense, the Zürich team reflects the ideas of Le Corbusier and the Athens Charter. The City assumes functions that were already ambitiously defined by the Declaration of La Sarraz: "The three essential functions whose fulfillment urbanism must ensure are: 1) inhabiting, 2) working, 3) re-creating the self. Its objects are: a) occupation of the land, b) the organization of traffic, c) legislation." The functions considered must be dissociated to the extent possible. For example, the modern urbanist will assign different traffic routes to automobiles and to pedestrians. Then, a subsequent project will reorganize the functions initially identified into a comprehensive whole. It is clear that the school of Le Corbusier has conceived and conceives the City as the sensible and tangible form of an essential content: the complete satisfaction of human needs. It seeks to create the conditions of a true community.

The programmatic approach thus defined comprises an ideology, which is itself supported by sociological arguments. More specifically, the sociological schema supports the technical project, the practical living program, and the implicit ideology. This schema is simple and clear. The development, conceived as a community, encompasses a hierarchy of levels or degrees. These levels or degrees can be easily integrated because they are already the constituent elements of the social totality: the individual (not the isolated or isolatable individual but the first element of the totality: *Einzelmensch*); the family; the immediate neighborhood (*Nachbarschaft*, approximately 200 persons on 0.9 hectares of land); the neighboring group (*Nachbarschaftsgruppe*, 600 persons on approximately 2.7 hectares); the small district (1,800 persons on 9 hectares); the district (7,200 persons on 40 hectares); the city (consisting of one or more districts).

It is a systematic approach based on the establishment of this hierarchy. Before it can be used technically to prepare grids, principles are formulated—for the integrated hierarchy, for the constitution of kernels (*Kerne*) at each level, and, finally, for the visibility or supervision of the whole from the summit, the integrated ensemble that becomes sensible, legible, and tangible in on-site construction projects (*Prinzip der Stufung, Prinzip der Überschaubarkeit, Prinzip der Kernbildung* [Principles of gradation, manageability, core formation], 32). As stated, these principles are not only the conceptual expression of the schema; they dominate it. They are operational and structural or, rather, "structuring." They must determine in the community, more and better than an organization or an institution, an equilibrium that is both stable and living, a kind of self-regulation.

Therefore, the functions of integration apply to all levels with perfect consistency: physical life, spiritual life, collective life, from the need for food to the need for political activity, including science, religion, and art. The structural integration, projected onto the land, incorporating a program of action as a life program, creates, for each degree and each function, an effective core, a kind of organizing center. As conceived by the authors, the ascending and descending scale of cores, zones of contact, and communication confers a living structure on the city. Partial cores are formed from small commercial or cultural centers intercalated between elementary groups and the principal center of the community.

In practice, this schema is more relaxed. It leaves room for the individual, whether isolated or seeking solitude; those human beings whom circumstances have cast into solitude or who prefer isolation are not considered "deviants."

Nonetheless, the concept of a hierarchy as strictly integrated with levels and cores causes some concern.

Methodologically, shouldn't we distinguish several approaches: the technical approach of the architect who considers the apartment, then the building, then the group of buildings before combining them; the analytic approach, which seeks to move from the simple to the complex; the dialectical approach, which seeks to grasp through concepts the general and the total in relation to "the elements" and the future?

The confusion between these approaches risks leaving gaps in our knowledge and masking them. According to the proposed schema, where do we find insertion into the overall society? Where do we find a way into totality? This schema represents a totality. It is sufficient in itself. The frequent reference to the landscape, to the country, to the Swiss as a people, culture, and nation cannot replace a comprehensive grasp of "industrial society" or a national variant of that industrial society.

The reader of *Die neue Stadt* remains unsated. It is unclear just who is going to work in the New City, nor how or why, in which branches of industry, with what standard of living, or with what salaries or benefits, budgets, possibilities, openings, or obstructions. How do these economic data affect the integration so deeply sought? One could reply that other, specifically economic, studies will eventually flesh out the project. Perhaps. But in thus bracketing the economic element in the outline of the program, we move without realizing it from an already questionable sociological schema to a kind of "sociologism" that is even more unilateral and questionable. In this hierarchy, so strongly integrated and structured into levels, other levels are erased: the economic and the psychic, the spontaneous, the informal. More specifically, how will the social ensemble act on the desires or opinions—or, if you will, on the attitudes and aptitudes and behaviors—of the members of a local community? How would the differences in professional categories, social layers and classes, manifest themselves? Couldn't we anticipate that industrial workers, laborers, or technicians might have specific needs or desires that are hardly dissimilar from those of other categories of inhabitant? In short, social man cannot be defined solely by habitat. The schema postulates this assumption without further explanation.

The hierarchical integration thus assumes a simplified theory of needs and functions. We populate the community with families the same way we orchestrate the functions of the city with elementary needs attributed to the different levels. Is it certain that this "federalist" and hierarchical construction is the tangible expression, in everyday life, of the freedom and style of democratic life?[6]

The ideology of hierarchical integration is apparent in physical construction. Those who designed the project know that monotony would have to be avoided if they wished to prevent boredom. They discovered that shortcuts to addressing the problem, for example, by alternating horizontal lines (blocks) and vertical lines (towers), did not succeed. They then made use of all the known types of houses and high-rises, small and large, low and high, straight and curved (*Punkthäuser, Kulissenhäuser, Turmhäuser,* etc.). On the site, they juxtaposed a variety of forms that risked becoming mechanical or simply "plastic," and failed to break the monotony. Didn't the desire for surprise and variety, especially important in modern life, demand bolder initiatives? And to determine its potential satisfactions, wouldn't it be necessary to escape what those involved claim to be "desirable" and what sociological methods of empirical and subjective investigation tend to overestimate? When consulted, the inhabitants want to find the things they are accustomed to. At the same time, and more profoundly, they want surprise, diversity, novelty.

There is a certain naivete in Le Corbusier's early projects. He grouped buildings around "civic centers." Today, we know all too well that such centers could easily become the functional and operational "core" of a bureaucracy that would closely monitor the integration of the community.

Do we not find a similar naivete in the idea of "crowning" the New City with an Academy that would provide spaces to members of the community with artistic vocations (65–66)? Of course, the project is not absurd and reveals an extreme sense of goodwill, entirely deserving of our esteem. Could such a "crowning" effort play the role of the Acropolis, the Temple of Jerusalem, the Mozarthaus in Salzburg? Would it be the soul of the City or the animator of souls?

In historical cities, monuments possess such complex functions that the concept of "function" cannot exhaust them. They remind us and call out to us. They make present a past and a future. They unite and combine: cathedral, palace, theater, various edifices. They are covered in symbols, generally poorly understood, and fading from generation to generation, but so rich that the so-called aesthetic perception most often achieves merely the shadow of such symbolism. The tourist who admires the beautiful proportions of a cathedral does not see it as a microcosm, a summary of the world, of history, and of the human drama according to Catholic doctrine. For such a "function," we make use of words like "transfunctional" or "suprafunctional." Such monuments are not useless. If they no longer serve a purpose, they overflow their functions (gathering together, organizing) as well as the institutions they represent locally (authorities, agencies, etc.). To turn to the theory of information, we can say that monuments in a historical city rise above redundancy, repetition, the systems of signs and signals that govern routines. They sit on top of the semiologic systems that constitute the fabric of the everyday social text: discourse, clothing, gestures, street theater. They say more. They have greater meaning. They express the inexhaustible.

Just as the idea of "crowning" the City with a monument seems proper and profound, the idea of giving a too clearly defined cultural building this "suprafunctional" task appears questionable. To resolve the problem, shouldn't we reinvent or imagine several monuments or several types of monuments? Shouldn't we differentiate the City in ways other than by homogenous districts? Shouldn't we create the polycentric city? Because *Die neue Stadt* alluded to the ancient city and its "monumental crown," we should bear in mind that it organized social time and space around several centers of activity: the agora, the stadium, the temple or acropolis, the theater. Cyclical and rhythmic time was regulated by the most widespread forms of collective interest.

This solution no longer has meaning. Cyclical and rhythmic time, in industrial society, has not disappeared; it has become subordinated to the linear or discontinuous time demanded by technology. Its rhythms and cycles no longer possess the regular and regulating character they had before industrial society. Neither the ancient city, in spite of its beauty, nor the medieval city, in spite of its prodigious vitality, can supply us with models. This does not mean we can ignore the suggestions they provide, however: polycentrism, dynamic structuring, the complementarity of elements rather than their segregation.

I have criticized the project in some detail to emphasize its interest, although it appears to leave aside the social importance of play. In a way I would once again call naive, it leads us to believe that nature, both controlled and developed—green spaces, forests, walks—is sufficient to satisfy the desire for variety and play.

Le Corbusier's earlier projects go further. They distributed, among all the spaces and sectors of the planned town, basketball courts, tennis courts, soccer fields, pools, and tracks. From the point of view alone of sporting activities, a stadium outside the town is inadequate. Similarly, it is not enough to plan areas for local festivities (although this concern is to the credit of the authors of *Die neue Stadt*).

Play is multifaceted and multiple. Leisure and play are not exactly the same. And isn't it play that completes and is the culmination of sociability? It distributes its diversity and inventiveness among activities that are integrated into everyday life, within the family, and in getaways to distant places, departures, vacations, camping trips to mountainside and seashore. There are countless intermediaries: games of skill or chance, games in cafés (cards, pool, jukeboxes) or clubs, games serious (chess) and frivolous (betting, etc.), as well as window shopping, derided by many urbanists, simple gossip, and many others. Play doesn't correspond to any elementary need, although it presupposes them all. Rather, it corresponds to refined and clearly differentiated desires, based on the individual and the group, desires that are quickly extinguished by monotony and the lack of possibility.

Following the paradigm constructed around the family as social cell, members of the community do not get much or frequent amusement; they rarely play. A terribly serious form of culturalism reigns over this ensemble, integral with functionalism, structuralism, paternalism, and possibly a certain technocratic ideology as well. Along with this culturalism we find a disturbing sense of moralism, which exists not only in Switzerland and Zürich. Technicians, in their disdain for leisure and their wish for a better organized social life, forget that the café serves less for the purpose of intoxication than for friendly get-togethers and games. There are very few cafés in the new towns and large-scale developments. It is in this way that "operative" schemas, which are theoretically questionable because they are unilateral, produce conformity in practice and that hierarchical integration is accompanied by a moral danger as well as boredom.

This leads us to, or leads us back to, the fundamental question of children and adolescents. Is it possible to set aside certain experiences for the sake of a sociological paradigm said to reflect reality and the ideal of democratic freedom? In Israel especially, although to a lesser degree than the countries of the East, there is an attempt to provide children with a specific social life, without separating them from the family or society as a whole. This is justified by the activities that are characteristic of children and adolescents (especially games) as well as their place in the overall society as distinct groups with their own problems. We know that children and adolescents, when they have a relatively autonomous life, connect other partial groups instead of separating them.

Perhaps these experiments have not yet resulted in entirely satisfactory results. Still, we need to take them into account. They do not destroy the family as often claimed; they do alter the accepted paradigm, which fetishizes the family and the neighborhood and transforms them into social entities, into basic elements and the foundations of the integrated whole, baptized a "community."

As well, this sociological paradigm risks confusing an important question, that of the *optimum*. A remarkable study recently conducted in cities in northern France suggests the existence of norms that are quite different from those accepted by the authors of Die neue Stadt. Based on this research, the optimum resulting in the smooth operation of large-scale collective services (well-equipped hospitals, universities, theaters) is found when there are approximately 300,000 inhabitants, with an active and productive population, workers for the most part, of approximately 60 percent. Only a structure of this kind would provide the essential resources needed to prevent the urban complex from constantly having to rely on outside funding. "The optimum agglomeration was sought solely as a function of the population alone. Yet, we have shown that the social structure played a more important role than population."[7]

Which is to say that the problematic of new towns is yet to be resolved.

Notes

[*Revue Française de Sociologie* 2, no. 3 (1961): 191–98, reprinted in *Du rural à l'urbain* (Paris: Anthropos, 1970), 129–40.—Eds.]

1. The work of Le Corbusier and his team, assembled for the International Congress of Modern Architecture (CIAM [Congrès Internationaux d'Architecture Moderne]), in Athens in 1933. Preceded by the Déclaration de la Sarraz (Vaud, Switzerland, 1928). Published in 1941 in Paris, during the occupation, without the author's name. Republished in 1958 by Éditions de Minuit.

2. *Die neue Stadt: Eine Studie für das Fürttal* (Zurich: Bauen und Wohnen, 1961).

3. See [*La*] *Lecture de l'expérience* (Paris: Presses Universitaires de France, 1955), 43, especially the section on "psychological transductors." [This book was co-authored by Mandelbrot with A. R. Jonckheere and Jean Piaget, and was actually published in 1958.—Eds.]

4. [Lefebvre would edit the collection *Actualité de Fourier: Colloque d'Arcs-et-Senans sous la direction de Henri Lefebvre* (Paris: Anthropos, 1975).—Eds.]

5. It would be useful to compare these infrastructure grids with those published in France by the review *Urbanism* (62–63, 1959). The Swiss team advanced quite far in the analysis of services (business, medical, dental, etc.) and the surface areas needed for streets, traffic, parking, and so on.

6. *Die neue Stadt*, 32.

7. P. Pinchemel, A. Vakili, and J. Gozzi, *Niveaux optima des villes: Essai de définition [d'après l'Analyse des Structures Urbaines du Nord et du Pas-de-Calais]* (Lille: Ceres, Faculté de Droit, 1959).

CHAPTER 12

The Valley of Campan

A Study in Historical Sociology

Introduction

The Valley of Campan is of definite interest for the historical and sociological study of the peasant community (agro-pastoral).[1]

The valley itself comprises several villages and hamlets (Campan, Sainte-Marie-de-Campan, la Séoube, etc.); these villages have always been and remain organized as a solid unit, with its center in Campan. In this case, the federation of villages, the valley community, coincides in Campan with the village community. The Valley of Campan itself stands against the Pic du Midi and Pic du Néouvielle. These two chains separate it from the Spanish valleys. Campan is the last French community in these mountains in the direction of Spain. For a long time, it has benefited from being a *march* or border community, without having suffered the drawbacks or borne the costs (nor has it had the strategic importance), since the nearly uncrossable summits separate it from the other slope. The navigable pathways pass through the neighboring valley, known as the Vallée d'Aure. Campan, therefore, has had certain privileges as a *borderland community* without having lost its pastoral nature and without having been subjected to a permanent military authority (and consequently without having had the benefits and misfortunes of "trails" placed near an important passage or pass [*col*]).

Finally, the Valley of Campan is largely open to the influences of the plain, the village itself being roughly five kilometers from Bagnères-de-Bigorre, a hot spring dating from Roman times, with a market located at the foot of the mountains as they meet the plain. The Valley of Campan reveals a remarkable intermingling of customary law and written (Roman) law, of montagnard traditions and the influences that are dissolving them.

For centuries the valley held an originality and independence that were nearly complete. It remained a kind of quasi-autonomous pastoral republic, a "free valley," one of those small, archaic Pyrenean states of which Andorra is the last living example. But at the same time, it was never isolated, never separated from the general history of the province (Bigorre and Navarre), the region (Southwest France, source of the ancient parliaments of Toulouse and Pau), or of the *généralités* of Auch and France.[2]

For these reasons, and others that will become clear, it is worth individual study (in connection with the study of Pyrenean communities and the peasant community in general).

The community of Campan is located at the limit of the primary axial zone of the Pyrenees. Blocks of ancient rocks (Hercynian) rise on either side of the Adour but, primarily, to the south of the valley. Consequently, it offers a highly varied terrain: granitic rock, mediocre pasturage (schist, sometimes favorable, primarily on the highlands of the Tourmalet, which connects Campan to Barèges), and areas of Devonian limestone, which harbor magnificent prairies, especially on the Col d'Aspin, connecting Campan with Arreau (Vallée d'Aure).

The valley is part of a broad syncline known as the "Arreau syncline" and, along its length (about twenty kilometers), runs parallel to the general direction of the upthrust. But the succession of basins and defiles that it reveals has no direct relation with the upthrust. The relief has been profoundly disturbed and shaped by glaciers and by water. Between the valleys, we find "mature" surfaces affected by erosion, ridges with shallow or almost horizontal slopes (high-altitude plateaus). Thus, between Aure and Campan, at the foot of the Arbizon, there is no significant natural obstacle. This led to secular disputes over the possession of summer pasture lands [*estives*].

Henri Cavaillès has written that in Campan we find "the appearance of a valley, structural and rather open, in carboniferous shale, between the exterior front and the ancient massifs."[3]

The river has nearly eliminated the structural valley; the soil, hollowed out by the glaciers of the Arbizon, the Pic du Midi, Pic du Néouvielle, and the Adour, has been raised. Campan (and Bagnères) are found very much above the nearest neighboring valley, that of Arros. In the Valley of Campan itself, the important hamlet of Séoube is located on a glacial alluvial cone near the mouth of the Aspin peak. Nowhere does the attraction of glacial deposits "appear as evident as in the high valley of Campan. The morainic cone extending before Sainte-Marie—between the two branches of the Adour—is invested on all sides by homes and barns."[4]

These morainic beds, these deposits spread over the hillsides or accumulated in the bottoms, provide the best land for a predominantly pastoral existence. This is especially true of Campan.

> None of these deposits has been better utilized than this one. The glacier that produced it was not very powerful but it was easily able to develop its bottom moraine in a broadly hollowed-out basin, in soil consisting of carboniferous shale, between the large crystalline massifs of the south and the calcareous peaks along the border. In the deep and gently inclined confined groundwater between Gripp and Payole and Sainte-Marie-de-Campan, extend prairies that are likely the largest and best maintained in the Pyrenees.[5]

Here, we have to ask about the qualities of those who were able to take advantage of this favorable soil; and we have to seek the historical and sociological conditions in which those qualities appeared.

The Valley of Campan, therefore, provides a great variety of features in a relatively limited physical span: highly varied altitudes from the bottom of the valley (606 meters) to the Pic du Midi, contrasting climates that vary with the terrain, the exposure, and the corridor. To the south, the ancient high rocks have lost all plant soil, which the runoff from melting snow has washed away into the valley over the course of the years. Above these bare surfaces we find a zone of nutrient-poor grassland, pine trees, beech (Niclade pine forest, the forest of Mourgoueilh), followed by a region of rich, irrigated prairies.

To the north, a high limestone peak, blindingly white and dry (the Haboura Peak), slopes toward magnificent natural grasslands (in the direction of the Col d'Aspin).

Above Sainte-Marie (900 meters), the harvest doesn't begin until August 8, that is, two weeks after the bottom of the valley. Corn, on well-exposed slopes, grows at elevations that can reach 1,200 meters. Overall, the climate of the valley is characterized by extreme humidity (nearly 1,500 centimeters of rain near the Pic du Midi, with the maximum rainfall occurring near 1,800 meters). The humid winds from the northwest sweep the Valley of Campan and the Col d'Aspin. Whereas the vegetation in the Aure Valley still has southern or Mediterranean plants (thyme), the Valley of Campan is clearly Atlantic: apple trees, beech trees, pine, English oak, ash. This results in a clearly defined pastoral lifestyle. "The Valley of Campan produces butter and cider, just like Normandy."[6] Because of the humidity, the forests and prairies are always threatened by the invasion of epiphytes and mosses. This is especially true in the midlevel regions, which receive the most moisture, essential in spring and autumn pasturage and frequently providing hay meadows. Unusable plants and trees rapidly replace the grassland with heaths (blueberries, heather). This danger, coupled with the number of cattle, made the strict organization of pastoral life necessary—essentially collective or "communitarian."

It should be noted that lower-level pasturage determined the formation of villages that are currently partly abandoned (village of Peyras). The same variety, and the same contrasts that make the Valley of Campan so remarkable, are found in its hydrography.

The white limestone peaks in the south have been barely affected by stream beds, which are almost always dry. In the north, on the contrary, floods have cut and shaped a series of ridges, where each argilo-siliceous area gives rise to a forest. The Adour (a very old generic name) is formed by the meeting at Sainte-Marie of the branches of the Adour that run

The Valley of Campan

through La Séoube and Cabadur (Caput Adurris), which are joined by the Adour of Lesponne where they emerge.[7]

For centuries the Valley of Campan has been celebrated for its beauty, the originality of the houses (with their terraced roofs), its organization, and by the character of its inhabitants.[8] Travelers to the region have used expressions such as "the Happy Valley," "the Valley of Tempe," or "the New Arcadia" to describe the area and have been eager to recount their impressions at the very moment the voyage appeared most difficult, most distant (from Paris), and almost as exotic as the ascent of Anapurna today. Below we reproduce some of those accounts, but only those that have a documentary interest.

Chapter 1. Traditional Organization

Rather than returning to the general problems of the peasant community, I will simply note that it is characterized by the following:

(a) the combination, in variable proportions, of collective ownership and individual ownership (proportions that vary quantitatively and qualitatively, that is, in terms of the rights of the collective or community to various forms of private property and fixed assets).

(b) collective disciplines governing the schedule of work, crops, pastoral life, irrigation, the use of forests, and so on. In the case of agro-pastoral communities like that of Campan, these disciplines are both very simple and very complicated. They always involve allowing livestock access to pasturage at low, medium, and high altitudes on specific dates, of closing them on other dates (*vètes*), and preventing overgrazing.

(c) autonomous or quasi-autonomous administration, generally involving the appointment of agents who, without a division of power, have an authority that is administrative, judicial, fiscal, economic, and political but remains subject (more or less) to the direct control of the community.

The importance of collective ownership in Campan remains considerable in spite of the takeover, removal, and sale of communal assets. Based on the data gathered on site and the figures prepared by specialists, the territory of Campan covers roughly 9,535 hectares.[9] Of this total surface area, 25 percent, 2,400 hectares, belongs to individuals and is privately held, and 75 percent, 7,135 hectares, belongs to the commune. Given that the takeovers and dispossessions date back to the eighteenth century and beyond, we can state that collective ownership has, since time immemorial (as the saying goes), taken precedence over private ownership in Campan. This is an essential, even a primordial, feature of a peasant community; all the other features follow from and are related to this form of ownership; possession and collective use effectively require an administration, an organization, a police, and discipline.

The traditional organization of Campan, its local customs, are summarized in a series of texts, the most important of which is a census from 1629:

> "The King of France, Sovereign Lord and Count of Bigorre, has ordered the review, inspection, recounting, reform, and renewal of his rights across all domains." The Chambre des Comptes of Navarre, therefore, will investigate and collate "said neglected domains, prepare a cadastral survey, and recognition of all lands held by His Majesty as fiefs or commons," upon the "receipt of a statement of enumeration" throughout the extent of his holdings.

Under the stimulus of an already authoritarian and powerful central power, these inspections became much stricter than in previous periods.

They were carried out carefully but slowly. After two years, two "commissaires généraux" were appointed to reform the region, coupled with threats and "proceedings for negligence," a year after the convocation began of "vassals and long-term leaseholders in possession of assets belonging to His Majesty." In fact, the search did not actually begin until two officials, a farmer general and a sub-farmer general, took matters into their own hands.

But it was only in 1629 that Campan rose up following a feudal seizure carried out on July 2 by the crown's prosecutor of all the assets belonging to the crown—which is to say, the collective properties of the community—so that all benefits became illegal or illegitimate from that moment on. There then assembled, "convoked by the sound of the church bell according to custom," the guards and municipal magistrates (or *consuls*; both titles were in use) as well as a number of inhabitants of high standing (it should be pointed out that the leaders of the community didn't feel it was necessary to convene a general assembly; rather, they called a special meeting, which bore the official name of "Conseil juré"). The members of this assembly agreed "jointly for the entire community and renouncing division and discussion," which seems to indicate that the controversy was a matter of great concern. They appointed, before the royal notary of Campan, two syndics, that is, two official delegates with clear instructions for a specific purpose. These two syndics, "special and general, neither of whom could override the other," were responsible for settling the matter as best they could. They were Marc Perrier, guard, and Guilhaume Carrère, notary and first consul, who were provided with a "syndical" legal instrument giving them full authorization to act. They traveled to Pau to obtain relief of the feudal seizure, make a signed declaration listing the assets belonging to the crown, and pay all taxes, fees, and fines. Two surgeons, François Ducay and Jean Lafforgue, served as guarantors and pledged their own assets as surety.

The procedure says a great deal about the resistance of local traditions and franchises to the orders and encroachments of centralized power, about the feudal nature of the means of action and certain resources of the monarch and the new state, and on the workings of the community in the seventeenth century, already dominated by a rural bourgeoisie and, therefore, already in decline and disposed, in spite of its reticence, to submit. There follows a detailed assessment beginning with determining local boundaries, a description of the limits of the community of Campan, determination of its possessions as a community, and the rights and possessions belonging to it in the territory of the neighboring communities: Bagnères, Asté, Baudéan (we have not reproduced this tedious enumeration).

This document (along with the attached entitlements, serving as a catalog of privileges, freedoms, and franchises, and a description of the "customary" usages of the community) requires comment. It is striking because of its ambiguity and incompleteness.

In terms of its ambiguity, the bureaucrats of Campan patently developed this to serve as a legal instrument in their silent struggle against royal power, but one they fought only procedurally, having, as members of a bourgeoisie integrated into the ranks of the new centralized state, already abandoned all other forms of resistance.

They manipulated the multiplicity of jurisdictions, not only to exploit the rivalry between judges from Tarbes and Bagnères but especially that of the parliaments. There is some hidden irony in the fact that the Campan representatives reminded the commissioners of Navarre that they were making an appeal before the parliament of Toulouse.

The representatives of the community of Campan recognized the king, their immediate lord, as the source of high, medium, and low justice. The consuls of Campan, therefore, would have access to only a portion of that low justice, corresponding to basic policing activities (minor infractions up to 65 sous in damages, according to custom). But how then would they have the right to imprison the guilty? How would these consuls have the right to apply the so-called major law? The text masks this expropriation with a clever pretext—only in cases of nonpayment of taxes or fraud would they have recourse to the King's services. In fact, it's clear that the inhabitants of Campan were accustomed to assuming responsibility for their own administration. They cleverly defended this self-administration of the community and even more cleverly made sure that the magistrates and merchants who had assumed responsibility for it would benefit.

The incomplete character of their approach is typified by the fact that there is nothing about the organization of pastoral life or the irrigation syndicates. For the inhabitants of Campan, these were internal matters about which the king (a direct but distant master) had nothing to say. Nor was anything said about the distribution of taxes, concerning which the king was the foremost interested party. We have to consult other texts, notably the "Cahiers de Délibération" of the community, to obtain information about such matters.

Having said this, the document does establish the situation of the community. The community is a collective seigneury of commoners [*seigneurie roturière et collective*]. Not only did it possess (through the influence of the king, its immediate and direct lord, whose vassals they were—as was the entire kingdom, for that matter) all of its lands, but it owned them "nobly," which is to say, without any fiscal obligation, a mountain purchased with all the rights of a nobleman. As their immediate lord, they paid the king a fee and held long-term leases [*affièvements*] with him. The community had the right or power to intervene in the armed conflicts among the lords and could point to a kind of contract of alliance entered into in 1604 with the neighboring lord, Baron de Castelbajac.[10] As a seigniorial domain, the community had certain rights, rather poorly defined, of jurisdiction, policing, and administration. In principle, all the powers belonged to the *véziau*, the general assembly. There was either no or a very imprecise division of powers. The consuls were judges, administrators, political leaders, representatives of the community before the higher political bodies (the États de Bigorre). Although the "guards" were mostly tax collectors and treasurers (in fact, this function already required a suitably wealthy candidate, one with sufficient working capital, which the position enriched), these "guards" shared their responsibilities and powers with the consuls. They appointed a "manamenté," a representative with permanent powers who served to carry out seizures and make arrests.

The terms negotiated with royal power were quite ingenious. The king was represented in the community by a *baile*, or administrator, who purchased the position. But the *baile* had to swear an oath before the general assembly of all the members of the community. The Cahiers reveal that, in spite of certain conflicts of interest, the *baile* in question bought and paid for his position with the approval of the representatives of the community. In general he was an inhabitant there. For greater certainty, a *sous-baile* was appointed to serve under him, functioning in the *baile*'s place if he were absent or refused to act, that is, in case of a conflict of interest.

The guards and consuls enacted seigniorial rights on behalf of the community. They owned mills (for flour and to full cloth). They approved the appointment of the parish priest by the bishop but appointed the *marguilliers* (administrators of the Church's assets) as well as the school principal, and awarded the prebendary with a small benefit (chapel) located in Campan. They housed the curé and the vicars, taxed merchandise, and owned the taverns, butcher shops, and mills. In this way, the seigniorial community of commoners controlled local commerce and industry, although there wasn't much of it. It closely controlled the local market. Outside the holdings of the community, production (agricultural, pastoral, the production of bread, clothing, etc.) was strictly familial and artisanal.

Of course, it is, at least theoretically, the community, that is to say, the general assembly of neighbors, or *véziau*, that held these powers and assets. Guards and consuls were simply delegates, appointees, representatives.

As for the individuals, they are also "fiévataires," or leaseholders. Their rights are included in the terms of the fief and general long-term leases. In their case, the word "fief" refers only to the right of ownership, limited by the seigneury of the community and that of the king: perpetual ownership (leasehold). The lords held the eminent property, the direct domain being superimposed on the "utilitarian" one, and upon the condition that usage taxes (*droits de fief*) and transaction fees ("lods et ventes," known as "Capsos" in the region) were paid.

The usage tax was paid collectively, which implies that the community, as such, represented all the asset owners and through them held their rights. Here, we can observe the entanglement of titles and rights typical of feudal and customary relations, one that was incompatible with ownership as defined by Roman law and the modern civil code. Each parcel of land belonged simultaneously to an individual (more specifically, a family), to the community, and to the seigneur (here, the king), but for various reasons and under different modalities.

The community held all its territory, collective assets, and private assets, but among the latter its rights were reduced and tightly limited by individual appropriation (more precisely, familial).

The great skill of the petit bourgeoisie (notaries, lawyers, merchants, doctors and surgeons) who governed Campan lay in integrating the community into the system of feudal and seigniorial relationships that remained the backbone of the Ancien Régime. In so doing, they preserved within the community as such a degree of cohesion, an existence, and a reality that was already somewhat reduced and would continue to slowly diminish. In this way, they also integrated themselves as a local bourgeoisie into this system. In spite of the frictions and conflicts, they became its support; they applied and would increasingly come to apply the laws. They became the instrument of a kind of *refeudalization* of relationships following the great upheavals of the previous centuries (especially the sixteenth and the first half of the seventeenth), upheavals that resulted in an absolute monarchical State. It was as if this local bourgeoisie had purchased offices, including noble offices (guards and consuls in Campan had the right to wear the robe and cap by a decision of the Parliament of Toulouse of April 9, 1633). But it was the community that gave them—freely—these functions, which were both honorific and lucrative. However, they often became costly, even overwhelming, when the king forced them to pay and sought among high-ranking citizens those who would assume responsibility for an increasingly heavy tax burden. In return for these advantages, they put their talents, activity, and sometimes their assets at the service of the community.

This document, therefore, determines the traditional organization of the community only as a function of a clearly determined group of intersecting interests.

Below, I'll illustrate certain features of this arrangement by situating these economic and political interactions within the general history of the community. It is primarily the Cahiers de Délibération that provides the documentation on the internal and concrete life of this pastoral republic, one engaged in a secular struggle for its integrity and autonomy.

Chapter 2. The Struggle for the Integrity of the Territory

For centuries, perhaps millennia, the members of the community struggled to occupy the space comprised between their "natural borders," that is, to remain masters in their valley and also to escape those borders and invade their neighbors, who behaved similarly. The struggle was as complex as the struggle of peoples and nations. With the proviso that we are deflecting the word from its precise, modern meaning, we could speak (for lack of something better) of a kind of imperialism of the agro-pastoral community.

There is a concrete basis to this: because the pastures were rapidly being degraded by the large number of livestock, the extent of the high mountain pastures and especially the intermediate zones (spring and autumn pasturages, which are reduced in the Pyrenees because of the shape of the sloping hills) determine the quantity and quality of livestock.

Feed had also to be found for the livestock in winter, and the amount of this feed is determined by the surface area of the hay meadows. In 1813 the prefect, Laboulinière, correctly noted the importance of an appropriate balance between winter and summer resources as well as the fact that the montagnard always fails to recognize this balance, raising too many livestock on the high mountain pastures and expecting too much from summer pastures. The "pastoral imperialism" I referred to above assumes its most violent form when the community succeeds in overturning these balances and limits, in acquiring rights on the plain and organizing winter (or "reverse") migration. This was not the case in Campan, which quickly found that every passage to the open plains was closed off by other powerful communities (including Bagnères). This pastoral imperialism, with its long and sometimes bloody conflicts, can be found in the history of the Bearnese valleys more than in Campan. We know that Béarn was one of the places that provided support for the power and government of the princes of Béarn, who used and subjugated the city.

Therefore, the struggle of the inhabitants of Campan was essentially one for the integrity of their territory, threatened by less-favored communities and by the activity of their leaders. There were two aspects to this struggle for integrity: to hold the territory found between the valley's natural borders, the slopes, in other words, the entire valley; and to become its masters and freely exercise the customs and collectively organized practices of pastoral life, together with a small amount of agricultural production. Those two aspects cannot be separated.

It would be wrong to think that this struggle was always pacific, diplomatic, or legal. It resulted in serious incidents where enterprising leaders, consuls, or seigneurs took control of the management of neighboring communities. This was especially true when conflict broke out with the four federated villages known as the "Quatre Véziaux" over the large but poorly defined pasturages found between the Aure Valley and that of Campan. The conflict became violent when a hotheaded seigneur, the Sire de Castelbajac, got involved in the quarrel, leading to a pitched battle (in 1599). The concept of a "natural border" played the same role in this bit of local history as it did in the larger one: partly justified, partly arbitrary, its meaning was largely determined by a specific economic and political structure.

We should not dismiss the struggles between these small communities. It was only belatedly that the illustrious quarrels between Rome and its neighbors assumed a heroic grandeur. There is no inherent difference between the combat of the Horatii and the Curiatii and a legal battle between Campan and the Quatre Véziaux of Aure other than that the first has been magnified and transformed by legend, whereas the second has become no more than an obscure memory in the local folklore.

The conflicts of Campan with the neighboring communities or authorities have a more than anecdotal interest, however; to an extent, they inform us about the evolution of the concept of land ownership, of vacant land, of pasturage and forests.

The oldest document held by the Archives of Campan is a cadastral document (*bornage*) from 1083 for the Comté de Bigorre in the south.

These are likely apocryphal documents, put together by bureaucrats in the sixteenth or early seventeenth century, difficult times, characterized by the onset of great economic and political troubles for the community.[11] Not only were the powers of the state beginning to be organized, but the development of agriculture and grazing on the plain were beginning to deprive the montagnards of a portion of their markets for livestock, butter, and cheese.

Because of the failure to reach a political understanding against common enemies, the difficulties degenerated into conflicts between neighboring communities. Each party tried to resolve its problems by extending its territory, by increasing the size of its herds. It was at this time that the people of Campan first became allies and then enemies of the Lord of Castelbajac, subsequently engaging in battle with their neighbors from the Quatre Véziaux over "transport" meadows. The beginning of the document reproduces the initial arguments of the *Fors de Bigorre*.[12] Moreover, in 1080 Centulle, Vicomte de Béarn, became the Comte de Bigorre through marriage with an heir. He subjugated the seigneurs and peasant communities of the valleys while also bowing before the power of the King of Aragon. He died around 1088, assassinated by one of his vassals. The first version of the customs and Fors of Bigorre is from 1097 or 1098, and probably written in Latin.[13] (There is no critical edition of this compilation, which has been modified several times, as was the Fors de Béarn.) The authorities responsible for the first edition of the Fors were most likely appointed when the document was first written. But it is hard to accept that a ground rent in cash would have been stipulated at this time. The term "albergue" generally refers to the purchase in cash of a feudal right, the right of the seigneur to reside for a given number of days a year on the vassal's lands, together with his entourage. Therefore, the *albergue* should not be confused with a long-term lease (*affièvement*), that is, with a (feudal) ground rent. These concerns, these findings, relatively accurate, appear to be foreign to the people of that time. The documents in question, moreover, are accepted by [Pierre] de Marca, whose erudition remains undisputed and who is said to have accepted their authenticity.

Even if the documents are not authentic, they are still of interest. They demonstrate that the people of Campan believed they formed a border community and knew how to make use of this situation. The peak for which they served as guardians was not of very great importance, though; it looked out over the neighboring valley on the French side, not toward Aragon. No matter. The goal of their tenacious diplomacy was to extend their authority to the "eau versante," that is, to the natural borders of their valley, and to remain masters there.

They experienced assaults from all sides. The strong community of Bagnères extended to the Pic du Midi, but to reach the high mountain pastures (poorly delimited), flocks had to cross Campan. But Bagnères had a town charter as the county seat of the district, known as a "quarteronnage," as a result of which challenges continued to arise repeatedly. Baudéan, caught between Bagnères and Campan, had few pastures and sought to expand to the high mountain beyond the Adour of Esponne. Asté, ruled by the powerful Viscounts of Asté (the family into which the "belle Corisande" was born), possessed only mediocre prairies at low altitude on the Lhéris and acquired, by force or negotiation, rights to the high mountain prairies and forests of Campan.[14] The inhabitants of Quatre Véziaux, a federation comprising four villages (in the Aure Valley), sought the magnificent "transport" pastures. These complicated relationships, by turns violent and bureaucratic, culminating in conflicts or transactions, continued until the decline of agro-pastoral life. In all likelihood, all the organized communities experienced similar difficulties, which left behind traces of undisclosed antagonism: conflicts, local wars, and legal actions were gradually replaced by fights, brawls among the young at local celebrations, sporting or verbal rivalries, sarcasm, name calling, and quarrels among children, the unconscious heirs of centuries of bitterness.

According to local tradition, Campan has always escaped feudalism. This claim is as false for Campan as it is for the other communities of the Pyrenees, whether "free valleys" or allodial lands, principalities or states that retained a certain degree of autonomy for many years (like Andorra until today). It eludes historical truth, namely the bitter and sometimes successful struggle of the local communities, valleys, and principalities to preserve their relative independence. The inhabitants of Campan held or claimed to hold a very ancient concession from the Counts of Bigorre for the possession of their lands (collective or individual). In fact, it is certain that the agro-pastoral community existed well before the Counts of Bigorre, and long before the establishment of feudal relations of production, ownership, and subordination. The lords, here the Counts of Bigorre, began by declaring themselves the sole masters and owners of the land, in particular, communal lands. Having done so, they negotiated a transaction with the actual owners, the users. Both parties—under the ritual forms of homage and the legal forms of contracts—engaged in a bitter struggle to maintain or expand their rights. It would be impossible, as well as tedious, to provide a detailed reconstruction of this struggle, sometimes hidden, sometimes overtly violent. We can assume that the texts signal periods when feudal domination weakened (never well established in southern France and the Pyrenees); when the local lords needed the help of their vassals in terms of manpower, money, or goods; and when this marked a turning point. Unsure, in spite of the strength of custom, of seeing their momentary advantage become customary, the vassals demanded a written document. This document—although still relying on custom—therefore manifests a change in customs, generally to the benefit of the subjugated. Concerning the relation between the community of Campan and their lords, we have a document (unquestionably counterfeit) from 1093 as well as traces of its findings in 1177, 1300, 1341, 1446, 1541, 1582, and so on. Throughout this period, the situation of the community improved. It was recognized as a community. Its assets grew: mills, markets, fairs, the trade in wine and meat were added to the property it held. It paid its debts collectively and had recognized authorities. I want to analyze this process of emancipation, which also has a general significance.

But the community had to worry about not only its own lords but those of the neighboring villages. These, acting in the name of the community they ruled over (and which they dominated feudally), always behaved with the interests of their community and themselves, of their class, in mind. How did the Lords of Asté, of Baudéan, and of Aspin become owners of vast tracts of land in the territory of Campan? Through violence, purchase, or simply by taking control of lands whose use their own community had held from time immemorial, the result of a compromise that had been customary among the montagnards? It's impossible to say. No doubt all of these played a role. Every seigneur sought to extend his domain and increase the number of his subjects (for his resources in kind, in species, and in taxes, that is, in feudal rents, were proportional to the number of subjects, families, of "homesteads" that the lord rules over). They also wished to extend their domains, whether in vacant lands, pastures, or forests, so they could "grant" lucrative concessions to their subjects, whose number increased naturally along with these new resources.

The Valley of Campan

The Vicomtes d'Asté (or Aster) held, along the mountains in the territory of Campan, various cantons: Empiège, Entrecueu, and so on. Similarly, the communities of Aster, Gerde, Liés, and Banios had joint ownership of the area of Mourgoueilh, where the inhabitants of Campan retained rights of use (flax fields and forest pastures). The people of Campan never accepted the domination of the Lords of Asté over a portion of their territory. There followed a series of conflicts, arbitration hearings, transactions, and legal decisions. The oldest preserved text is from 1328. At that time, the Sénéchal de Bigorre, on behalf of the king of France and the procurer, appointed two well-to-do citizens from Bagnères as arbitrators.[15] This was a clever means of introducing the outlook of the bourgeoisie into feudal challenges, of humiliating the Vicomte d'Asté, and of enhancing the prestige of the town, equipped with a charter and supported by the king; as well as being a skillful way to finally force insubordinate montagnards to submit to the town.

There appeared before the arbitrators the Vicomte d'Asté and two *vicini* (neighbors, inhabitants of Campan). The procedure was open and amicable. Both parties promised the arbitrators, negotiators of the agreement (of the compromise), that they would put an end to the current state of affairs. Anyone who infringed the peace that had been agreed upon would pay two hundred Tours pounds. They would submit any new dispute to the arbitrators.

The arbitrators decided that men from the community (of Campan) could, at any time, together with their animals, use the disputed mountains, that is, have the ability to graze, shelter [*gistre*], and *acabaner* (to construct cabins or barns but not houses), and use the *coral* (a shelter for shepherds and livestock). Any livestock that had strayed would not be seized directly (*pignoré,* or *carnalé*). The people of Campan would bring their livestock out two weeks before the feast of Saint John (June 24) and would not bring them in until the feast of the Assumption (August 15). Additionally, they would have the right to graze (but not to shelter) on all the lands and woods belonging to the vicomte, except if there was a risk of damage to the wheat and hay, as was the custom. The pledges carried out by the vicomte were restored. These were pledged against an annual payment of butter, a day's stay on the mountains in question, and fifty Tours pounds, forty of which went to the vicomte and ten to his children. The parties swore on the Bible, touching it with their right hand, to confirm the transaction.

This text informs us of the actions carried out by the people of Campan for the preservation of their rights and customs against the rights or claims of feudal lords. They defended them and they counterattacked. When they could do nothing else, they paid. But we can draw other interesting conclusions from this text, which can serve our purposes without returning to the previously mentioned document.

In 1328 the community (commune) was already recognized as such. Taking advantage of favorable conditions, it negotiated with a powerful feudal lord as an equal. However, it did not yet have any consuls, only syndics. So the general assembly, which approved the arbitration decision, appointed six permanent syndics for five-year terms. These were de facto authorities, mandated by and standing in for the community before the higher authorities. The residents of the community served as guarantors, "constituentes se insuper fidéjussores," using their assets and those of the community. Making use of conflict and a relatively satisfactory outcome to this conflict, the community managed to obtain recognition of its existence and that of its representatives, although they still did not have the status of consul.

The general assembly, or *véziau,* remained supreme [*souveraine*]. It was convened for every matter of importance, for every exceptional event. Its representatives could do nothing without its backing. It approved or disapproved the actions of its representatives, ratified them or failed to do so. Its absolute decisions appear on official documents, alongside the official documents of its appointees, whose mandate was limited, imperative, and controlled. In principle, not only could all the "neighboring" members of the community participate; they were required to do so. But this was not essential provided that the best and greater part of the community, that is, the elders, appointed representatives, and heads of families attended. These individuals were authorized to make commitments on behalf of "the local community."

The text informs us of the transition between the de facto community and the de juris community recognized as such. It illustrates the passage from the community of practice to the organized community, producing—within the framework of feudalism, but relying on the activities of urban communes or, at least, making use of the plurality of forces and formal bodies—its legal and political bodies. That is, relying on the transition between practical custom and recognized (customary) law.

These institutions were produced in the context of the struggle against the feudal lords, a struggle for freedom or, rather, for *specific* freedoms, the exemptions, customs, and traditions that would become "privileges," that is, customs guaranteed by a written document.

The conflict between Campan and the lords of Asté, which hadn't been resolved but was attenuated by the 1328 transaction, returned later for unknown reasons (possibly an increase in the population and a drive by the local communities seeking to extend their pasture lands, an attempt that the lords were able to use to benefit their own interests). In 1440 there was a new arbitration agreement and, consequently, a new judgment; it was issued by representatives appointed and accepted by both parties, without cost, and immediately enforceable.

The judgment maintained the rights of forest pasturage for Campan. However, between the feast of Saint Bartholomew (August 24) and Christmas, the people of Campan could occupy the cabins and pasture lands vacated by the people of Asté. The people of the house of Asté (the community or, more specifically, the village of Asté, whose leaders, representatives, and substitutes were their lords, for there was no question of a community as far as they were concerned) committed themselves and their assets, as did the community of Campan, to respect this transaction. The vicomtesse stated she would not benefit from the *senatus-consulte* or the Loi Julia.[16] The appeal was made before the seneschals, before the "small royal seal of Montpellier," the parliament of Toulouse, the Pope and his official representatives in Tarbes and Auch.

Based on the text, we see how the lords of Asté energetically defended the rights of their subjects against the strong invading community of Campan. The villagers of Asté comprised their "homes," their people.

The lords appear as representatives of these subjects, assuming responsibility, pledging to uphold the agreement, and committing their assets in any litigation. But it was the lords who received any fees that were owed.

Lords on one side, syndics on the other (along with the consuls, guards, counselors, and assembly members) acted as substitutes for their respective agro-pastoral group. Upon them, in them, were concentrated the rights and powers of the group together with its assets.

The notion of the delegation of power—of all powers—therefore is still very strong. It implies a genuine substitution of persons. The syndics (later the consuls) *are* the community from which they emanate, body, soul, and worldly goods.

In 1449 justice hadn't yet lost its simple, direct, and free nature. The arbitration decision issued by the representatives (arbitration, as we know, replaced the *ordalie,* the judgment of God) still had a sacred aspect, guaranteed by a ritual oath of a magical nature. The right hand was placed upon the holy book.

Primitive customs hadn't disappeared, but they were transformed. God's judgment, following the sworn statement of witnesses—in the event of contradictions between these witnesses—became a divine arbitration award issued by wise and venerated men. Similarly, the ancient "fidejussores," witnesses, guarantors, surety, participating personally and with their property in the sacred agreement, became recognized as permanent authorities. Thus, we find a continuity in these community institutions between 1328 and 1449. But by 1449 major changes were underway.

The community had its institutions, its organization, recognized and already well established, as it remained until the end of the Ancien Régime and, therefore, for several centuries, consisting of guards, consuls, *manamentés* (representatives), and counselors. Already we find a certain depreciation of the general assembly, or *véziau.* The act of 1328 stipulated that the assembly was to meet every two weeks; and a codicil discussed this meeting and the authorization it issued. Nothing of the kind occurred in 1449, however. The limited assembly that had appointed the syndics functioned as a general assembly that approved their decisions. Within the small context of the village community, established power already had a tendency to separate itself from its base, its organic and social foundation, and to constitute itself a political power.

Although justice retained its simple and straightforward character, it had already become organized into a complicated and interconnected system of official bodies and appeals (a naive system that, theoretically, reached all the way to the Pope). The community's struggle against the lords was increasingly waged on the judicial plane. It was no longer a question of pledge obligations and, therefore, the direct and necessarily violent seizure of assets, but of a careful trial resulting in a judicial decision.

The struggle for the integrity of the territory, inseparable from the struggle for freedoms and customs, changed its nature, lost its acuity. In one sense the community triumphed. It was now a "seigniorial commons," capable of pursuing the feudal lords before well-established formal bodies and, therefore, their equal. It consolidated into one moral, material, administrative, and political personality its members, persons, and assets. It was no longer a simple de facto power, able to assert itself through direct action (pledges or extralegal seizure). Its entrance into the monarchical state system was underway. But at the same time, it sowed within itself the first seeds of its future dislocation, precisely because the de facto community, the group founded on customary practice, organized and armed to defend itself—the primitive or quasi-primitive group of pastoral peasants attached to the land—was no longer the essential and determining element of the situation. Therefore, at the very moment of its triumph (and official documents and long-term leases attest to this), the community lost its functions and already had begun its decline.

Once a social formation associated with conditions predating feudalism, which continued even after later modes of production, were in force, it appeared outwardly as a body designed for action and struggle against these new formations. But to the extent that they penetrated the community, it lost its meaning and function. Having become a seigniorial domain overseen by its representatives, the community saw itself threatened by its victory from within.

The disputes with the house of Asté resumed in the sixteenth and seventeenth centuries, the heirs of the vicomte, the Marquis of Montpezac, and the Dukes of Grammont having conceded a mountain to the neighboring community of Bulan. The people of Bulan, as neighbors, had the traditional right of passage through the neighboring lands until the third steeple, therefore, through Asté and Campan. But already distant from these mountains, their right had no value if they were unable to construct temporary shelters and use the corrals or *cortals* (shelters with a milkroom).

The people of Campan stubbornly refused to give them this right, which meant their right to passage was worthless.

The heirs of the house of Asté, after payment of a fee, claimed only to have provided the right of passage to the inhabitants of Bulan. We can see here the complications associated with the reciprocal rights and obligations of agro-pastoral groups, aggravated by the presence of the feudal lords. The rights were inextricably interconnected: passage (limited to daylight hours only), forest pastures (permanent between the dates—established by custom and controlled by the authorities—of the introduction, departure, or passage of various kinds of livestock—cows, sheep, goats, pigs), construction of temporary shelters, construction of *cortals, glandage* (the right to graze pigs in the oak forests where they fed on acorns), foresting, *affouage* (the right to collect foliage, which was added to the feed for the animals; the right to cut wood for heating and construction).

The "useful" domain dissociated into a series of rights that the feudal lords sought to negotiate or concede individually, each of them against the payment of fees. Further complicating this intertwining was the difficulty of boundary marking on the mountainside and the bad faith of the parties, who did not hesitate to transgress, or even move, the existing boundary limits. What's more, the custom or primitive customary right ("soft law"), in this case direct seizure, pignoration, did not disappear, although it grew weaker and became incorporated in juridical laws, in the rights that appeared in documents, in the interconnection of formal bodies, of appeals, and of legal jurisdictions. This led to such lengthy and complicated legal proceedings that on June 4, 1742, a committee of lawyers and jurists from the Parliament of Toulouse met to examine the dispute between the community of Campan and the dukes of Grammont. The committee acknowledged that, legally speaking, it was unable to understand anything about the nature of the dispute. It proposed to Parliament that it rule on the facts and not on the texts. They stated that "either the terrain is large enough for the various communities to graze their livestock on or it is not." In the first case, the communities could "cumulatively" remain users of the mountain areas they were disputing; in the second, the inhabitants of Campan had priority based on the decision of 1328.

After 1510, the texts—transactions, decisions, payment of fees, operations, appeals—followed one another inextricably.

The cost of legal disputes, fees, and fines came to have a powerful negative effect on the fate of the community, both with respect to the financial contributions of its members and the crystallization of the local bourgeoisie around the group of bureaucrats, lawyers, notaries, court prosecutors, syndics, and so on.

It is worth pointing out that the persistent feudalism, here represented by powerful lords, the dukes of Grammont, continued to weigh on the life of the community, becoming increasingly burdensome. The feudal lords, "inherent" owners of lands that the communities had a right to use (in perpetuity, the useful domain), began to consider themselves as owners in the full sense of the word. Such long-term leasing (*inféodation*) gradually began to lose, almost imperceptibly, its medieval characteristic of co-ownership, of coexistence between a perpetual usufruct and a "fundamental" right that remained abstract, becoming concrete only by means of a fixed perpetual rent regardless of the value of the currency.

The fief had become a simple title of ownership through a very slow and very ancient evolutionary process. Likewise, the rent binding the tenant to the land as to the person of the lord became a monetary rent, representing the transition between feudal rent and capitalist rent. Likewise, long-term leasing tended to become a rental. It is clear that from the sixteenth century and later (documents from October 2, 1510, May 27, 1568, April 23, 1663, October 11, 1698, August 17, 1716, May 15, 1719, December 5, 1741, May 23, 1761, September 16, 1769, etc., which it would be impractical to reproduce with their interminable therefores and whereases), the heirs of the Vicomte d'Asté sought to become masters in their domain. As renters of the land, pushed by the depreciation of fixed fees, they felt they had a right to rent their lands to whomever they saw fit, that is, to the one who could pay the most. But the concepts of ground rent, of rental, of property only came into focus gradually. What could these lords sell: clearly defined rights of use already in the possession of the community by customary right? They could only transfer them to other communities, preferably to their vassals, if they wished to remain within the existing, customary legal context—or, more exactly, the context of *legitimacy*—while taking into account existing customary relations between those communities, relations they bent to their own interests. Therefore, the feudal lords tended to isolate the concepts and practices relative to capitalist ground rent: to ownership of the land, pure and simple. But at the same time, they were unable to do this. They remained enclosed within the framework of feudalism, of their seigniorial rights. The feudal lords used all their power, all their persistent influence, extending as far as the monarchical state, to maintain rights that began to assume a meaning quite different from their original meaning, for those rights were increasingly becoming liberated from the personal relations between the lord and his vassals, between the feudal lords and the communities of which they were the lords and masters. They became abstract rights capable of being bought and sold. They were transformed into an object of commerce, into ground rents in the capitalist sense, with the owner renting the land that belonged to him absolutely against the payment of money.

It is remarkable that the legal proceedings and judgments multiplied throughout the seventeenth and eighteenth centuries. The situation became so convoluted that, at one point, specialized legal scholars of the time gave up trying to understand it. How, indeed, could they have understood the internal contradictions of this situation: new relations of ownership being formed within earlier relations, growing within but in conflict with them? We know that this contradiction would be resolved and cut short by the Revolution of 1789 and the promulgation of a code based on absolute private property, exclusive of custom and community rights.

However, the new code didn't resolve all the difficulties because the legal disputes continue until today, as shown by a recent text that appeared in the record of legal proceedings (*Juris-Classeur*).

Here, we begin to approach the concept of a refeudalization of relations over the centuries. This refeudalization cannot be understood in France and in the situations under review without examining the nonfeudal relations this form contained, relations that both predate feudalism (deriving from the community and custom) and postdate feudalism (ground rent, ownership, rental, unfettered sales).

The Ancien Régime tried, in its own way, to resolve the question. After 1666, that is, with the formation of the Office of Waterways and Forests (of which Monsieur Froidour was the promoter in the Midi Pyrenees), the state carried out a process of breaking up ownership, of "triage" and "cantonment." The lords, for their part, received a third of the disputed territory (triage). This was a partial solution that failed to satisfy anyone. As far as the lords were concerned, the conflict between possession and ownership, between customary usage and the sale of rights for cash, was being repeated. The communities felt they had been wronged, the lords as well. Whatever the case, between 1666 and today, a series of triages and cantonments led to the creation of various properties in the territory of Campan. The situation was simplified in the sense that it was now quite clear what had transpired.

Thus, the dukes of Grammont remained owners of a portion of the territory of Campan but, as before, the inhabitants of Campan had the use of the land against payment of a fee.

Likewise, the federation of some of the communes of the former Viscountcy of Asté (Asté, Gerde, Liès, Banios) continued to hold, in common with Campan, the mountain of Mourgoueilh (780 hectares, including 462 of pine woods in Mourgoueilh). But the people of Campan had the right of (daytime) passage and the right to collect deadwood (*lignerage*). This was based on a document from 1593, subsequently confirmed by a decision of the parliament of Toulouse on September 11, 1782.

On the other hand, the commune of Campan held 87 hectares of the territory of Asté.

Earlier, I referred to the interminable quarrels between Campan and the communities of the Aure Valley, the Quatre Véziaux, supported intermittently by the lords and sires of Castelbajac. These quarrels had begun in the distant past, the inhabitants retaining a hazy memory of a legendary legal duel between the champion of Aspin (who played the role of David) and that of Campan (identified with Goliath by analogy with the size of the villages involved in the dispute).

Later texts allude to a long-term leasing or rental agreement from 1147, granting the people of Campan the use of woods and pastures located near the sources of the Adour, Payolle (or the Séoube), and an arbitration agreement of 1292. But these documents appear to be impossible to locate. Two documents, dated April 30, 1470, and July 27, 1491, assign to Campan, on behalf of the sires (barons) of Castelbajac, the usage rights for these pastures and forests referred to by terms in the local dialect (*péchence* for forest pasturing and *jacence* for "gistre," or sheltering, for example). Which also happened to reserve to the lords in question the direct, fundamental ownership, the dependency associated with these lands.

Being highly active, the lords of Castelbajac considered or claimed to consider themselves the lords of Campan, who now found themselves to be collectively (as commune or community) vassals of an asset that belonged to them. This resulted in an inextricable series of disputes, quarrels, struggles, and legal proceedings. The result of each conflict depended on the existing relations of force. A document (deteriorated and whose date is illegible) shows the people of Campan as supplying wood for the reconstruction of a château belonging to a feudal family, the château of Séméacq. On May 15, 1511, the lords of Aspin confirmed the earlier concessions but reserved the rights of their subjects in Quatre Véziaux. The Lord of Castelbajac demanded from the people of Campan the *ost*, that is, their military service. The community of Campan avoided this by contracting for a kind of military alliance with this turbulent lord at the time of the wars of religion. However, in 1599, there was an actual pitched battle with the Lord of Castelbajac's own men and, finally, in

The Valley of Campan

1602, a transaction.[17] On February 10, 1602, the Lord of Castelbajac agreed to "release" the inhabitants of Campan, that is, to renounce the fee, which had the feudal characteristic of a recognition of sovereignty, and submit any litigation to the jurisdiction of the Count of Bigorre, who was also the King [Henri IV] (whereas the Aure Valley was considered part of a separate property, Nébouzan, with its own states and tribunals). This lord and the people of Campan became allies and good friends.

Do we attribute this revival of an old conflict to a growth in population or to the troubled times and turbulence of the lords of Aspin and their subjects? It's impossible to say.

It is odd, however, that the most serious conflict of the community with the feudal lords—an armed conflict—dates from the early seventeenth century. It signaled a resurgence of feudalism strictly speaking, with its private wars and conflicts that fell outside ordinary judicial constraints, a resurgence that was distinct from the "refeudalization" previously examined and which fell within the framework of the monarchical state.

Once the matter of feudal dependency was settled with the Lord of Castelbajac, a legal document of February 28, 1608, ordered the boundaries to be marked and another from June 12, 1609, attempted to determine the reciprocal rights of the communities. Consequently, Campan, having acknowledged the possession of a right of transport through the Quatre Véziaux of Aure (Ancizan, Cadéac, Guchen, and Grézian), agreed to pay 500 livres a year for the livestock its inhabitants led through those lands. Afterward, the position of the people of Areau was as follows: the 1609 document established an "association of reciprocal rights," specifically, grazing rights between neighbors; but because Campan's participation in this association was predicated on the payment of fees, the people of Areau enjoyed a legitimate possession that was not subject to limitations.

But it was at this time that jurists from Campan discovered—or invented—the texts of 1083 and 1096. This led to an inextricable succession of quarrels, legal actions, transactions, and judgments before the various tribunals, and appeals courts, where the rights of forest pasturage (with or without the rights of sheltering and temporary residence), of the right to collect deadwood (with or without the right to graze pigs on acorns, the right to cut wood for buildings and carriages or make "plow harnesses"), were separated and combined in different ways. This interminable proceeding did not have any consequential general significance. Note, however, that it illustrates the difficulty of coherently establishing relationships between neighboring communities, the apparently simple rights of use on adjoining lands fragmenting into a series of rights meeting diverse and changing needs. It is also worth pointing out that at every period of tension, up until year V of the Republic [September 1796], there reappeared the customary right of pledging, or pignoration (*Plaidoyer pour les habitants de Campan,* chez Roquemaurel, Tarbes, Year V of the Republic).

Earlier I referred to the archaic nature of the Pyrenees. It doesn't arise from its isolation. On the contrary, ever since prehistoric times, the Pyrenees have been crossed by many human groups and have been subject to a variety of influences. The inhabitants have experienced and understood events, assimilated technologies, languages, and social transformations, but always as a function of their own concerns and, therefore, as a function of a quasi-primitive economic base and social formation: a predominantly pastoral agricultural existence, the peasant community and its continuation. We see them at every period attempting to interpret the facts and orient circumstances in their own way, in the direction of regionalism and a localism both narrow and tenacious.

With the collapse of the monarchy, the people of Campan saw an opportunity to resume the secular quarrel with the Quatre Véziaux. They drafted a "petition to the national assembly" signed by the community's notables and the heads of local families.

This text illustrates the continuity of a community that had become a commune through changes of political regimes in spite of its gradual dislocation. Interpreting the new republic in terms of ancient peasant democracy, the general assembly that had fallen into disuse now went into action with renewed vigor. The community attempted to take advantage of the circumstances; paying a feudal tax to the nation, it asked the national assembly for a special favor. However, the petition does not appear to have achieved the hoped-for results. With the Revolution,

Campan fell under the single general law that eliminated privileges and local borders. Questions regarding communal assets would be examined and settled on the basis of national laws within the unified and indivisible Republic.[18]

The process of setting aside reserved areas did not succeed in eliminating the quarrels. On November 28, 1666, a "triage" of the contested lands took place. Campan had received a third, the inhabitants of the Aure Valley received a third, and the final third remained undivided. Litigation ensued concerning this last third as well as over the various rights associated with grazing and passage through the other two lots. The dispute became so confusing that the decisions of the Parliament of Toulouse (1725 and 1771) were annulled by the Parliament of Pau, which then had to annul its own decision.

The portion that remained undivided with the inhabitants of Aspin (or Quatre Véziaux of Aure) comprising 31 hectares was divided by a ruling issued by the Tribunal of Bagnères on December 11, 1862, based on the oldest method of division: the number of hearth fires lit. On May 15, 1871, Campan received an area of 29 hectares, 91 ares, containing 1,009 fires. The people of Aspin, with 50 fires, received only one hectare and 42 ares.[19] New challenges ensued.

In fact, even today, usage rights are intermingled. In the forests and pasture lands known as "Mourgoueilh," the right to pasturage is held by Campan together with the communes of the former Viscounty of Asté. Baudéan, which formed a separate seigneury under the control of Baron de Baudéan, even today enjoys the right of pasture on Mourgoueilh in the area assigned to Campan following the division into reserved areas. This is based on a document dated March 10, 1500, and a decision of the Parliament of Toulouse of September 11, 1782, where the parliament ruled on the facts (the needs) rather than existing texts. In addition to its forests and its (approximately) 4,500 hectares of grassland, Campan enjoys rights of transit and grazing (including livestock that were leased, that is, animals that did not belong to the inhabitants who grazed them) on Piet and Béziau, mountains belonging to the commune of Cieutat—on Teillet, which belongs to Asté, on Arizes, which belongs to Bagnères, on 224 hectares of forests and 320 hectares of grassland in Mourgoueilh, in addition to its own lot and a lot on which, apparently, Campan no longer had rights, and on 496 hectares of forests and 2,860 hectares of grassland belonging to Quatre Véziaux, lands confined to its territory or situated on its territory. (The right to pasturage only applies to forests populated with deciduous trees; fir trees are excluded.) Additionally, Campan possesses, though assigned to different uses, 87 hectares outside its own territory in Asté and 2,404 hectares in Bagnères.

We cannot understand the current situation of such a commune without looking back at the Middle Ages (even beyond). In the entanglement of possessions and rights, we discover the entire history of rural life, customs, and ownership under the Ancien Régime, under feudalism, and under earlier modes of production (the quasi-primitive community). In other words, in a place such as the Valley of Campan, the historian, the sociologist, and even the simple observer can feel, at every moment, the presence of the distant past. This gives the impression of an especially well-preserved "sociological fossil" still in the last stages of its death throes.

To study the lengthy adventure of the Campan community in detail, we would also need to discuss its difficulties with the Monastery of Escaladieu. Initially established in the high valley of the Adour, the monks then moved to Escaladieu, in the pre-Pyrenean valleys, but they preserved their domain of Cabadur.[20] In 1524 they granted "ad novum accapitum sive emphiteosin perpetuam," a new fief and perpetual lease, the largest part of this domain to the people of Campan. The guards and consuls agreed "pro se ipsis corum et ujuslibet ipsorum heredibus et totius universitatis." This is one of the earliest documents in which the concept of possession and perpetual use is clearly tied to that of inheritance (individual and collective) in Campan. The abbot and his successors carefully preserved, on the lands on which a concession was granted, direct ownership, rights of transfer, and the prevalence of long-term rents, in short, the feudal rights compatible with possession or "ownership" to the benefit of the people of Campan (collectively and individually).

We would also need to summarize the relations of Campan with the town of Bagnères. Endowed with a charter, a tribunal, and a district leader,

Bagnères extended its territory all the way to the Pic du Midi as well as owning property and having rights in Campan. The high mountains of Bagnères are accessible only by the road from Tourmalet, that is, through Campan. This led to a tiresome series of agreements and disagreements, although their history doesn't lack in general interest. For at certain moments the peasant community relied on the nearest town. We have seen how the bourgeoisie of Bagnères, already possessing a charter (in 1171), served as an arbitrator between the community of Campan and their feudal neighbors. This charter gave the people of Bagnères long-term ownership (*emphytéose*) of their assets with the right to bequeath, sell, and dispose of them in a variety of ways. It granted them the right to appoint legal advisors and judges. It organized a transition between the primitive regime (including investigations into complaints by an injured party or family of the victim; oral proceedings with oaths, bonds, respondents or sureties, and witnesses; arbitration decisions or legal disputes; financial compensation; banishment and, therefore, a breach of the peace and blood vengeance) and the activities of a regular tribunal. It is clear that this charter served as an example, a model, and a political objective for the people of neighboring peasant communities. But Bagnères was also a peasant community with its own lands, livestock, and usage rights. In upholding these rights, it made use of its power as a town. It sought to bring Campan into its jurisdiction from the administrative, criminal, economic, and political points of view. The people of Campan could never accept this type of control without resistance. The result was a complicated policy, subject to sudden reversals, sometimes resulting in heated disputes. The people of Campan were unable to avoid becoming part of the "quarteronnage," then the arrondissement of Bagnères, under the jurisdiction of its court, dependent upon its market, its craft and commercial agencies, and later its industry and capital. They defended themselves for many years with varying degrees of success.[21]

In short, the secular struggle of the community for the integrity of its territory (and the free exercise of its own customs) obtained certain results but never achieved its complete objective.

With respect to ownership and possession, in Campan we need to distinguish the following:

(a) The overall territory, granted or let by the landowner, the Comte de Bigorre, then the king of France (documents from 1083 and 1096, if authentic, from 1177, 1300, 1351, 1446, 1541, 1582, and various judgments by the commissioners responsible for reforming the domain). From these documents we see a bipartite form of perpetual possession, increasingly equivalent over the centuries to the right of ownership but always limited in some sense by the Ancien Régime and its feudal structure or its remnants. On the one hand, the people of Campan, as a community, collectively owned their territory or at least their land to the extent that it was not encumbered by other rights (individual or collective). This ownership was itself divided into two parts, one inalienable (public buildings, roads, etc.), the other alienable but subject to certain customary or legal restrictions.[22]

On the other hand, each inhabitant as an individual or, rather, as a head of a family held, in addition to a house, parcels of arable land, meadows, and usage rights on collective possessions, rights otherwise attached to the fact of being a "neighbor," a member of the *véziau,* of having a home and *hearth* and, therefore, of being a member of the community or collectivity.

(b) The lands (mountains, forests, pastures) formerly owned, to some extent, by feudal neighbors and that became private properties of their descendants, although still encumbered by certain rights of usage subject to payment of a fee.

(c) The lands or territories belonging to the neighboring communities of Campan (today communes) on its territory or belonging to Campan on the neighboring territories. On all these lands, ownership is not absolute. It continues to be broken down into distinct rights of usage governed and distributed by traditions and customs that are still in force even though they have gradually fallen into disuse and no longer give rise to once-bitter disputes.

As incompatible as this might seem (or might effectively be) with the concept of ownership found in Roman law and taken up in the Napoleonic code, it is a fact and it is this fact that is of particular interest here.

We have only summarized the complicated vicissitudes that have led to this situation, vicissitudes that are enormous on the local scale but miniscule on a larger scale. A detailed study, which would be tedious, to say the least, would require an entire volume and require the publication of a register of title deeds. This summary seeks to identify the overall aspect, which is to say the aspect by which the history of the community of Campan connects with general history. Unquestionably, the systematic exploration, using a method that is both historical and sociological, of the past of these Pyrenean villages and a large number of French villages generally, would reveal similar vicissitudes. The interest of Campan, or any other village in the Pyrenees, consists in the proximity of an often-distant past. We can conjecture that such comparative studies would confirm the general findings I have attempted to identify here. Until that confirmation, until similar work has been conducted on a sufficient number of communities, such studies of course remain subject to possible revision.

Notes

[Originally published as Henri Lefebvre, *La vallée de Campan: Étude de sociologie rurale* (Paris: Presses Universitaires de France, 1963), 83–116. The first half of the book is a presentation of historical documents; the second part is titled "Étude de sociologie rurale," which is also the book's subtitle. We have included the brief introduction and the first two chapters of the second part, which are the most sociological and geographical parts of the study. The following chapters are more historical.—Eds.]

1. These words indicate a dialectical movement between historical research and research that reflects sociological reality.

2. [A *généralité* was an ancient financial and administrative unit of France intended to assist with the collection of taxes. Originally four in number, there were approximately thirty-three in the late eighteenth century.—Trans.]

3. Henri Cavaillès, *La vie pastorale et agricole dans les Pyrénées des Gaves de l'Adour et des Nestes: Étude de géographie humaine* (Paris: A. Colin, 1931), 22.

4. Cavaillès, *La vie pastorale et agricole*, 59.

5. Cavaillès, *La vie pastorale et agricole*, 19.

6. Cavaillès, *La vie pastorale et agricole*, 40. See also [Daniel] Faucher, "La viabilité de quelques grands cols pyrénéens et leur enneigement," *Revue Géographique des Pyrénées et du Sud Ouest* 3, no. 2 (1932): 195–201, 198. [We have completed and corrected Lefebvre's reference.—Eds.]

7. Toponymic issues are beyond our competence and will not be addressed here. [The Adour is a river in southwestern France that flows down from the Pyrenees.—*Trans.*]

8. This construction, where the "loges," large pieces of slate, prevent water from flowing into the roof beams and the thatch, is found elsewhere, but only in Campan has it produced a distinctive style.

9. "Statistique de la propriété dans la zone montagneuse," a report by Georges de Roquette-Buisson for the Congrès international pour l'aménagement des montagnes, Bordeaux, 1907, and, by the same author, *Les vallées pyrénéennes* (Tarbes, 1921).

10. This text appears in the *Archives communales* but in very poor condition.

11. This does not eliminate the fact that older documents, possibly deteriorated, may have been modified or reworked.

12. [*For(s)*: a privilege or custom.—*Trans.*]

13. M. A. Davezac-Macaya, *Essais historiques sur la Bigorre, Bagnères de Bigorre*, vol. 2 (1823). But it appears that the date should be pushed forward to the start of the following century, around 1110.

14. [Diane d'Andouins, Comtesse de Guiche, known as "la belle Corisande," was the royal mistress of Henri IV.—*Trans.*]

15. Sequestration or feudal seizure of the Count of Bigorre by Philippe Le Bel in 1293 following a lengthy and complicated series of challenges concerning the inheritance and suzerainty of this fief.

16. The *senatus-consulte Velléien* and *Loi Julia* are documents that exempted the assets of married women from the agreement.

17. Documents archived in 1849 at the Bibliothèque Municipale de Tarbes, according to documents belonging to the Parliament of Toulouse: *Relations du traitement fait aux gens de Campan par le seigneur de Castelbajac.—Transaction entre la communauté et le seigneur en 1602*. (Copy of this latter document in Campan.)

18. Decision issued by the Assembly on November 10, 1792, acknowledging the Court of Cassation's examination of similar cases. Judgment issued on II Frimaire [third month of the Republican calendar, corresponding to late November] year II, releasing Campan from the deadline, held to be null and void in consequence of a law of 9 Ventôse [mid-February] of the same year.

19. [One *are* is equivalent to 100 square meters.—*Trans.*]

20. Davezac-Macaya, *Essais historiques sur la Bigorre*, 217.

21. Very recently a secular dispute between Campan and Bagnères was settled concerning the Mongie, where a winter sports facility was built. Bagnères prevailed.

22. We understand the difficulty in formulating in "modern" terms the concept or the *fact* of collective ownership. Certain jurists do not even acknowledge

it as such any longer. [Maurice] Hauriou (*Précis de droit administratif et de droit public,* 12th ed. rev. [Paris: Recueil Sirey, 1933], 1072), defines collective ownership as the sum of the individual rights of the inhabitants "ut singuli," an unacceptable definition because it attempts to translate a fact from one period of time into the language of another. [We have corrected and completed Lefebvre's reference.—*Eds.*]

Publication History

"Introduction to *From the Rural to the Urban*" was originally published as "Du rural à l'urbain: Introduction," in *Du rural à l'urbain* (Paris: Anthropos, 1970), 7–20. Copyright 1970, Éditions Économica.

"Problems of Rural Sociology: The Peasant Community and Its Historical–Sociological Problems" was originally published as "Problèmes de sociologie rurale, la communanauté paysanne et ses problèmes historico-sociologiques," *Cahiers internationaux de Sociologie* 6 (1949): 78–100. It was subsequently published in *Du rural à l'urbain* (Paris: Anthropos, 1970), 21–40. Copyright 1970, Éditions Économica.

"Social Classes in Rural Areas: Tuscany and the *Mezzadria Classica*" was originally published as "Les classes sociales dans les campagnes, La Toscane et la Mezzadria classica," *Cahiers internationaux de Sociologie* 10 (1951): 70–93. It was subsequently published in *Du rural à l'urbain* (Paris: Anthropos, 1970), 41–62. Copyright 1970, Éditions Économica.

"Perspectives on Rural Sociology" was originally published as "Perspectives de la sociologie rurale," *Cahiers internationaux de Sociologie* 14 (1953): 122–40. It was subsequently published in *Du rural à l'urbain* (Paris: Anthropos, 1970), 63–78. Copyright 1970, Éditions Économica. An earlier translation, with a few short omissions, appeared in Henri Lefebvre, *Key Writings*, ed. Stuart Elden, Elizabeth Lebas, and Eleonore Kofman (London: Continuum, 2003), 111–20. The translation here is new.

"Social Relations, Population Phenomena, and Labor Problems in the Agricultural Sector of Underdeveloped Countries" was originally published as "Les relations sociales, les phénomènes de population et les problèmes du travail dans les pays sous-développés, secteur de l'agriculture," in *Atti del Congresso internazionale di studio sul problema delle aree arretrate, Milano, 10–15 ottobre 1954*, 4 vols. (Milan: Dott. A. Giuffrè, 1954–56), 2:823–33.

"The Village Community" was originally published as "La communauté villageoisie," *La Pensée*, no. 66 (1956): 29–38.

"The Theory of Ground Rent and Rural Sociology" was a contribution to the International Congress of Sociology, Amsterdam, August 1956, originally published as "Théorie de la rente foncière et sociologie rurale," *Transactions of the Third World Congress of Sociology* 2 (1956): 244–50. It was subsequently published in *Du rural à l'urbain* (Paris: Anthropos, 1970), 79–87. Copyright 1970, Éditions Économica. Translated by Matthew Dennis and first published in English as Henri Lefebvre, "The Theory of Ground Rent and Rural Sociology," *Antipode* 48, no. 1 (2016): 67–73. The text has been translated into Spanish twice: "La teoría de la Renta de la Tierra y la Sociología Rural," translated by Óscar Uribe Villegas, *Revista Mexicana de Sociología* 27, no. 1 (1965): 7–14, reprinted in *La renta de la tierra: Cinco ensayos,* by Henri Lefebvre, José M. Caballero, Oscar González, and Werner Kamppeter (Mexico City: Editorial Tlaiualli, 1983), 11–18; and "Teoría de la renta de la tierra y sociología rural," in *De lo rural a lo urbano*, trans. Javier Gonzalez-Pueyo, ed. Mario Gaviria (Barcelona: Ediciones Península, 1971), 77–84. Both translations have been consulted in producing this version, with the subheadings deriving from the 1983 reprint.

"The Marxist–Leninist Theory of Ground Rent" was originally published as "La teoría Marxista-Leninista de la renta de la tierra," in *Estudios sociológicos sobre la Reforma Agraria* (Mexico City: UNAM, 1965), 129–54. This publication consists of papers delivered at the Fifteenth National Sociology Congress of Mexico, held in Tepic/Nayarit, October 19–24, 1964. Translated by Sîan Rosa Hunter Dodsworth.

"Introduction to the Psychosociology of Everyday Life" was originally published as "Introduction à la psycho-sociologie de la vie quotidienne," in *Encyclopédie de la psychologie* (Paris: Fernand Nathan, 1962), 102–7. It was subsequently published in *Du rural à l'urbain* (Paris: Anthropos, 1970), 89–107. Copyright 1970, Éditions Économica.

"The New Urban Complex: Lacq-Mourenx and the Urban Problems of the New Working Class" was originally published as "Les nouveaux ensembles urbains: Un cas concret: Lacq-Mourenx et les problèmes urbains de la nouvelle classe ouvrière," *Revue Française de Sociologie* 1, no. 2 (1960): 186–201. It was subsequently published in *Du rural à l'urbain* (Paris: Anthropos, 1970), 109–28. Copyright 1970, Éditions Économica.

"Experimental Utopia: For a New Urbanism" was originally published as "Utopie expérimentale: Pour un nouvel urbanisme," *Revue Française de Sociologie* 2, no. 3 (1961): 191–98. It was subsequently published in *Du rural à l'urbain* (Paris: Anthropos, 1970), 129–40. Copyright 1970, Éditions Économica.

"The Valley of Campan: A Study in Historical Sociology" was originally published as *La vallée de Campan: Étude de sociologie rurale* (Paris: Presses Universitaires de France, 1963), 83–116. Copyright 1963, PUF/Humensis, 1963.

Index

absenteeism, 43, 82
absolute rent, xxxii, xxxiii–xxxiv, 107, 118, 120, 128–38, 141–45
abstraction, xxiii–xxv, 12, 117, 123, 133, 152, 168, 194
administration, 21, 30, 43, 46, 48, 53, 70, 82–83, 178, 209, 210, 212–14
adolescents. *See* youth
Adventures of the Dialectic (Merleau-Ponty), 96
advertising, 152
Aebli, Werner, 193
Aesop, 151
aesthetics, xv, 157, 166, 168, 200
agrarian capitalism, xxxi, 61, 130, 132, 138, 142. *See also* capitalist farms
agrarian communities. *See* peasant communities
agrarian reform, xiii, xxv–xxvi, 4–5, 60, 67, 71, 72, 87, 99, 100–102, 106, 131–32
agrarian regimes, 64–66
agriculture: agricultural era, 8, 18–19; agricultural labor, 23, 29, 37–57, 62, 81–85, 87, 105–6, 110–11, 115, 120, 128, 134, 136, 137, 141; agricultural production, 3, 8, 38, 49, 55–56, 60, 65–66, 70–72, 77–87, 95, 98, 105, 116, 119–45, 214; agricultural revolution, 19, 67, 71; agricultural towns, 72, 105; archaic remnants, xxix, 61, 62, 69, 100; capitalist farms, 23, 32, 44, 45–46, 61, 67, 109–10, 112, 116, 128–30; cooperative approaches, 23, 26, 51, 61–62, 72; crop rotation, 22, 26, 27, 53, 54, 65; and ground rent, xv, xxx–xxxii, 39, 69, 71, 82, 105–12, 115–45; industrialized agriculture, 32, 71, 72, 109, 110, 111, 116; irrigation, 51, 70, 71, 80, 209; large-scale agriculture, 23, 32, 40–42, 72, 84, 112, 116; livestock, xv, 26, 29, 44, 49–50, 52–56, 116, 122, 208, 209, 216, 221, 226, 231; mechanization, 45, 61, 65, 69, 71, 72, 78, 81, 110, 111, 115–16, 136, 137; origins of, 29; owner-operators, 45, 48; product prices, xxxii, 107, 110, 118, 119–22, 126, 129, 131, 133–35, 141–42, 144; sharecropping, xxvi, xxvii, 37–57, 66–67, 69, 73, 78, 81, 83, 85, 112, 116, 118, 135, 137; small farms, 40–42, 45, 48, 72, 73, 107, 109, 112, 124, 144;

specialization, 60–61, 78, 111–12, 116; tenant farming, 38, 45, 63, 66, 69, 71, 73, 78, 84, 111; traditional methods, 78; in underdeveloped countries, 61, 72, 77–87, 116–17; vegetable crops, 44, 111, 116
Aix-en-Provence, 178–80, 181, 189
Algeria, xiii
alienation, 2, 154, 167–68
analytic-regressive moment, xxix, 13, 69
Ancien Régime, 32–33, 214, 224, 229, 234, 236
Anderson, James, 107
Andorra, 206, 219
appropriation, 6, 24, 81, 152
arable land, 17, 90, 125, 236
arbitration, 28, 54, 221, 223–24, 230, 235
archeo-civilization, 67–68
arch lands, 82–84
aristocracy, 37–38, 39, 165
art, 19, 73, 96, 152, 154, 177, 188, 197
artisans, 44, 47, 62, 71, 80, 83, 180, 181, 214
Asiatic feudalism, 71, 80, 109
Aspin, 220, 230, 231, 233
Asté, 211, 219, 220–21, 223–24, 225–26, 229–30, 233–34
Athens Charter, 193, 196
Aure Valley, 208, 217, 219, 230, 231, 233
automation, 60, 187, 189
average profit, 107, 110, 118, 121, 127–29, 131, 133–34, 139–40, 143
Aztec civilization, 92

Baden-Powell, Robert, 21
Bagnères-de-Bigorre, xxi, 205–6, 211, 212, 216, 218–19, 221, 233–35
Balzac, Honoré de, xx, 19, 163
banality, 156, 157, 158–59, 164
Banfi, Antonio, 77

barbarians, 30, 33, 67
Basque country, 27, 31
Baudéan, 211, 219, 220, 233
Béarn, 27, 31, 216
Berdoulay, Vincent, xxii
Bigorre, xxi, 31, 206, 213, 218, 219
Bladé, Jean-François, 19
Bloch, Marc, 23, 64–65
border communities, 205, 218
boredom, 5, 153–54, 157, 161, 164–65, 171–72, 176, 181, 184, 186, 190, 199, 202
boundaries, 27, 211, 215, 217, 218, 226, 231
bourgeoisie, xxxiii, 2, 8, 19–20, 68, 69, 82, 92, 107, 116, 123, 138, 141–42, 165, 211, 215, 221, 227, 235
bourgeois society, 97–98, 118, 130–31
bourgeois thought, 95–96, 98–99, 117, 128
braccianti, xxvii, 45–47, 49, 50–52, 56
Brazil, xiii, 61, 86
Brittany, xii, 110, 145
Bruhat, Jean, 101–2
Brühlmann, Eduard, 193
Brunner, Edmund de S., 22
Brutails, Jean-Auguste, 19
Bulan, 226
bureaucracy, 163, 167, 188, 190, 199, 219, 227
Byzantine law, 92

Caesar, Julius, 30
cafés, 163–64, 177, 201, 202
Cahiers internationaux de Sociologie, xii, 59
Campan Valley, xii, xxvi, 205–37
Capital (Marx), xv, xxiv, xxxi, 95, 117, 118–19, 123
capitalist farms, 23, 32, 44–46, 61, 67, 109–10, 112, 116, 128–30
capitalist ownership, 63, 81–82, 83–85

Carrère, Guilhaume, 211
Castelbajac, Baron de, 213, 217, 218, 230–31
Castro, Fidel, 4
Catalonia, 19, 33, 67
Catholicism, 98–99, 111, 200
Cavaillès, Henri, 207
cemeteries, 182, 185
Cenac-Moncaut, Justin, 19
censorship, xiv, xv
Centre national de la recherche scientifique (CNRS), xii–xiii, xvi, 3
Châtelet, François, 96
Chen Po-Ta, 108
children, 26, 33, 73, 152, 154, 165, 167, 183, 186–87, 202
Chile, xiii
China, xiii, xxv, 4, 60, 99, 108
choice, 152, 157, 162, 165
Chombart de Lauwe, Jean, 61
Christ, Rico, 193
clans, 24–25, 29, 81, 124
class: class consciousness, xxvii, 96, 180, 181, 189; class relations, xxiv, xxvi–xxix, xxx, 77; class strategies, 5, 6; class struggle, xxx, xxxiv, 96; emergentist theory of, xxvii; landowning class, xv, 37–38, 43, 45–48, 51, 82, 108–9, 121, 134, 138, 140, 142; and peasant communities, xii, xxvi–xxvii, 37–57, 73, 85, 108; as process, xxvi–xxix; and the state, 102; and the street, 161; subaltern classes, xxvii–xxviii, xxx; and urban development, 179–81, 187–90, 199; working class, 135, 142, 166, 179–81, 187–90. *See also* aristocracy; bourgeoisie; lumpen-proletariat; petit bourgeoisie; proletariat
classical economics, xxiv, 112, 117–18, 119–20

climate, 42, 193, 207–8
clothing, 152, 200
collective disciplines, 26–27, 70, 72, 209
collective ownership, xxix, 24–25, 31, 61, 80, 81, 82–84, 90–91, 97, 124, 209–10, 213, 236
colonialism, xxxii, 62–63, 72, 78, 82–87, 102, 116–17, 124, 141
commercial capitalism, 78, 80–81
commercialization, 60
commodities, 6–7, 11, 123, 135, 162
common sense, xxx, 158
communication, 158–60, 168
communism, xii, xiv–xv, 1, 101
communitarian cities, 174–75
competition, 5, 70, 121, 123, 125–29, 134, 136, 138–41, 144, 145
complexity, xviii–xix, 61–62
concentration of ownership, 60, 63, 71, 115–16, 142
concrete abstraction, xxiii–xxv
conduits, 6–7, 166–67
consanguinity, xxix, 70, 73, 80, 91
Conscience mystifiée, La (Lefebvre and Guterman), xii
constant capital, 55–56, 134, 139
consumer goods, 5, 28, 152, 162, 173
consumption, xxiv, 5, 6, 24, 162, 165
contracts: labor contracts, 24; law of, 93; rental contracts, 129; sharecropping contracts, 43, 44, 49, 57
contributions, theory of, 54–57
cooperatives, xxviii, 23, 26, 31, 51, 61–62, 72
co-ownership, 178, 180, 227
cost of living, xxiv, 158
credit, 133
Critique of Dialectical Reason (Sartre), xviii, 12–13

Critique of Everyday Life (Lefebvre), ix, x–xi, xxi, xxxiv
crop rotation, 22, 26, 27, 53, 54, 65
Cuba, 4
culture, 22, 63–64, 73, 99–100, 152, 165, 177, 182, 196, 202
Curi-Seimbres, Alcide, 19
customary law, 21, 30, 71, 82–83, 93, 94, 206, 214, 223–30
cyclical time, 201

dead, the, 182, 185
dead abstraction, xxiii
Declaration of La Sarraz, 196
deep objectivity, 97
De l'État (Lefebvre), x, xiii
Delisle, Léopold, 19
de Marca, Pierre, 218
democracy, 28, 87, 101, 132, 144, 188, 199, 232
depopulation, 42, 111, 112
Descartes, René, xiv
descriptive moment, xxix, 69
desires, 9, 152, 153–54, 159–60, 162, 166, 176, 199, 201–2
Development of Capitalism in Russia, The (Lenin), xxxi, xxxiii
dialectical humanism, 176–77
dialectical materialism, xxiii–xxiv, 2, 5, 89–90, 96–97
Dialectical Materialism (Lefebvre), ix, xxiv
dialectics, xi, xix–xx, xxiii–xxiv, 1–2, 10, 12, 96–97, 168, 198
Diderot, Denis, xiv, 163
differential rent, xxxii–xxxiv, 107, 118, 120, 126–36, 138, 141–44
disalienation, 168
dissatisfaction, 5, 161, 172, 177
distribution, 5, 107–8, 110, 118–19, 131–32, 152

division of labor, xxxii, 23, 165
double monopoly, xxxiv, 109–10, 124–25, 127–28, 129, 136, 140
Ducay, François, 211
Dürer, Albrecht, 195
Durkheim, Émile, 26, 173
Du rural à l'urbain (Lefebvre), x, xiv, xv, xvii–xviii, xxi–xxii, 1–14

ecology, xix, xxviii, 62
economic growth, 8, 63
education, 152, 186, 196
Egli, Ernst, 193, 195, 196
Egypt, xxv, 60
Elements of Rhythmanalysis (Lefebvre), ix, xxxv
emigration, 67, 111, 112. See also migration
empiricism, 20, 64, 96, 112, 194, 196
Empoli, 51, 52–54
Engels, Friedrich, xxiii, 30, 89–91, 93, 95, 96, 100, 106–7, 122, 132
England, 46, 66, 71, 82, 106–7, 117, 123–24, 137
entrepreneurship, 44, 82, 125, 127, 138–40
Entrikin, Nick, xxii
equality, 25, 31, 130, 131–32
Escaladieu, monastery of, 234
Espace et politique (Lefebvre), xvii
ethnographic methodologies, 67
Ethnological Notebooks of Karl Marx (Marx), xxxi
European feudalism, 71, 80, 109
everyday life, x, xx–xxi, 3, 5–6, 151–68, 173, 176, 183–85, 196, 200, 201
Everyday Life in the Modern World (Lefebvre), ix, xxxiv
exchange relations, 23, 70, 130
exchange value, 117, 123, 162
existentialism, xiv, 12

Index

"Experimental Utopia" (Lefebvre), xxi, 193–203
exploitation, xxvii, xxxiv, 5, 38, 42, 82, 107, 109, 111, 115, 124–29, 131, 132, 136, 140–42
Explosion, The (Lefebvre), ix
expropriation, xxv, xxxii, xxxiii, 83–85, 212
extractive industries, xvi, 122

fallowing, 65
family, 20, 22–26, 29–31, 44, 51–52, 70, 90–91, 93, 159, 168, 197, 202
farming. *See* agriculture
farms, small, 40–42, 45, 48, 72, 73, 107, 109, 112, 124, 144
fascism, xii, 1
fattorie, 42–45, 47–54
fattorie committees, 48–54
fertility, xxxii, 107, 118, 119–20, 125–26, 133
fertilizer, 39, 52
festivals, x, 27, 201
fetishism, xxi, 119, 158, 162
feudalism: Asiatic feudalism, 71, 80, 109; in the Campan Valley, 210–11, 214–15, 218–31, 234–36; cultural manifestations, xxix, xxxiii; European feudalism, 71, 80, 109; feudal rent, 13, 122, 218, 220; feudal rights, 84, 218, 234; feudal seizures, 210–11; Muslim feudalism, 71, 80, 83, 109; and nationalization of land, 131, 132; persistence of, xxvii, xxix–xxxi, xxxiii, 18, 39–42, 80, 116, 118, 135, 140; refeudalization, xxvi, 215, 229, 231; semifeudal systems, xxx–xxxi, 39, 40, 43, 69, 78, 80, 81, 111, 116, 131, 135; and sharecropping, xxvi, xxvii, 39–42, 69, 78, 81, 116, 135; in underdeveloped countries, 80, 81, 83, 84, 135

finance capitalism, 81, 82, 86, 111, 138
Fin de l'histoire, La (Lefebvre), x
fishing, 25
fixed rent. *See* ground rent
Florence, 37, 40, 42, 50, 54, 55
folklore, xxix, xxx, 33, 72, 159, 217
food, 85–86, 135, 152, 196, 197
forests, 17, 25, 94, 122, 208–9, 217, 220–21, 223, 226, 230, 233–34, 236
formal logic, 10, 21
Fors de Bigorre, 218
Fourier, Charles, 195
French law, 83–84
French Revolution, 109, 228, 232–33
Freud, Sigmund, 1
Friedmann, Georges, xi
functional cities, 175–76
functionalism, 172, 175–76, 184, 190, 200, 202
Fustel de Coulanges, Numa Denis, 93

games, 176–77, 190, 201, 202. *See also* play; sport
gangs, 187
Gaviria, Marco, xv, 14
genetic structuralism, 13
Germanic law, 30, 94–95
Germany, 94
gestures, 59, 152, 153, 155, 200
ghettos, 173, 174
Giraudoux, Jean, 193
globalization, xxxv
Goldmann, Lucien, 13
gossip, 153, 167, 201
governing functions, 27–28, 211–15, 222–25
Grammont, dukes of, 226, 227, 229
Gramsci, Antonio, xxvi, xxvii–xxviii, xxix–xxx
grazing, 209, 217, 221, 226–27, 231–32, 233. *See also* pasture

Grosseto, 40, 42
ground rent, xiii, xv, xix–xx, xxiv–xxv, xxx–xxxiv, 4, 13, 39, 69, 71, 82, 98, 105–12, 115–45, 218, 228
Gurvitch, Georges, xii, 3, 89
Guterman, Norbert, xi, xii, xxxiv
Guttman, Louis, 186

habous, 83, 84
Hagetmau, xii, xxxv
Halbwachs, Maurice, xii
Halfacree, Keith, xxii
Haudricourt, André-Georges, 89
health, 85
Hegel, G. W. F., xi, xii, 1–2, 59, 93, 94
Hegel, Marx, Nietzsche (Lefebvre), ix, xxxv
Heidegger, Martin, 1
Hess, Rémi, xiii, xiv, xvi
hierarchies, 44, 73, 189, 197–99, 202
historical-genetic moment, xxix, 13, 69
historical law, 94
historical materialism, xxiii–xxiv, xxvi, 2, 99, 122
historical method, 95–99
historical sociological method, xviii–xix, xxviii–xxix, 33, 69–74
historico-cultural theory, 68
Hitler au pouvoir (Lefebvre), xii
home, 18, 25, 154, 155, 160, 163, 176
horizontal complexity, xviii–xix, 61–62
housework, 153, 165, 187
housing, xvi, 18, 20, 53, 85, 86, 152, 174, 175, 177–81, 183–85, 195–96, 199, 209
human geography, x, xix, 21, 62, 65
Hungary, 106
hunting and gathering, 24–25
Husserl, Edmund, 1

ideology, xx, xxvii–xxviii, xxix, 2, 4–7, 11, 19–20, 46, 73–74, 172–73, 197

inalienable rights, 83, 84, 93, 236
Inca civilization, 92
incorporated comparison, xix
India, xxv, 60, 80, 108
individualism, 23–24, 26, 31, 33, 44, 66, 70, 71, 172–73
industrial capitalism, 78, 86, 111, 137, 138, 141–42
industrialization, xvi, 3, 7–8, 32, 71, 72, 85, 109, 111, 116
industrialized agriculture, 32, 71, 72, 109, 110, 111, 116
industrial labor, 49, 85, 86, 87, 134, 137, 141, 165, 187–88, 189, 199
industrial production, 105, 134, 189
industrial revolution, 19
inequality, xx, 25–26, 31, 78–79, 117
infrastructure, 174, 196
inheritance, 31, 60, 91, 234, 235
Institut de sociologie urbaine (ISU), xvi
institutions, 4, 6–7, 10–11, 223, 224
integral history, xxviii–xxix
integral philosophy, xxiii, xxviii
integration, 8, 197–99, 202
"Introduction to a Critique of Political Economy" (Marx), 97–99
Introduction to Modernity (Lefebvre), ix, xi, xvi
"Introduction to the Psychosociology of Everyday Life" (Lefebvre), xxi, 151–68
investment, xxxi, xxxii–xxxiii, 39, 43, 49–51, 79, 107, 116, 120, 125–30, 134, 139–40, 142, 143
Iran, xiii
irrigation, 51, 70, 71, 80, 209
Islamic law, 82–83
Israel, 102, 202
Italy, xiii, xxv, xxvi, xxvii, 4, 37–57, 60, 62, 66, 67, 71, 78, 105, 106–8, 138

Jansen, Cornelius, x
Japan, xiii, xxv, 60
"Junker" economy, xxxiii
justice, 100, 132, 212, 224, 225

Kautsky, Karl, xxiii, 130
Key Writings (Lefebvre), ix, x, xxii
khammès, 83
kibbutzim, 102
Kojève, Alexandre, xii
Kolb, John H., 22
kolkhoz, 61, 72, 99, 100–102
kulaks, 100, 116, 132

labor: agricultural labor, 23, 29, 37–57, 62, 81–85, 87, 105–6, 110–11, 115, 120, 128, 134, 136, 137, 141; and automation, 60, 187, 189; division of labor, xxxii, 23, 165; housework, 153, 165, 187; industrial labor, 49, 85, 86, 87, 134, 137, 141, 165, 187–88, 189, 199; intensification of, 38–39, 43; jobs for women, 187; labor contracts, 24; land–labor–capital formula, xv, xx; productivity of, 38–39, 43, 62, 69, 120, 134, 136, 137; seasonal labor, 48, 61, 111; slave labor, xix, 23, 29, 71; social labor, 117; supplementary work, 50; unemployment, 48, 49, 50–51, 77, 79, 82, 85, 86; unpaid labor, 43; wage labor, xix, xxiv, xxv, 27, 51, 52, 56, 107; wages, xxiv, 51, 52, 56, 86, 110, 128, 198
Labouret, Henri, 21
La Bruyère, Jean de, 19
Lacq-Mourenx, xi, xvi, xx, xxvi, 7–8, 177–87
Lafforgue, Jean, 211
La Fontaine, Jean de, 19
land clearance, 29, 33, 51, 70
land improvement, xxxi, xxxii–xxxiii, 49–51, 53, 120

land–labor–capital formula, xv, xx
landlords, xxxi, xxxiii, 107–12, 118, 123, 137–38, 144–45. *See also* landowning class
landowning class, xv, 37–38, 43, 45–48, 51, 82, 108–9, 121, 134, 138, 140, 142
land quality, 125–26, 127–28, 133, 144. *See also* fertility
land redistribution, 25, 109
land reform. *See* agrarian reform
land sharing, 90
language, 6, 151, 152, 155, 156–57, 158–60
large-scale agriculture, 23, 32, 40–42, 72, 84, 112, 116
latifundia, 23, 67, 71, 92, 105, 107, 109, 135
Laveleye, Émile de, 29
law of decreasing productivity, 107, 118, 119, 130
laws of becoming, 96–97
Lazarsfeld, Paul, 185
leases, 92, 210, 213, 214, 227–28, 230, 234
Le Corbusier, 174, 196–97, 199–201
Ledoux, Claude-Nicolas, 195
Lefebvre, Georges, 23
Lefebvre, Henri: at CNRS, xii–xiii, xvi, 3; cofounds ISU, xvi; doctoral theses, xii, xxi, xxii; and the Parti communiste français, xii, xiv–xv, 1, 4; teaching, xii, xvi; translations of works, ix–x, xv, xxii; work on everyday life, ix–x; work on Marx, xi, xiv–xv, xxxiv; work on rural issues, xii–xiv, xv–xxiii; work on urban issues, xv–xvii, xx–xxii, xxxv; and World War II, xii, xxi
legal personhood, 83
leisure, 154, 168, 173, 184, 187, 196, 201–2
Lenin, Vladimir Ilyich, xi, xv, xxiii, xxxi, xxxiii, 95, 99, 100, 108–10, 122–36, 140

Le Péage-de-Roussillon, 173
Le Play, Frédéric, 20, 22, 30, 93
Lewin, Kurt, 177
Limousin, 42
linear time, 201
literature, 18–19, 166
livestock, xv, 26, 29, 44, 49–50, 52, 53–56, 116, 122, 208, 209, 216, 221, 226, 231
living standards, 81, 85–86, 198
logic, 10, 21
Logique formelle, logique dialectique (Lefebvre), xiv
long-term leases, 92, 210, 213, 214, 227–28, 230, 234
Lourdes, 90
Lucca, 37, 40, 42
lumpen-proletariat, 86, 179, 180

McMichael, Philip, xix
Madagascar, 21, 102
Mandelbrot, Benoît, 194
Manuel de sociologie rurale (Lefebvre, planned), xiii, xx, 72–73
marginalism, 107
market economy, 6, 20, 32, 44, 60–61, 68, 70, 72, 80, 125, 130
marriage, 91
Marx, Karl: on alienation, 2; brought to French audience, xi, xiv; *Capital*, xv, xxiv, xxxi, 95, 117, 118–19, 123; correspondence, 99; dialectical materialism, xxiii, 2, 5, 89–90, 96–97; on distribution, 5, 107–8, 118–19; early works, 1–2, 94; *Ethnological Notebooks*, xxxi; on ground rent, xxxi–xxxii, 4, 98, 106–8, 117, 118–23, 128–29, 130; on historical method, 97–99; interest in Balzac, xx; "Introduction to a Critique of Political Economy," 97–99; laws of becoming, 96–97; Lefebvre's work on, xi, xiv–xv, xxxiv; methodological approaches, xi, xviii, xxix, 13, 89–90, 96–99; on peasant communities, 91–95, 99, 108; on production, xxiv, xxxi, 5, 97–98, 119–22; on surplus value, xxiv, 5, 118–19, 121; "On the Theft of Wood," 94
Marxism, xi, xviii, xxix, 2, 4–5, 12, 13, 21, 63, 89–90, 93–95, 96–99
Marxisme, Le (Lefebvre), xiv
"Marxist–Leninist Theory of Ground Rent, The" (Lefebvre), xix–xx, xxiv–xxv, xxx–xxxiv, 115–45
Marxist Thought and the City (Lefebvre), ix, xv, xvii
materialism, xxiii–xxiv, xxvi, 2. See also dialectical materialism; historical materialism
Materialism and Empirio-Criticism (Lenin), xxiii
maternity, 164, 165
matriarchy, 91, 166
maximum profit, 138–39, 141–42, 143, 145
mechanization, 45, 61, 65, 69, 71, 72, 78, 81, 110, 111, 115–16, 136, 137
melk lands, 83
Menshevik law, 130
Merleau-Ponty, Maurice, 96
Metaphilosophy (Lefebvre), ix, xxxiv
Méthodologie des sciences (Lefebvre), xiv
Mexico, xiii, xxv, 60
mezzadria classica, xxvi, xxvii, 37–57
Midi, 19, 33, 60, 185
migration, 67, 77, 81–82, 85, 111, 112, 171, 216
migratory herding, 26, 85. See also nomadism; seminomadism
military service, xii, 184, 230
mills, 213, 214, 220

mining, 122, 173
mir, 22, 25, 29–30, 99, 100–101
misery, 153, 158, 184
modernity, xi, xxx, 1, 5, 7–8, 18, 160, 164, 165, 189–90
Molière, 19
mondialisation, xxxv
monetary economy, 23, 26, 68, 72
money, 23, 70, 80, 130, 135, 162, 228
monographs, xxviii, 68, 92, 93
monopolies: and competition, 125–26, 128, 129, 136, 138–41; double monopoly, xxxiv, 109–10, 124–25, 127–29, 136, 140; of exploitation, xxxi, xxxiii–xxxiv, 109–11, 124–25, 127–29, 131, 132, 136, 140–42; of land ownership, xxxi–xxxiv, 109–11, 121–22, 124–25, 127–29, 131, 134–35, 140–42, 145; monopoly capitalism, xxxiii–xxxiv, 108, 136–45
monuments, xx–xxi, 155, 159, 182, 200–201
moralism, 163, 174–75, 202
morality, 20, 83, 99, 101, 174–75, 196, 202
Moreno, Jacob L., 22, 177
Morhange, Pierre, xi
Morocco, 102
Mossé, Claude, 89
mountains, 25, 40, 44, 90, 205–37
Mourgoueilh, 208, 221, 229, 233–34
Mouvement républicain populaire (MRP), 93
Muslim feudalism, 71, 80, 83, 109
Musset, Alfred de, xiv
mutual assistance, 27, 99, 100
myth, xxix, 33, 72, 73–74, 152

Naples, 163
Napoleonic code, 83, 236
Narodniks, 131, 132

Nationalisme contre les nations, Le (Lefebvre), xii
nationalization, xxxii, xxxiv, 99, 130–32
natural environment, 68
natural law, 94
natural resources, xv, xvi, 79, 85, 122
Navarrenx, xii, xvi
needs, 9, 152, 153–54, 160, 166, 176, 185–86, 196, 197, 199
neighborhood relations, 72, 73, 91, 173–74, 183
neighborhood units, 173–74
Nelson, Lowry, 64
neoliberalism, xxxiv
networks, 166–67
Neue Stadt, Die, 193–203
"New Urban Complex, The" (Lefebvre), xvi, 171–90
new urbanism, 11, 193–203
Nietzsche, Friedrich, x, 1
nomadism, 23, 29, 62, 82, 85, 106
Normandy, 19, 208
"Notes Written One Sunday in the French Countryside" (Lefebvre), x–xi, xxi

objectivism, 96–97, 117
obligatory gifts, 43, 50
Office of Waterways and Forests, 229
"On the Theft of Wood" (Marx), 94
organic communities, 23–24, 174
overpopulation, 86, 186
overproduction, xxxi, 116
Owen, Robert, 195
owner-operators, 45, 48

Parain, Charles, 89
Paris, xii, xiii, xxi, 18, 66, 79, 109, 111, 115, 155–56, 162, 163, 172
Parti communiste français (PCF), xii, xiv–xv, 1, 4

passage, rights of, 226, 229, 233, 229, 231, 233
pastoral imperialism, 216
pasture, 17, 25, 26, 40, 61, 206, 208–9, 216–36. See also grazing
paternalism, 43, 172–73, 176, 202
patriarchal families, 18, 19, 22, 30–31, 44, 52, 70, 163
Pau, xxxv, 206, 211, 233
Paulme, Denise, 80
Paysans, Les (Balzac), xx
peasant communities: aspirations, 131, 133; in the Campan Valley, xii, xxvi, 205–37; and class, xii, xxvi–xxvii, 37–57, 73, 85, 108; collective disciplines, 26–27, 70, 72, 209; complexity of, xviii–xix, 61–62; culture and traditions, 63–64, 73–74; defense against outside forces, 23, 28, 32; defining, 22–28; evolution of, 29–31, 66–67, 70–73, 92; governing functions, 27–28, 211–15, 222–25; Marx on, 91–95, 99, 108; organic nature of, 23–24; origins of, 28–29; ownership types, 24–26, 31, 80–85, 90–91; political functions, 28; problems related to, 28–33, 59–61; proletarianization of, xxvi, 77, 82, 85, 86; relation to higher forms of economy, 32; relation to the state, 32–33, 92, 95, 210–12, 215, 217, 229, 232–33; and revolution, xxv–xxvi, xxxiii, 3–5, 32; scarcity of literary texts on, 18–19; scientific studies of, 19–22, 60; transition to socialism, 99–102; typology of, 73; in underdeveloped countries, xii, 61, 72, 77–87; wisdom of, 17, 33
perpetual rent, 84, 227
Perrier, Marc, 211
Perroux, François, 177
"Perspectives on Rural Sociology" (Lefebvre), x, xix, xxv, xxix, 59–74
petit bourgeoisie, xxx, 132, 214
Phenomenology of Spirit (Hegel), xii
Philosophies group, xi, xiv
physiocrats, 19–20
Pignon, Éduoard, xiv
Piketty, Thomas, xx
Pisa, 37, 40, 57
Pistoia, 37, 40
plains, 40, 44, 57, 106, 205–6, 208, 216, 217
planning, 61, 86–87, 142, 171–90, 193–203. See also urban development
play, 176–77, 184, 186, 187, 201–2
plows, 61, 66, 68
poderi, 42–43, 47–48, 53
Poggibonsi, 48–49, 52
political economy, xii, xv–xvi, xix–xx, xxiii–xxv, xxviii, xxix, 2, 21, 62, 98, 106, 117–18, 152
political functions, 28
Politzer, Georges, xi
population movements, 62, 77, 81–82, 171. See also migration
population size, 29, 39, 79, 81, 85, 86, 136–37, 178, 231
positivism, 20, 117, 154, 172, 176
poverty, xxi, 153, 158, 162
prices, xxxii, 60, 107, 110, 118, 119–22, 126, 129, 131, 133–35, 141–42, 144
primitive accumulation, xxv, xxxii, 3
primitive communities, 28–30, 80, 83–84, 87, 89–93, 99–101, 234
primogeniture, 31
privacy, 183
private property, xxix, 8, 24–25, 31, 68, 70, 72, 81, 83–85, 91, 93, 94, 126–27, 209–10, 229
privatization, xxxii, xxxiv

Problèmes actuels du marxisme (Lefebvre), xv
"Problems of Rural Sociology" (Lefebvre), xx, xxv, xxix, 17–34
production: agricultural, 3, 8, 38, 49, 55–56, 60, 65–66, 70–72, 77–87, 95, 98, 105, 116, 119–45, 214; of consumer goods, 162; and everyday life, 152; industrial, 105, 134, 189; Marx on, xxiv, xxxi, 5, 97–98, 119–22; means of, 8, 24, 81, 120, 125; modes of, xxvi, xxx–xxxi, 23, 59, 70–72, 80–82, 95, 225; overproduction, xxxi, 116; relations of, xxvi, xxviii, 5, 6, 8, 97–99, 101, 140, 219; specialization of, 60–61, 78, 111–12, 116
Production of Space, The (Lefebvre), ix, xv–xvi, xviii, xxii, xxv, xxxv
productivity, 38–39, 43, 62, 65, 69, 72, 81–82, 107, 118–20, 125–26, 129–30, 134, 136, 137, 144
profit, xxiv, xxxi–xxxii, 60, 107, 110, 118–19, 121–22, 127–29, 131, 133–35, 138–45
profiteers, 110, 111, 128
programmatic approaches, 193, 194–95, 197
progressive-regressive model, xviii–xix, xxix, 12–13
proletariat, xxxiii, 5, 8, 77, 82, 85, 86, 115, 123, 131, 132–33, 179–81
Provence, 19, 178, 189
proximity relations, 26–27
psychology, xi, 86, 152
Pyrenees, x, xii, xiii, xvi, xxi, xxii, xxvi, xxxv–xxxvi, 4, 7–8, 20, 33, 61, 67, 89–93, 205–37

Quatre Véziaux, 217, 218, 219, 230–34

Rabelais, François, xiv
raw materials, 79, 85, 138

rebaa, 83
refeudalization, xxvi, 215, 229, 231
Régulier, Catherine, xxii
relativism, xxiii, 165
religion, xxx, 63–64, 74, 83, 182, 197
religious communities, 175
religious property, 67, 124, 234
rent. *See* absolute rent; differential rent; feudalism: feudal rent; ground rent; perpetual rent; technical rent
repetitiveness, 153, 156, 157, 160, 163, 165, 168, 200
resettlement, 81, 84–85
Restif de la Bretonne, Nicolas, 163
reverse strikes, 51, 53–54
revolution, xxv–xxvi, xxxiii, 3–5, 32, 99, 109, 130–31, 228, 232–33
rhythmic time, 201
Ribbe, Charles de, 19
Ricardo, David, xiv, 93, 107–8, 117–18, 119–20, 129
Right to the City, The (Lefebvre), ix, xv
ritual, 27, 33, 219, 224
Rivière, Georges-Henri, xxi
Rodinson, Maxime, 89, 100
Roman civilization, 30, 42, 92
Roman law, 21, 24, 25, 30, 33, 71, 93, 94–95, 206, 214, 236
Roussillon, 19, 33, 67
Rousseau, Jean-Jacques, 19
Rural Life in the United States, 62–63
rural sociology, x, xvii, xix, xxiii, xxviii–xxix, 12, 17–34, 59–74, 105–12
rural–urban transition, xvi–xvii, xxv–xxvi, 7–8
Russia, xiii, xiv, xxxi, xxxiii, 4, 22, 23, 29, 60, 61, 99, 100–102, 123, 130–32
Russian Revolution, 99

salaries. *See* wages
San Gimignano, 47–48, 50–51

Sand, George, 19
Sartre, Jean-Paul, xiv, xviii, 12–13
satisfaction, 5, 152, 161, 172, 177
Schelling, Friedrich Wilhelm Joseph von, xi
seasonal labor, 48, 61, 111
Sée, Henri, 23
segregation, 8, 181
semantics, 156–57, 158
semifeudal systems, xxx–xxxi, 39, 40, 43, 69, 78, 80, 81, 111, 116, 131, 135
seminomadism, 23, 29, 62, 85, 106
Senegal, xiii
serfdom, xxxiii, 38, 67
Serres, Olivier de, 19
sex, 152, 158
sharecropping, xxvi, xxvii, 37–57, 66–67, 69, 73, 78, 81, 83, 85, 112, 116, 118, 135, 137
shelter, rights of, 221, 226, 230, 231
shopping, 162, 201
Sicard, Harald von, 21
Siena, 37, 40, 42
signals, 155–57, 159, 168, 200
signs, 155–57, 159, 161, 200
slavery, xix, 23, 29, 71
slums, 85, 184
Smith, Adam, 107, 117, 118, 119
Smith, Lynn, 64
Soboul, Albert, xiii
"Social Classes in Rural Areas" (Lefebvre), xxvii, 37–57
socialism, 3, 4, 23, 72, 99–102, 109, 130, 132
socialization, 8, 130, 152, 188
social labor, 117
social mobility, 77, 81–82, 167
social psychology, 152
"Social Relations, Population Phenomena, and Labor Problems" (Lefebvre), xiii, 77–87

social structures, 32, 37–57, 61–62, 73, 78–87, 92, 193
social texts, 7–8, 157, 158–59, 160–61
Sociology of Marx, The (Lefebvre), ix, xxxiv
soil, xiv, xxxii, 39, 49, 51, 54, 107, 193, 207–8
solidarity, 24
Somme et le reste, La (Lefebvre), x, xv
Sorel, Charles, 19
Soviet Union. *See* Russia
sovkhoz, 23, 32, 61
space: comparison across space, xix; and everyday life, 151, 154, 155, 156, 162, 163; organization of, xvii, 28, 33; political economy of, xv–xvi, xix–xx; production of, xv–xvi, xviii–xix, xxxv; rural as production of space, xv, xviii–xix; and urban development, 173, 185, 200–201
Spain, xiii, 61, 92, 105, 108, 138, 205
specialization, 60–61, 78, 111–12, 116
spectacle, 160–62, 168
spontaneity, 21, 153, 163, 173, 174, 176, 177, 178, 183, 187, 188, 198
spontaneous cities, 172, 173, 180, 181, 184, 189
spontaneous sociability, 173, 177, 183
sport, 188, 190, 201, 219
Stalinism, xiv, xv, 2, 139
Stanek, Łukasz, xxi
state, the, xxviii, xxxii, xxxiv, xxxv, 6, 8, 11, 32–33, 61, 92, 94–95, 102, 130, 142, 144, 163, 210–12, 215, 217, 229, 232–33
State, Space, World (Lefebvre), ix, x
statistics, xix, 62, 63, 186
stem families, 93
Stolypin reforms, 101
Strabo, 91
streets, xxi, 153, 155, 156, 158, 160–63, 200

strikes, 51, 53–54
structuralism, 11, 13–14, 202
structure, 13–14, 17–18
subaltern classes, xxvii–xxviii, xxx
subjectivism, 96–97
subsidization, 145, 179–80
sugar beet, 138, 145
Sumner Maine, Henry James, 21
superstructures, 6–7, 59, 100, 101
supplementary work, 50
surplus profit, xxxi, xxxii, 110, 127–29, 131, 134–35, 138
surplus value, xxiv, 5, 118–19, 121, 134–35
surrealism, xi
Survival of Capitalism, The (Lefebvre), ix
symbols, 155–57, 159–60, 168, 200

tacit communities, 22, 29–30
taxes, 80, 83, 212, 214, 220, 232
technical environment, 68
technical rent, 110, 143, 144
technocracy, 175, 176, 202
technology, 33, 34, 60, 61–62, 65, 69, 70, 86, 116, 119–20, 134, 151, 153, 164
television, 160, 168
tenant farming, 38, 45, 63, 66, 69, 71, 73, 78, 84, 111
terrain, xiii, 40, 206–7
territoriality, xxix, 70, 73, 91
theater, 175, 190, 200, 201, 203
"Theory of Ground Rent and Rural Sociology" (Lefebvre), x, 105–12
Thompson, E. P., xxvii
time: comparison across time, xix; cyclical time, 201; and everyday life, 151, 154, 155, 156, 162, 163; and historical method, 95–96; linear time, 201; organization of, 27–28, 33; rhythmic time, 201; and urban development, 173, 185, 200–201

tools, 23, 39, 45, 49, 50, 55–56, 61, 86, 153, 189
Toulouse, 78–79, 112, 206, 212, 223, 226–27, 229, 233
Toward an Architecture of Enjoyment (Lefebvre), ix, xv
tractors, 61, 116, 136
trade unions, xxviii, 188
traffic, 196
transport networks, xxxv, 120, 126, 128
tribes, 80, 81, 83–84, 124
triviality, 5, 153, 156, 158–59
Trotsky, Leon, xxvi
Trudoviks, 131, 132
truth, xxiii, xxiv, 12, 96
Tunisia, xiii, 80–81, 82–87
Tuscany, xiii, xxvi, xxvii, 37–57, 67

underdeveloped countries, xii, 61, 72, 77–87, 116–17, 135, 137, 178
undivided property, 24–25, 233
unemployment, 48, 49, 50–51, 77, 79, 82, 85, 86
uneven development, xxv–xxvi, xxx–xxxi, xxxv, 33, 78–79, 109, 116, 117, 138
United States, xiii, 21–22, 60, 61, 62–64, 124
unpaid labor, 43
urban aristocracy, 37–38, 39
urban development, xvi–xvii, 7–8, 171–90, 193–203
urbanization, xvi–xvii, xx, 6, 7–8
urban markets, 37–38, 69, 112
Urban Revolution, The (Lefebvre), ix, xv, xvii
utopianism, 194–95
utopian socialism, 100, 132, 195

vacant lands, 83–84, 217, 220
Vallée de Campan, La (Lefebvre), xii, xxi, xxii, xxvi, xxx, 205–37

variable capital, 56, 134, 139
Varloot, Jean, 89
vegetable crops, 44, 111, 116
vertical complexity, xviii–xix, 62
vicinage relations, 70, 91
Vienna, 163
"Village Community, The" (Lefebvre), xxi, xxx, 89–102
Visigothic law, 30, 91

wage labor, xix, xxiv, xxv, 27, 51, 52, 56, 107
wages, xxiv, 51, 52, 56, 86, 110, 128, 198
warfare, 29, 216–19, 230–31
water, 25, 71, 80, 122, 193, 208–9. *See also* irrigation

Weulersse, Jacques, 21
window shopping, 162, 201
Winkler, Ernst, 193, 196
women, 26, 29, 33, 73, 153, 161, 162, 164–66, 167, 187
working class, 135, 142, 166, 179–81, 187–90. *See also* proletariat
World War II, xii, xxi
Writings on Cities (Lefebvre), ix, xvii

youth, 163, 166, 167, 186–87, 202

zadruga, 22, 29–30
Zambotti, Pia Laviosa, 68

HENRI LEFEBVRE (1901–91) was a leading French philosopher, sociologist, and urban theorist. Many of his more than sixty books have appeared in English translation, including *Dialectical Materialism; State, Space, World; The Urban Revolution; Toward an Architecture of Enjoyment;* and *Marxist Thought and the City* (all from University of Minnesota Press).

STUART ELDEN is professor of political theory and geography at the University of Warwick, UK. His books include *Terror and Territory* (Minnesota, 2009), *The Birth of Territory,* and *Shakespearean Territories*. He has been involved in editing several previous collections of Henri Lefebvre's writings and has coedited or edited books on Kant, Foucault, and Sloterdijk.

ADAM DAVID MORTON is professor of political economy at the University of Sydney. His books include *Unravelling Gramsci: Hegemony and Passive Revolution in the Global Political Economy; Revolution and State in Modern Mexico: The Political Economy of Uneven Development*; and *Global Capitalism, Global War, Global Crisis,* coauthored with Andreas Bieler.

ROBERT BONONNO has translated fiction and nonfiction, including René Crevel's *My Body and I* (a finalist for the French-American Foundation Prize) and works by Michel Foucault, Henri Lefebvre, Albert Memmi, and Isabelle Stengers.